Trade Unions and Politics

Trade Unions and Politics

Ken Coates and
Tony Topham

Basil Blackwell

© Ken Coates and Tony Topham 1986

First published 1986

Basil Blackwell Ltd
108 Cowley Road, Oxford OX4 1JF, UK

Basil Blackwell Inc.
432 Park Avenue South, Suite 1505,
New York, NY 10016, USA

British Library Cataloguing in Publication Data

Coates, Ken
   Trade unions and politics.
   1. Trade-unions — Great Britain
   I. Title   II. Topham, Tony
   331.88′ 0941   HD6664

   ISBN 0-631-13752-1
   ISBN 0-631-13753-X Pbk

Library of Congress Cataloging in Publication Data

Coates, Ken.
   Trade unions and politics.

   Includes index.
   1. Trade-unions – Great Britain – Political activity.
   2. Unemployment – Great Britain.   3. Manpower policy –
   Great Britain.   I. Topham, Tony.   II. Title.
   HD6667.C63 1986   322′ .2′ 0941   85-22959

   ISBN 0-631-13752-1
   ISBN 0-631-13753-X (pbk.)

Phototypeset by Dobbie Typesetting Service, Plymouth, Devon
Printed by T. J. Press Ltd, Padstow

Contents

Acknowledgements

As teachers in university adult education, we are always in debt to our students, who are responsible for our continuing education, and who also save us from many errors we would otherwise commit.

Among our other friends and colleagues, we wish especially to thank Graham Allen, Tony Benn, Steve Bodington, Frank Cousins, Bernard Dix, Royden Harrison, Stuart Holland, John Hughes, Michael Meacher, Lewis Minkin, Tony Simpson, Mike Somerton, Ron Todd, Daniel Vulliamy, Larry Whitty and Bob Wright. All have helped us considerably, while, of course, none is responsible for our mistakes and misjudgements.

We owe a particular debt to Michael Barratt Brown, the master pedagogue of a whole generation, whose steady encouragement has been an unfailing inspiration as well as a challenge. We are also deeply grateful to Ken Fleet, who not only gave us enormous practical help, but also his deep experience and the knowledge won from a hundred grass-roots campaigns. And without Rita Maskery's tireless work, this manuscript would have remained more opaque than Etruscan runes. We should like to record our affectionate thanks to these three comrades, certainly for their untiring work, but also for their example.

We also owe our thanks to René Olivieri and Elaine Leek, who so promptly and carefully readied our finished text for publication.

Abbreviations

Trade Unions

ACTT	Association of Cinematograph, Television and Allied Technicians
APEX	Association of Professional, Executive, Clerical and Computer Staff
ASLEF	Associated Society of Locomotive Engineers and Firemen
ASTMS	Association of Scientific, Technical and Managerial Staff
AUEW	Amalgamated Union of Engineering Workers
AUEW/TASS	(Technical, Administrative and Supervisory Staff)
BFAW	Bakers, Food and Allied Workers
COHSE	Confederation of Health Service Employees
CPSA	Civil and Public Services Association
EETPU	Electrical, Electronic and Telecommunications and Plumbing Trades Union
FTAT	Furniture, Timber and Allied Trades
GMBATU	General, Municipal, Boilermakers' and Allied Trades Union
ISTC	Iron and Steel Trades Confederation
NACODS	National Association of Colliery Overmen, Deputies and Shotfirers
NALGO	National Association of Local Government Officers
NATSOPA	National Society of Operative Printers, Graphical and Media Personnel
NATTKE	National Association of Theatrical, Television and Kine Employees.
NCU	National Communications Union
NGA	National Graphical Association
NUAW	National Union of Agricultural and Allied Workers
NUGMW	National Union of General and Municipal Workers
NUGSAT	National Union of Gold and Silver and Allied Trades
NUM	National Union of Mineworkers
NUPE	National Union of Public Employees
NUR	National Union of Railwaymen
NUS	National Union of Seamen

PLCW/TW	Power Loom Carpet Weavers/Textile Workers
POEU	Post Office Engineering Union
SLADE	Society of Lithographic Artists, Designers, Engravers and Process Workers
SOGAT	Society of Graphical and Allied Trades
TGWU	Transport and General Workers' Union
TSSA	Transport Salaried Staffs Association
UCATT	Union of Construction, Allied Trades and Technicians
UCW	Union of Communication Workers
UPW	Union of Post Office Workers

Other Organizations

CBI	Confederation of British Industry
CLP	Constituency Labour Party
ETUC	European Trade Union Confederation
GCHQ	Government Communications Headquarters (Cheltenham)
ICFTU	International Confederation of Free Trades Unions
IMF	International Monetary Fund
IWC	Institute for Workers' Control
NCEO	National Council of Employers' Organizations
NEB	National Enterprise Board
NEC	National Executive Committee
NEDC	National Economic Development Council
PLP	Parliamentary Labour Party
TUC	Trades Union Congress
TULV	Trade Unions for a Labour Victory

Tables and Figures

For Maja

1 Entering the Age of Unemployment

Mass unemployment produces two kinds of victims – the direct and the indirect.

The direct victims enter poverty, for long periods of time and, in some age groups and regions of the country, permanently. This poverty pushes them to the margins of society, where they normally live a kind of twilight existence, without hope of betterment in personal life, and without those social links that could offer collective improvement.

The indirect victims consist of a whole population, in as much as we are 'members of one another'. But very large categories of people suffer more than others, because they live and work in exposed situations. Low paid workers in declining industries feel the draught of unemployment, and moderate their claims, even when their wages are too small to permit decent existence. Workers in the public services are similarly squeezed. As the economy declines, public spending cuts are pressed remorselessly, only to be followed by further decline. Few low paid public servants can stand on their rights in such circumstances.

But above the lowest levels, much larger groups of people also suffer. The conditions of trade union activity are transmuted in the political economy of mass unemployment, and with this, even the maintenance of the political institutions of democracy becomes more and more difficult. Nothing is more divisive than enforced idleness, concentrated within one sector of a population. To restore hope to those who are deprived of work, it is necessary to restore unity among those who still retain their (sometimes) slippery grip upon employment. This is not easy; fear divides more than it unites. It can all too easily excite a purely selfish competition, even if it sometimes imposes defensive solidarity.

British unemployment, running at above 4 million in real terms, is the direct result of governmental policies which base themselves on an appeal to 'sound money'. The dread of inflation, the determination not merely to avoid, but actually to counter policies of public intervention in protection of jobs, these things have justified the most ferocious attack on the standards of the poorest people in society.

1

At the beginning of the decade J. K. Galbraith pinpointed it with controlled irony:

> Britain has, in fact, volunteered to be the Friedmanite guinea pig. There could be no better choice. Britain's political and social institutions are solid, and neither Englishmen, Scots nor even the Welsh take readily to the streets . . . There are other advantages in a British experiment. British Social Services and social insurance soften what elsewhere might be intolerable hardship. British phlegm is a good antidote for anger; but so is an adequate system of unemployment insurance.[1]

However, the longer the experiment continues, the more strain is put upon both the phlegm and the social institutions. It was entirely foreseeable, even in 1980, that, Scottish and Welsh pacifism notwithstanding, it might be prudent to strengthen and centralize the police forces. Such actions were discreetly taken, and turned out to have been very necessary from the point of view of the Government, during the sombre days of 1984.

The anticipated benefits of monetarism have not followed: but that is another argument. Yet the ill effects are only beginning to come home in their full and desperate meaning. Even the fall of the pound, which at the beginning of 1985 was sliding towards parity with the dollar, could do nothing serious to increase the volume of British manufacturing exports, for the very simple reason that so much of British manufacturing capacity had been devastated during the preceding years while the pound was overvalued to as much as $2.40. It takes several years, even in a favourable climate, to construct a new industry, starting from scratch. The elimination of what was seen as the slum sector of the British economy has not of itself produced bright new factories. This means that a falling pound produces little or no economic benefit. Where there was a dearth, there remains, simply, a dearth. Within this context, it is entirely likely, whatever happens to the oil prices which have hitherto, almost coincidentally, sustained the British Government through the longest period of untrammelled folly ever endured by its citizens, that within a short period of time there will be renewed and intransigent crises in the balance of overseas payments.

It is a time of extremes; but it is also a time in which it is desperately urgent to restore the capacity for agreed, democratic social action. The basis for this must be an alternative labour economics. This begins by insisting on a universal right to work, which is prepared to guarantee employment to all who seek it. Two roads to such a goal exist: the expansion of the economy and the creation of new jobs on the one hand, and the sharing of existing employment on the other. A complex variety of options exists in both avenues, but an alternative polity demands a sustained attempt to welcome all our people back from their exile beyond the margins of rejection, misery and loneliness. Such an alternative implies a great increase in democratic participation at every level of the political economy, and is founded on the axiom that the unused creativity of the people is not only a prime political resource, but also a potential economic force.

This is the context within which trade unions must consider the development of their policies and actions for the rest of a decade that will certainly prove to have been the most difficult in their histories. It is also the context within which democratic politics will reassert their central place in British life if democracy itself is not to be extinguished. Above all, it is the context in which the limits of nationalism will have to be understood, if we are to build an economic framework in which choice again becomes possible.

The Effects of Unemployment on the Unions

Before we can sensibly discuss the contemporary political role of our trade unions, we must examine the effects of mass unemployment upon their general capacity to defend, represent and advance the interests of their members. Before we can do this, we need an estimate of just how many people are unemployed.

We do not have in this country a generally accepted and reliable tally of the total number of unemployed people. The monthly figures published by the government are rightly regarded with total scepticism, and not only by trade unions and the political opposition. Official massage exercises are transparent, and can be briefly summarized.

The official monthly figure of the unemployment level is merely an instant snapshot of those unemployed people claiming benefit at unemployment benefit offices. It amounts to some 3¼ million. This figure is a byproduct of the unemployment benefit system; it has nothing to do with accurate labour market analysis. An estimate by the Institute of Policy Studies suggested that it contains only three-quarters of the real unemployed. Amongst those missing from the figure we can list:

1 250,000 women who, according to a Department of Employment estimate, are seeking work but not able to claim unemployment benefit.
2 The substitution of voluntary registration at the Job Centres means that the unemployment count was switched from Job Centres to unemployment benefit offices, with a resulting disappearance of between 150,000 and 200,000 from the figures of jobless.

3 From August 1983, men over 60 receive the higher rate of supplementary benefit straight away, and do not, therefore, have to sign on at unemployment benefit offices. Some 40,000 men are removed from the count thereby.
4 Men over 60 no longer need to sign on in order to qualify for National Insurance credits – a loss to the jobless figure of some 107,000 men.
5 Government special employment and training measures reduce the number of claimants by 340,000.[2]

By January 1985 this last figure of 340,000 represented the numbers involved in the Youth Training Scheme alone. In addition, 130,000 people were involved in the Community Programme, 79,000 in job release schemes, 63,000 in the Young Workers Scheme and a total in all of 662,000 people were covered in these and related special employment and training measures. The Department of Employment estimated that 475,000 of these people would have been able to claim unemployment benefit had they not been participating in the schemes in question. The remainder would have been deemed ineligible for benefit for one reason or another.

Some of these schemes show the direct influence of Mr Gradgrind. The Young Workers Scheme, which began in January 1982, 'is designed to encourage employers to take on more young people at realistic rates of pay': 'realistic' means 'low'. Employers get £15 a week compensation from the government for a period as long as a year for each young person they employ at wages lower than £50 a week. Such young people must be under 18 and in their first year of employment.[3]

The total of these 'missing persons' from the unemployment figures is some 900,000. This confirms the repeated assertions of bodies like the TUC that the real unemployment total is 4 million not 3 million. But there is more. Even this revised figure does not represent an acceptably accurate count. The journal *Labour Research* examined this problem and made the claim that there were, as early as June 1982, more than 4.6 million real unemployed, compared with the then government figure of 3 million. The same journal calculates that subsequently the total has exceeded 5 million.[4] This estimate includes, as well as those categories of unemployed excluded from the count and detailed above, a further substantial group of 'hidden unemployed' who have simply disappeared from the labour market. Since 1979, although the population of working age has risen by over half a million, the numbers of employed plus registered unemployed have *fallen* by over half a million. One million people have therefore been 'driven . . . into economic exile'.[5] On this analysis, the unemployment rate in December 1982 was 19.2 per cent, compared with the government's figure of 13.3 per cent. Figure 1.1 gives the picture at this point, disregarding the further deterioration of 1983.

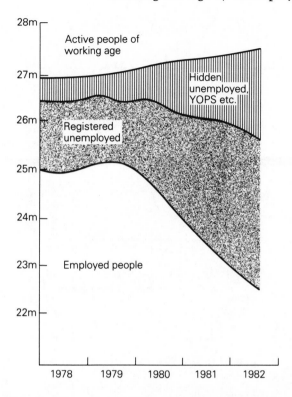

Figure 1.1 The unemployment gap (*Source: Labour Research*, December 1982).

Within these total figures, three groups suffer most. The percentage of women active (at work or seeking work) in the labour market grew from 55 per cent in 1971 to 64 per cent in 1979. But by 1981 the trend had been reversed – only 61 per cent were active. Young black people are known not to register for work so frequently as whites, and older men are increasingly dropping out of the job market as they abandon the hopeless pursuit of non-existent jobs. All of these constitute a large part of what the Americans call officially 'the discouraged'.

If today then we are confronted by 5 million people out of work, the future prospect held out to us is no less bleak. In the new cycle, if slump prevails, so will the levels of unemployment. But where the slump is overtaken by a 'recovery' in the orthodox sense of a revival in private market investment, this very investment will displace further labour as it pursues the high productivity of new technology, robotization and similar innovations.

The effect of the trade cycle is not difficult to see in the official graph (figure 1.2) of unemployment and vacancies from 1965 to 1984. At the

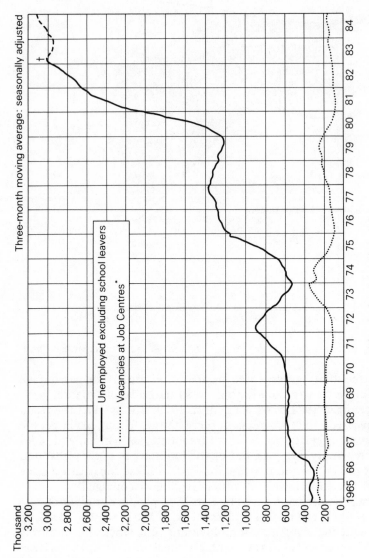

Thousand

Three-month moving average: seasonally adjusted

Unemployed excluding school leavers

·········· Vacancies at Job Centres*

*Vacancies at Job Centres are only about a third of total vacancies.
†Figures affected by Budget provisions for men aged 60 and over.

Figure 1.2 Unemployment and vacancies: United Kingdom 1965–84
(*Source*: Department of Employment press release).

beginning of the period, while unemployment ran at not much more than 300,000, economic upturn would reduce even that number. The gap between the number of vacancies and the number of people needing work was a mere crack. At the end of the period, this gap is a terrific void, of more than 3 million according even to these fictionalized statistics. The official graph shows how recent 'recoveries' have produced no real diminution in the number of unemployed. The graph comes more and more to resemble a staircase, in which attenuated 'booms' are the flat treads, while the vertical rises mark out the slumps. If the restricted 'recovery' of 1983/4 and 1985 leaves us with substantially more than 3 million people officially recorded as being out of work, we must anticipate a truly horrendous increase at the end of this relatively prosperous period.

The government was claiming success in its employment policies during 1985, on the strength of figures showing an increase in the employed labour force of 343,000 during 1984. This overall figure conceals a continued fall in manufacturing employment of 40,000, and hence a substantial shift towards the service sector. This is a virtuous and permanent trend in the eyes of the government. But how many of these services are exportable, to fill the huge balance of payments gap which will appear as the oil dries up? Moreover, these overall employment figures do not reveal that much of the rise has been in part time women's jobs concentrated in the southern regions, as well as the clear trend towards more self-employment, much of which is precarious and small scale. None of these trends is favourable to wages, or to trade unionism.

In this chapter, our concern is with the effects of this sustained mass unemployment upon the trade unions. The most obvious and immediate effect has been upon the levels of trade union membership. Data covering all unions, whether affiliated to the TUC or not, are only available to the end of 1983. Even so, they already record four successive years of falling trade union membership (table 1.1).

The all-time peak membership of trade unions in Britain was reached in 1979, when 13.289 million people belonged to 453 distinct trade unions. Of these, 112 were affiliated to the Trade Union Congress, which had a total membership of just over 12 million. Between 1979 and the end of 1983 the number of trade unions had shrunk to 393. A fierce rationalization had been imposed with many mergers and takeovers: worsening economic conditions squeezed the smaller and middle sized organizations, which found that increasingly expensive central and specialized services were harder and harder to maintain. Naturally, there are considerable economies of scale in trade union organization, as elsewhere, but the actual membership of these 393 organizations was down to 11.338 million, a reduction of 15 per cent since 1979.

Table 1.1   Trade unions: numbers and membership 1973–83

Year	No. of unions at end of year	Total membership at end of year (thousand)	Change in membership since previous year (%)
1973	519	11,456	+0.9
1974	507	11,764	+2.7
1975	`501	12,193	+3.6
1975ª	470	12,026	—
1976	473	12,386	+3.0
1977	481	12,846	+3.7
1978	462	13,112	+2.1
1979	453	13,289	+1.3
1980	438	12,947	−2.6
1981	414	12,106	−6.5
1982	408	11,593	−4.2
1983	393	11,338	−2.2

ªThirty-one organizations previously regarded as trade unions are excluded from 1975 onwards because they failed to satisfy the statutory definition of a trade union in section 28 of the Trade Union and Labour Relations Act, 1974. To help provide a link in the series, two sets of figures are given for 1975. The first gives the figures on the original basis for comparison with earlier years, while the second gives estimates for comparison with later years.
Source: Department of Employment Gazette, January 1983.

Table 1.2   Membership of TUC affiliated unions

Year	No. of unions affiliated	No. of members affiliated
1976	113	11,036,326
1977	115	11,515,920
1978	112	11,865,390
1979	112	12,128,078
1980	109	12,172,508
1981	108	11,601,413
1982	105	11,005,984
1983	102	10,510,157
1984	98	10,082,144

Source: TUC Annual Reports.

Employment had been reduced by 8 per cent, so that trade unions had been shrinking faster than the workforce. Of course, the virtual collapse of manufacturing industry in a number of sectors implied a sharp reduction in union membership, while the extension of new employment opportunities took place, to a considerable extent, in the service sector, where it generated a large number of part time jobs for women workers. These people are much more difficult to organize than their full time colleagues. The discrepancy for the year 1983 shows union membership down by 2.2 per cent as compared with the previous year, while the labour force had actually grown by 0.5 per cent.[6]

The Certification Officer publishes his report in April, and it refers to data collected more than a year earlier.

We can come closer to an up-to-date picture from the returns covering TUC affiliated unions only (table 1.2).

Table 1.3 Trade unions: analysis by industry 1982–3

Industry in which most members were deemed to be employed	Standard Industrial Classification (1980) (Division)	Membership (thousand)		Change (%)
		1982	1983	
Agriculture, forestry and fishing	0	0.5	0.4	− 22.3
Energy and water supply	1	413	359	− 13.1
Extraction of minerals and ores (not fuels); manufacture of metals, mineral products and chemicals	2	144	140	− 2.4
Metal goods, engineering and vehicles	3	1,819	1,779	− 2.2
Other manufacturing industries	4	686	713	+ 3.9
Construction	5	267	265	− 0.6
Distribution, hotels and catering: repairs	6	460	445	− 3.2
Transport and communication	7	742	701	− 5.5
Banking, finance, insurance, business services and leasing	8	337	343	+ 1.8
National government	9	552	540	− 2.2
Local government	9	1,521	1,562	+ 2.7
Education	9	745	726	− 2.5
Medical/health	9	658	675	+ 2.5
Other	9	151	152	+ 1.0
Membership of unions covering several industries	—	3,097	2,937	− 5.2

Source: Department of Employment Gazette, January 1985.

It can be seen that since 1979 the TUC has been losing members somewhat faster than all the British trade unions taken together: 17 per cent of affiliated membership have now disappeared from the figures, a drop from 12.1 million to 10.1 million. Among these losses, those of the TWGU, APEX and UCATT are particularly severe, while some public sector unions, such as NALGO, NUPE, COHSE and the POEU have actually gained increases in membership.

The Department of Employment offers a breakdown of trade union membership, industry by industry, with comparisons between the years 1982 and 1983 (table 1.3). This shows swingeing reductions in membership in energy and water supply, and, to a lesser extent,

Table 1.4   Changes in union membership, 1979–82[a]

Union	1982 membership (thousand)	Loss since 1979 (%)	Paying political levy (%)	Affiliated to Labour (%)
TGWU[e]	1,502	28	98	73
AUEW-(ES)[d]	1,001	18	79	83
GMBATU[c]	825	15	91	75
NALGO[c]	784	+4	N/A	N/A
NUPE[b]	702	+2	98	85
USDAW	417	11	92	95
ASTMS	410	16	30[d]	33
EETPU	380	10	83	46
UCATT	261	25	65	73
NUM	245	3	94[e]	94
COHSE	231	+8	92	59
SOGAT 82	225	13[a]	39[f]	32
NUT	221	11	N/A	N/A
CPSA	199	11	N/A	N/A
UCW	198	2	95	96
AUEW-TASS	172	15[b]	54	55
BIFU	151	+15	N/A	N/A
NUR	150	17	97	106
POEU	136	+9	73	68
NGA 82	132	4[e]	44[f]	15
NAS/UWT	120	1	N/A	N/A
GMBATU–Boilermakers section	114	11	53	63
APEX	109	28	71	84

[a]1979 figures include 1979 NATSOPA membership.
[b]1979 figures include NUGSAT membership.
[c]1979 figures include SLADE membership.
[d]Certification Officer's figure is for 1981.
[e]Ninety-four per cent of members affiliated to TUC, according to statistical statement.
[f]Percentage is for union before merger with SLADE.
Source: Labour Research, August 1983.

transport. (The figures in 'agriculture' presumably relate to a minority sector, since they list only a handful of union members in the sector as a whole, which was mainly organized by the NUAW, which had recently merged with the TGWU.) But, it shows an increase of 3.9 per cent in non-metal manufacturing industries, 2.7 per cent in local government and 2.5 per cent in medical and health care sectors. The major losses come from manufacturing: if the different categories of manufacturing were aggregated, they accounted in 1979 for a quarter of the workforce. Half the subsequent loss of union membership occurred in this savagely punished sector.[7] Taking this evidence union by union, *Labour Research* calculated the membership loss between 1979 and 1982 (table 1.4).

All this indicates a major, though not yet catastrophic, reversal of the whole post-war trend, particularly marked in the 1970s, of rising trade union membership. If the bulk of these losses have come about as a result of industrial contraction, which has fallen unevenly, there remains a serious potential threat of a different kind of loss, resulting from impediments to trade union efficiency. Some people fear that the closed shop might prove to be a Trojan horse for the unions. The runaway increase in trade union membership during the 1970s was certainly 'reinforced by the rapid spread of the closed shop',[8] but up to 1985 the changes in industrial law which have been brought in to hamper closed shops have not yet produced obviously identifiable large scale defections of conscripted members. Even so, Professor John Gennard estimated, on the basis of his research, that the number of employees in closed shops had fallen from 5.2 million in 1979 to 4.5 million by the middle of 1982.[9]

On the other hand, Tom Wilson of GMBATU, reports that 'there were actually more closed shops in 1983 than in 1978', although fewer of these were outside manufacturing industry.[10]

1 November, 1984 is now the deadline on this question, since dismissals arising from closed shop agreements are not thereafter immune from civil court actions unless those agreements have been previously validated in a ballot. Such a ballot must meet extremely onerous conditions and will not be deemed to have succeeded unless 80 per cent of those entitled to vote, or 85 per cent of those actually voting, express their support. Mr Tom King, Secretary of State for Employment, was no doubt recalling these conditions when he claimed that 'November 1st will virtually mark the legal extinction of the closed shop'.[11]

Hyman, writing earlier in 1984, anticipated difficulties:

The rise in the number of unionists in the seventies *despite* mounting unemployment, reflects not a sudden expansion of trade union consciousness, but the artificial accretion of paper membership. That so many of these paper unionists do not feel themselves to be 'part of the union' constitutes a genuine problem of union democracy – a problem that the Tories have effectively exploited.[12]

It remains to be seen whether the coming years will see a particular outpouring of members who were involuntary recruits to trade unions. Probably most of those who joined under closed shop agreements will agree with their 'voluntary' colleagues in applying rather practical criteria to their judgement of the effectiveness of their unions. In 1984, from tallies compiled the previous year, the TUC reported a gratifying set of statistics which seemed to show that membership was holding up.

What have been the combined effects of rising unemployment and falling membership on the ability of trade unions to carry out their functions? To evaluate this it is necessary to look at the evidence about resistance to redundancies and closures, the terms negotiated for redundancy, trends in pay settlements, trends in strikes and, of course, the evidence about the effect of government offensives against trade union and workers' rights.

Resistance to Redundancies

It was in 1969 that the first attempt was made, albeit unsuccessfully, to organize a major factory occupation – at the GEC/EE works in Liverpool – in resistance to mass redundancies.[13] Two years later, the Upper Clyde shipyard workers staged the first dramatic, substantially effective demonstration of the method of occupation and work-in, as a response to the threat of closure of their yard.[14] The self-confidence generated among workers by this example stimulated a wave of sit-ins and work-ins in the next few years.[15] Not all of these were concerned with closures and redundancies. The method was used with success in the Manchester engineering industry as part of a struggle for wage increases.[16]

The sit-in/work-in method acquired a new and political significance during 1974–5, when Tony Benn at the Department of Industry responded to sit-ins in three famous cases (Triumph Meriden motorcycles, the Scottish Daily Express and Fisher–Bendix) with financial support for the establishment of worker cooperatives to save these enterprises from closure.[17] This phase marks the climax of the widespread resistance of workers and their trade unions to the threat of unemployment. A fourth attempt, through the sit-in method, to obtain government support for a cooperative, by redundant workers at Imperial Typewriters in Hull, failed to move a government increasingly resistant to Benn's initiatives. After Harold Wilson removed Tony Benn from the Industry Department, his successor, Eric Varley, contributed substantially to the beginning of a process of demoralization among workers and shop stewards, who continued to resist redundancy but also continued mistakenly to expect assistance in their struggles from a Labour government and its instrument of intervention, the National Enterprise Board.[18] But during this period of stalemate, and through to the late 1970s, the movement invented another form of opposition to redundancies, that of the Lucas shop stewards' alternative corporate plan, based on the diversification of the company's product range into the manufacture of socially useful products.[19]

Since 1979, when redundancies and closures have multiplied apace in the private sector, when major state industries like steel, shipbuilding, railways and mining have experienced large rationalizations, and when public services such as education, local government and the National Health Service suffered heavy job losses following government cuts, there has been a marked decline in direct actions of any kind against dismissals. Of course, in the earlier period which we have reviewed, resistance was by no means universal; many groups of workers and their unions have from the outset of the crisis in the late 1960s accepted redundancy pay and signed redundancy agreements, rather than offering resistance. Ray Gunter's Redundancy Payment Act of 1965 was specifically designed to achieve this response, and to foster what could at that time be called unfeelingly, but without complete inaccuracy, 'labour mobility'.

In the 1980s repeated calls by the miners' leaders for strikes at first for wage increases, but more recently against pit closures, were all turned down by the members in a succession of ballots. The 1984 strike, in a category by itself, we discuss later. The steel industry has been reduced by deliberate government and EEC rationalizations, wiping out the plants in Corby and Consett and cutting huge swathes through the still surviving plants in Scotland, Cleveland, Scunthorpe and South Wales. Strike action by the steel unions in response has been sporadic and unsuccessful.

In other industries, longer structural declines have continued through to the present, with more setbacks in store. British Rail's most recent labour shedding has cut the workforce by 20,624 (11 per cent of the total numbers employed) between 1979 and 1983. In 1982, British Rail employed 145,000; the target set by the Serpell Report's most extreme option is for a further reduction to a total of 59,100. The docks industry's long running structural decline continues unabated; no industrial resistance has been offered by this once most militant group, which in the late 1960s went on strike for workers' control of their industry.[20]

Table 1.5   Number of registered dockers 1977–83

	No. of registered dockers	*Removed under severance schemes*
1977	29,470	999
1978	28,680	1,037
1979	26,898	2,080
1980	24,492	2,572
1981	21,022	4,784
1982	16,788	2,787
1983	15,340	1,494

Source: National Dock Labour Board

The docks industry's decline is recorded in statistical form in table 1.5.

Redundancy Terms

Levels of severance pay offered to redundant workers are widely blamed in the Labour movement for the collapse of industrial resistance. Yet one of the most generous schemes, in the docks industry itself, where compulsory redundancy is illegal, offers a maximum of £22,500 compensation to a docker with 15 years' service. This represents a mere 2½ years' pay at the present average wage for dockers of £185 a week. And in the current slump, the redundant docker's chances of alternative employment, or of establishing a successful self-employed business, in the depressed climate of East London, Liverpool or Hull, are increasingly remote. Invested, his lump sum gives him only a meagre income, even if he is one of the minority with 15 years' service; but unless he spends most of it, he does not qualify for supplementary benefit – catch 22!

The dockers of course can resist up to a point, by simply not applying for severance under what remains a voluntary severance scheme, in which case the government and the industry must bear the cost of increasing bribes, or of carrying the surplus labour. The flow of volunteers is beginning to dry up.

Elsewhere, the evidence of the past few years is grim. An important survey of redundancy terms[21] reveals that under the impact of the slump, many companies have cut severance payments from previous levels, have negotiated successfully to reduce or remove severance terms from their collective agreements with the unions, and are successfully bypassing not only the law, but also collective agreements and custom and practice, in the giving of notice of redundancy and in the selection of people to be made redundant. According to reports by trade union officials, more and more employers are practising the device of nominating up to nine individuals for redundancy at any one time. This evades the legal requirement to give minimum notice of redundancies, a law which applies only where ten or more redundancies are declared. Needless to say, the employer may then return on subsequent occasions to his longer term job cutting exercises.

In 1981 and 1982 over 1½ million individual payments were made out of the statutory Redundancy Fund, at an average of £1,284 per head. From the end of 1982 to June 1984, a further 800,000 payments were made, at an average rate of £1,153.[22] These figures stand in marked contrast to the more generous dockers' scheme, and to similar schemes in steel and other publicly owned industries. They can hardly be said to offer an inducement to accept voluntary redundancy. But some companies, perhaps in difficulties over their losses, or perhaps as a result of the changing balance of power in the bargaining relationship, are practising a hard form of blackmail in these days; they inform the union that if it does not agree to waive agreements on redundancy pay, then the numbers to be made redundant will increase, or there may be a complete closure. Unions have sometimes capitulated before this threat.

Employers' organizations now advise their members that severance terms should not form part of any agreement. Where agreements survive, the 'needs of the business' tend to override traditional 'first in, last out' rules, as the criterion for selection of redundant workers. The workers themselves are sometimes forced under duress to sign waiver forms exempting the employer from his legal obligation to serve 30 or 90 days notice of redundancies above specified numbers. This waiver procedure has also been extended in some cases to negate severance pay agreements. More often than not it is the shop floor members, rather than union officials, who insist most strongly upon capitulation to these onerous terms.

It is a tragic story. The more remarkable is the extent of opposition, often in extremely unpropitious circumstances. The seven month sit-in by (mostly women) workers at Lee Jeans in Greenock, or the series of actions by seamen to protect jobs with Cunard cruise ships, the ferries at Liverpool and Newhaven, or the Sealink services of Harwich, are good examples in the market sector of the economy, while a whole series of disputes in the National Health Service were able to join user protest to trade union action in defence of jobs and amenities. Early in 1981, there was an important action which prevented the closure of Storey Brothers' chemical plant at Brantham in Essex. Other actions were less successful, like that of the Resolven Aluminium Rolling Plant in the Neath Valley in South Wales.[23]

Pay Settlements

When we come to consider the evidence about pay settlements, this is more difficult. The interpretation of agreements is not always a straightforward business. Often efforts are made by employers to link pay concessions with changes in working practices. Sometimes unions may welcome this as advantageous, but sometimes this is quite evidently impossible. If a union signs such an agreement, what do we register: the gain in flat rate percentage rates, or the loss in job control or intensified work rhythms?

What, for example, are we to make of the deal at Perkins Engineers, Shrewsbury, concluded in November 1984? The new measured daywork rates are 12 per cent higher than those replaced: but in exchange the unions conceded 'bell-to-bell' working, job reductions across all grades, amalgamation of duties and reallocation of gradings, together with the pledge that 'all personnel will be required to undertake other work they are competent to perform, as required'.[24] Depending upon the rigour with which these measures are imposed, the value of 12 per cent could be a variable quantity.

Actual rates of increase have moved in a discernible pattern during the years of mass unemployment. During downward movements of the trade cycle they have tended to fall below the level of inflation, while on its upward courses they have nudged forward. Uncertainties about exchange rates can, of course, render inflation rather unpredictable, so that settlements made in the expectation of the continuance of present trends can go wrong.

Within this framework, the Labour Research Department analysis of settlements in the year 1981–2 showed that, out of 309 agreements considered, only eight ran at or in front of the rate of inflation. After the pre-election 'boomlet' the same source reported 'modest successes in a difficult year',[25] in which most rates rose by fractionally more than the rate of inflation. Perhaps this upswing had its own relationship to the fortunes of Prime Minister Margaret Thatcher in the 1983 polls. Taking the three years 1982–4, an Incomes Data Service comparison of pay settlements showed 'how the inflation rate has set a floor for most industry bargaining'.[26] But if this floor has been in place for a majority of the work people, for an important minority the rate of inflation has been, by contrast, a ceiling. In the public sector, especially the low paid groupings of local authority employees, stringent official intervention has restricted increases to much lower levels.

The official policy about public sector pay was, during Mrs Thatcher's earlier years, wrapped in a lot of talk about 'market forces'. But as the discrepancy between earnings in the private sector and those in welfare and public services widened, the potential for rumpus grew in the intervening space. Nurses were awarded 7¾ per cent on the basis of increases in the earnings index, while most public employees were denied recourse to the rewards of comparability.

The resultant ill feeling erupted in direct action by teachers and at the time of writing looks likely to produce other eruptions among civil servants and town hall staffs. Without doubt such ill feeling was intensified by the news of very high percentage increases for top civil servants, the judiciary and other members of the Establishment, announced in July. Even the House of Lords expressed their unease at this decision.

Within the private sector, 1984 brought difficult problems. Paradoxically, the implementation of new laws gave serious headaches to personnel managers who were struggling to introduce significant innovations. Insecurity about the closed shop can hardly have been welcomed at a time when management was preoccupied with other major changes in work organization. The miners' strike showed its initial influence in a tendency for other union claims to be pressed more fiercely, while the responses of the TUC became for a time less foreseeable. At the beginning of 1984 we saw the heyday of 'the new realism', but by the September Congress there was a quite different mood, reflected in the abrupt departure of Lionel Murray from the General Secretaryship, temporary suspension of participation in the National Economic Development Council and a flood of radical rhetoric in support of the NUM. How much these factors increased the level of settlements is open to doubt. Economic upturn, albeit restricted, seems a more plausible explanation for the better bargains agreed during much of 1984, over much of the private sector – and the ghosts of the unemployed were never far from the negotiating table.

Is it a pointer to a weakening of trade union influence that productivity payments and payment by results systems have been increasing? The proportion of men on payment by results (PBR) rose from 42.3 per cent in April 1980 to 46.5 per cent in April 1984. Among male non-manual workers, there was an increase from 12 per cent in 1980 to 19.1 per cent in 1984. The proportion of female non-manual workers on PBR more than doubled during the same period, from 6.5 per cent to 13.4 per cent.[27] Of course the context within which these developments take place is all-important. At times PBR goes along with enhanced job control at the local level: at other times its extension reveals an adverse shift in trade union influence. But with the emergence of 'no strike' agreements and other self-denying ordinances, it seems likely that unions have lost more in this particular process than is instantly apparent from the statistics of pay settlements.

If wages have been largely pacing inflation, the government's one economic 'success' has been its anti-inflation measures. What will they do if these policies themselves drift into crisis? The uncertainties of the pound against other currencies, above all the dollar; the world debt crisis which threatens major banking institutions with an explosion of default; and the dutch auction of interest rates which seems to have become epidemic during the early months of 1985: all these problems imply a worsening of inflation.

Given their reduced numbers, and the continued depressed state of the labour market, where there are 23 unemployed persons for every notified vacancy (using only the official unemployment figure), can the unions expect to respond effectively if they must seek to force up the settlement trends in pursuit of a higher inflation rate?

In addition to their relative weakness in the labour market, the unions must also contend with a government campaign to cut certain wages by decree, and to remove the traditional statutory supports for the lowest of all pay levels. The government, as we have noted already, subsidizes employers who pay young workers less than £50 a week. In addition, the abolition of the ancient Fair Wages Resolutions, which require government contractors to pay the 'going rate', was enforced in September 1983. This is a highly significant change in the climate of the labour market. Even the employers in the construction industry are alarmed at the prospect of an invasion of 'cowboy' companies which will follow. One company spokesman said that the abolition 'would take us back to the Stone Age'.

Wages Councils are a further target for government attack. In the somewhat overheated imaginations of Mrs Thatcher and her employment spokesman even such relatively toothless bodies offend against 'free market' principles and sustain wages at too high a level! In 1985, the government endorsement of the International Labour Organization Convention regulating statutory minimum wages expires; thereafter it will have a free hand for a wholesale butchery of the councils. Already the system of government inspection of Wages Council firms – never very effective – has been rendered derisory by cuts in the inspectorate. Confronting official policy on low pay, Opposition leader Neil Kinnock contrasted it with official attitudes to managerial incentives. The government's explanation for the crisis, he deduced, was that low wages were not low enough, while high wages were not high enough. This is a reversal of certain Conservative presumptions. Today, when the Secretary of State refers back, for downwards adjustment, wage rises proposed by Wages Councils, he gets away with it. In the consensual 1950s, one of his predecessors – the mild Sir Walter Monckton – caused a storm in and out of Parliament when he did the same; he was forced to withdraw his objections and allow the proposed increase.

Strike Action

The incidence of strike action further reveals an erosion of trade union militancy and bargaining influence. The number of work stoppages fell from 2,471 in 1978 to 1,154 in 1984. In no year between 1967 and 1979 had there been less than 2,000 strikes: but in 1980 there were 1,330. Strikes stayed very much at this level of frequency for the next three years, falling in 1984 to 1,154. Of course, one of these 1984 strikes was a truly gigantic event: the miners stayed out for almost exactly one year, and we discuss their struggle in detail in later chapters. But here we are concerned with another question, of how frequently workers have recourse to strikes serious enough to figure in the official statistics. And on this evidence we are bound to conclude that the strike wave of the 1970s is over. We argued a few years ago[28] that this wave was associated with the onset and first stages of economic dislocation and recession, a parallel period being that of the 1920s. At the depth of the slump in the 1930s, strikes were also at a very low level. In our view it was rather likely that there would be a similar outcome to any prolonged slump in the 1980s. This now appears to be the case.[29] Of course, the fact that strikes are less common by no means excludes particular explosions, which may again be very powerful. But when a volcano like the miners' strike erupts, nobody would argue that this was part of day-to-day collective bargaining. No: such eruptions are evidence that the bargaining system itself has been becoming an issue, a quite different matter.

In summarizing the historical evidence, we wrote in 1980 that 'those who desire "industrial peace" must, on this record, long also for the total defeat of the trade unions, as in 1926, and the thorough demoralisation of trade unionists which accompanied the mass unemployment of the 1930s'.[30] This is far from having been achieved, in spite of all reverses. But the ground on which the unions stand has been shifting, and shifting most uncomfortably.

Government Offensives

To complete this dark tale, we should also list the series of affronts which government has inflicted directly, by legal enactment curtailing workers' rights. These punishments have been administered without provoking anything more than token retaliation and a certain amount of recrimination. They include: reduced protection against unfair dismissal, reduced rights during illness, reduced health and safety protection, severely reduced rights to the closed shop, legal restrictions on the right to strike and to picket, reduced traditional training through apprenticeships, and reduced maternity rights. There is much more of this adversity to come. All these changes have been consciously fashioned by government, which has to some extent succeeded in attaching the blame for them to the very trade unions whose power has been impaired. In the eyes of their members, the unions are seen to have been damaged, but to a degree they are also actually held responsible for the weakening of their protective role at work.

It is with no pleasure that we have documented this story of adversity: it is alarming and dangerous for British democracy.

It is necessary to insist upon an honest appraisal of the extent of the crisis, however, in order to understand two points which are crucial to the analysis which follows, and to our prescriptions for appropriate trade union responses.

First, a change of this magnitude has its principal real effects upon workplace trade union positions, which are, to an alarming degree, shorn of power and function. The trade union leaders' apparently autonomous powers in their central offices have always rested on strength at the level of the workshop and it is at this base that adverse labour market forces erode power. The result is that relative power *within* the unions, which – it seems only yesterday – we were all proclaiming had gravitated under full employment to the shop floor, is now precipitated back upwards, towards the apex of the trade union hierarchy. But this is power only within the organizations. In reality, whilst some general secretaries may now dominate their union's internal structures and relationships, to the point where they can effectively withhold support from those remaining militants and pockets of industrial resistance struggling against the effects of the slump, their external power as measured by their influence over employers and government is close to zero. They may have the pull to ensure that prominent activists, such as Mike Cooley and Derek Robinson, remain victimized when dismissed by their employers, but they can often no longer deliver much more than token gains for their members. They may vote all kinds of sympathy to the mineworkers at big public conferences, but the same members are not listening, or, if they are listening, not hearing. Their behaviour in the face of government and employers is thus likely to seem increasingly irrelevant and sometimes, indeed, it may be seen as mere posturing. To engage active membership participation, new, realistic initiatives become vitally necessary.

This leads to our second point, central to the argument of this book. With bargaining inhibited, restrained by economic adversity, the primary trade union response to the present crisis must now be political. We have sought to monitor the effect of mass unemployment on the unions' industrial strength, and we are bound to conclude that it has been severe. Surely this is likely to remain so while the long slump prevails. Indeed things do not improve during minor upturns, as new technology threatens the structure of employment as we have known it. The postwar sellers' market for labour has gone, and in its passing has undermined the unions' traditional perception of their role. So far they have failed to define for themselves a new one.

Many of the forms of action which were proved to be effective in the past no longer produce beneficial results. It is for this reason necessary to examine the trade unions' political role, first as it is currently and traditionally expressed through the Labour Party, and then as it might be, if we were willing to think things through to their logical conclusion. Unless we do this we shall turn our backs on participatory democracy for the duration of the slump, which might quite literally take us, through the militarism it provokes, to the day when the world ends.

Mass membership involvement is far more possible in agreed and achievable political campaigns than in most forms of industrial pressure, while that slump exerts its icy grip on people's minds. But political campaigning which seeks to involve people in seeking solutions to their own problems, is quite different from the political pressures of yesterday, which were highly centralized, often relatively remote from the world of ordinary men and women, and based upon the real recognition by all those responsible for managing them of powerful forces lying latent, below. Yesterday was an age of what is now called corporatism, and to that we must now turn. Tomorrow will be different, and much worse, if the surviving ten million loyal trade union members do not find ways to generate a real crusade for jobs, peace and democracy.

Notes

1 J. K. Galbraith, *Observer*, 31 August 1984.
2 See *Labour Research*, December 1982, pp. 264–5.
3 Department of Employment, Press Release, January 1985.
4 *Labour Research*, December 1982, p. 264.
5 Ibid., p. 265.
6 *Department of Employment Gazette*, January 1985, p. 28.
7 Tom Wilson: 'The workers are fighting back', *Tribune*, 3 May 1985. For an account of the crisis in manufacturing, see John Hughes, *Britain in Crisis*, Spokesman, 1981.
8 Richard Hyman, 'Wooing the Working Class', in James Curran (ed.), *The Future of the Left*, Polity Press and New Socialist, 1984, p. 96.
9 This figure was cited in the House of Commons, 5 June 1984. Gennard's survey was commissioned by the Department of Employment. Cf. also W. W. Daniel and Neil Millward, *Workplace Industrial Relations in Great Britain*, Heinemann, 1983, pp. 60–81.
10 Tom Wilson, 'The workers are fighting back'.

11 This was reported in *The Times* on 31 October 1984. On 5 February 1985, Mr Bottomley replied to a Parliamentary Question that 'only a few thousand out of four million or so' members of closed shops had been balloted. This means that most closed shops 'have now lost any protection the law previously gave them'.

12 R. Hyman, 'Wooing the working class', p. 96.

13 *GEC/EE Workers' Takeover*, Institute for Workers' Control pamphlet series no. 17, 2nd ed., 24 September 1969.

14 See Jack McGill, *Crisis on the Clyde*, Davis-Poynter, 1973; Alasdair Buchan, *The Right to Work*, Calder, 1972; Frank Herson, *Labour Market in Crisis*, MacMillan, 1975; Robin Murray, *UCS – The Anatomy of Bankruptcy*, Spokesman, 1972.

15 See Ken Coates, *Sit-ins, Work-ins and Industrial Democracy*, Spokesman, 1981.

16 See Graham Chadwick, 'The Manchester Sit-ins', in Michael Barratt Brown and Ken Coates (eds), *Trade Union Register 3*, Spokesman, 1973.

17 See Ken Coates (ed.), *The New Worker Co-operatives*, Spokesman (for Institute for Workers' Control), 1976.

18 See *State Intervention in Industry, A Workers' Enquiry*, 2nd ed., Spokesman, 1982.

19 See chapter 8. Also Hilary Wainwright and Dave Elliott, *The Lucas Plan: A New Trade Unionism in the Making*, Allison and Busby, 1982.

20 See *Bulletin of the Institute for Workers' Control*, vol. 2 nos. 6–7, special issue on the docks industry, 1970.

21 Incomes Data Services, Study no. 280, December 1982.

22 Incomes Data Services, Study no. 327, December 1984.

23 All these cases are analysed in Hugo Levie, Denis Gregory, and Nick Lorentzen, *Fighting Closures*, Spokesman, 1984.

24 Incomes Data Services, Report no. 441, January 1985, p. 25.

25 *Labour Research*, September 1983, p. 237.

26 Incomes Data Services, Report no. 441, January 1985, p. 23.

27 *New Earnings Survey*, 1984.

28 Ken Coates and Tony Topham, *Trade Unions in Britain*, Spokesman, 1980, pp. 209–10.

29 This does not mean that strikes will be less important. To the extent that they become rarer, they will be more highly charged politically quite aside from the attentions of the Courts.

30 Coates and Topham, *Trade Unions in Britain*.

2 The Corridors of Power

HOW THESEUS WAS CHASED OUT BY THE MINOTAUR

The years of full employment have commonly been identified as years of consensus. 'Butskellism', a hybrid political philosophy alleged to draw equally upon the ideas of R. A. Butler, the prominent Conservative leader, and Hugh Gaitskell, the leader of the Labour Party, was the most explicit phase of this consensus, on the political level. It emerged in the 1950s.

But consensus was not restricted to a party convergence upon the 'middle ground'. There was also a more fundamental rapprochement in the field of industrial relations. At least in their political behaviour, leaders of trade unions entered 'the corridors of power'[1] and found themselves involved in a growing range of quangos and tripartite bodies. Even while there were sometimes stiff confrontations in strikes and other industrial conflicts, cooperation was the rule in the politics of national planning and regulation. This process gave rise to the notion of 'corporatism'.

Richard Hyman has argued that this term is imprecise, but that it implies a growing interrelationship between the state and a variety of producer groups or special interests. The interaction of these interests displaces certain effective Parliamentary controls. The most detailed and comprehensive presentation of this complex of arguments is to be found in Keith Middlemas' major work, *Politics in Industrial Society*.[2]

Stuart Holland, writing in the *Guardian*, said of this book that it 'is not only authoritative, persuasive and important in its own right, but of considerable significance for the politics of the Right today'. This remains true even though, six years after its publication, its central thesis of the existence of a 'corporate bias' in British politics has been dramatically challenged by the new Tory radicalism of Mrs Thatcher's Government: Since 1979 the trade unions have been expelled from influence in those corridors of power by successive measures which amount to an overall change in their status – the Employment Acts of 1980 and 1982, and the Trade Union Act of 1984, the GCHQ incident, the challenges to conventional state attitudes to wages and trade unionism in the public and Wages Councils sectors, and a variety of

23

lesser affronts. The stage was reached in April 1984, when the TUC itself, having striven by every imaginable contortion to uphold corporate tripartite relations with this Government and the employers, acknowledged the depth of the breach by symbolically, if temporarily, withdrawing from the National Economic Development Council. Nevertheless, for the Labour movement, the issues raised by Middlemas remain of high relevance. Indeed, its responses to his analysis are in some ways crucial for the politics of Labour today.

The book's central thesis is expressed as follows:

> Corporate bias is . . . a system which encourages the development of corporate structures to the point at which their power, divergent aims and class characteristics can be harmonised, even if that harmony involves a partial loss of class distinction, individuality and internal coherence. An element of representativeness remains, however, permitting constituents, whether on the shop floor or company boardrooms, to revoke consent: totalitarianism is logically impossible.[3] (See appendix 2.1.)

Middlemas offers a detailed historical survey in support of this thesis. Our own evaluation follows this in part, from a very different perspective. We reach different conclusions.

The growth of an enfranchised working class, organized in trade unions and eventually into a political party, had reached such proportions in the Edwardian era that the conventional view of Britain's political system, based on Parliamentary sovereignty reinforced by deference, had begun to break down. How was the new political force to be received? Overt opposition leading to its repression was a possible response, finding its strongest expression in the main employers' organizations during the major industrial conflicts of the 1890s, the 1910–14 period, and in the 1920s. Judicial judgments, such as those of Taff Vale and the Osborne case, tended in the same direction. But this option never won wholehearted state, Party or Parliamentary support. Instead, a complex and vacillating process of assimilation developed, combining educational, welfare and industrial relations reform in which governments invited the extragovernmental participation of industry and unions. This process was greatly accelerated during both world wars. It was reinforced by the pull towards the political centre operating in all political parties as they sought solutions to the tensions generated first by the inter-war slump, and then by the different crises of the post-war full employment period.

On the labour side of this convergence, the Trades Union Congress became involved in a growing network of institutions which expressed this corporate bias. But the TUC was intermittently subjected to a restraining force. The reactions of its constituent membership at critical moments helped to prevent full blooded and irreversible corporatism from supplanting the received political system. Dreams of a fully corporate state have found shadowy expression from time to time, ranging from proposals for an 'industrial parliament', and the calling of National Industrial Conferences in the early 1920s, through the Mondist tendency after the General Strike, to the concept of 'Great Britain Ltd' articulated by Lord Robens and other prominent industrialists in the 1970s.

The shop floor trade unionists have sometimes endorsed the leadership's participation in all this, and have also operated local versions of the assimilation model, from Whitleyism and joint consultation, to participation. At other times, they have revolted, and 'revoked consent', sometimes reinforced in their opposition by an alternative 'syndicalist' politics, more often by mass defensive responses as the gains of a preceding period were threatened. Thus, while there clearly exists a trend towards the ripening of corporate methods and practice (the NEDC has enjoyed a much longer and more established role than its pre-war forerunners), that trend is not crudely linear. Successive convergences by the TUC on corporate solutions have been followed by partial withdrawals, as in 1984.

An important corollary of this analysis is that, as corporatism waxes, so party political power wanes; its fluxes are like a film negative of the fortunes of corporatism. Over the whole twentieth century experience, however, the dominant trend in political parties has favoured corporatism. In the case of Labour, this trend has prevailed over an alternative vision of a class and community based democratic administration of economy and society, in which popular accountability would control central institutions and policies. In the Conservative spectrum, the relatively benevolent treatment of trade unionism and labour which was favoured by successive administrations, culminating in the influence of Macmillan and Butler, held at bay for long years more atavistic forces.

The 'Thatcherite' wing of Conservatism drew, more quickly than either wing of Butskellism, the lessons to be learned from the evidence that class tension was re-emerging between 1964 and 1975. In that climate, the TUC was compelled to respond to the political discontents of its members – a response expressed in the role of Jack Jones and Hugh Scanlon. Weakened in its corporate role in this upheaval, the TUC entered a phase of greater direct political involvement, through its central role in the TUC–Labour Party Liaison Committee (see appendix 2.2), and in its direct influence on Labour's legislative programme of 1974–6.[4] Class responses were not missing either, on the employers' side, for example in the CBI's inflammatory and militant responses to the Bullock Report and to the idea of compulsory planning agreements.[5]

The new Conservatism's response has been dramatic; it has thrown off the restraints of corporatism, reasserted the dominance of politics, and in general run as hard as possible against the long sustained process of assimilation.

The onslaughts on trade unionism, which we shall discuss below (see chapter 3), represent a clear commitment against both pluralist and corporatist ideals. The economic individualism preached by the Thatcher Government is accompanied by a parallel political individualism, which seeks to set persons free from the 'tyranny' of the groups to which they belong. Thus, individuals are to be liberated from constraints imposed by their unions. It hardly requires strong efforts of analytical imagination to see that the weakening or annulment of group pressures can only result in the strengthening of the role of government, and the removal of controls over state policy. This process is heavily reinforced when it is applied to such important sectors as that of local government, which has traditionally disposed of significant, if limited, real resources, with varying degrees of autonomy. The results of this entire process could be seen quite nakedly in the judicial summation of Mr Justice McCowan at the end of the Ponting trial, in which it was baldly insisted that the interest of the state was synonymous with that of the governing faction within it.[6] This is a crystalline form of the Thatcher doctrine if ever there was one.

Of course, the result of a curtailment of group and interest powers can only be, in the middle run, a further polarization of the political process, and a further strengthening of party antagonisms. To diminish the effective power of trade unions to act on a sectoral or local base is to incite them to seek to become effective in a more comprehensive way. That way lies through political action. Corporatism and syndicalism are no longer practicable responses. Here, too, there is no alternative.

The International Context of Consensus

Where we find Middlemas' analysis much more defective is within the international context. The framework within which corporate consensus had assumed maturity was that of full employment in the post-war Keynesian world settlement. It has been the collapse of that settlement which has skittled away so many of the national corporative mechanisms which it had earlier called into being in Britain, and damaged the politics of welfare and consensus far further afield.

The Keynesian revolution dominated the entire post-war generation. Continual growth in public expenditure, and continual expansion in welfare spending were written on the flag which Keynes handed to the post-war Western governments. They were seen as furnishing the ultimate answer to unemployment and poverty. Providing a large part of the underpinning argument of Butskellism, Keynes could show capitalists the benefits of government 'management' which could create conditions for continuous growth without requiring run-away nationalization or oppressive direct controls. He could show socialists such as Anthony Crosland what they thought to be an alternative road to tame the caprice of private greed and to establish benevolent social goals.[7] Public ownership in a few basic industries and services could be coupled with indicative planning to supplant the need for heavy intervention by the state in the management of production. By contrast, the state could flourish as patron–manager of demand, upholder of social standards and big spender.

This was the runway from which modern corporatism could take flight. For a long time this corporatism contained the institutions representing a majority of working people. There was great loss in this for the Labour movement, because it was impossible to conform to such rules without accepting the fundamental rule of wage slavery. Crosland was quite explicit about this: he mocked the old socialists who had condemned the very status of wage labour, and he spoke of the need to 'align the work group with the technological imperatives'.[8] [We must here declare an interest. We found this whole engagement to be an apostasy, because wage slaves remained in bondage even while their living standards increased and technology revolutionized even domestic life. For us, socialism was, is and will remain a call for freedom.]

The Keynesian settlement froze progress in industrial democracy,[9] while providing a warm micro-climate in which to nurture corporatism of the kind that Middlemas describes. Under it, workers' interests in the government of their enterprises were to be diverted, or, preferably to be transmuted, into wage demands. Within an epoch of full employment, employers found themselves competing for labour, and so the unions were working with the market trend when they presented their claims for wages and improved conditions. This provoked government fears of inflationary pressure, corporate mechanisms of wage control and resultant pressures on the workshop organization of trade unions to come into conflict with national trade union policies. Within this tension, a modest renewal of the impulse to workers' control could and did arise.[10] But it was not until the end of the Keynesian dispensation that unions learnt how to generalize their demands for industrial democracy in ways that might, had they emerged earlier, have been effective. To do this it was necessary first to legitimate workshop representation within trade union structure, and secondly to transform collective bargaining so that unions could pass from opposition to government.[11] In hindsight, we may say that if this process could have been brought to a head a decade earlier, the British political economy would have avoided a great deal of unnecessary pain.

Be that as it may, while Labour aspirations were frozen in the Keynesian model, those of capital were not. The Keynesian settlement was a world-wide affair, and it produced ideal conditions for the continuous growth of capital concentration. The fact that governments were separately managing demand enabled capitalists to combine to manage supply. More and more there were perceptible advantages to be had from doing this on a transnational scale. Within the post-war boom, concentration was a road to growth. Industrial organization polarized. By the beginning of the 1970s the British construction industry could be divided in half: at the bottom, a hundred thousand small firms competed; at the top, five giant companies presided. By 1970, the largest hundred companies in Britain, in the field of manufacturing, controlled half the manufacturing output. When these large companies were multinational, they were increasingly capable of evading the restrictions imposed by nation states in the interests of demand management. A growing proportion of international trade was taken up by exchanges which were *internal* to these major companies. The manipulation of the prices involved in these exchanges, and the device of 'transfer pricing', meant that companies could move their profits across frontiers at will, and maximize their returns in the most beneficial areas from the point of view of taxation. They could also minimize their profits in areas in which trade unions might be more demanding.

Paradoxically, states that sought to implement Keynesian techniques sought also, at the same time, to increase productive efficiency by encouraging mergers and concentration. Since it was clear that economies of scale improved the power to compete, Butskellite governments in Britain and their analogues outside, did everything possible to encourage this kind of corporate growth. None of this was entirely new, and indeed the process was already clearly discernible in the United States before the turn of the century. Vain attempts at anti-trust legislation date back to 1890.

But the process is a fundamental one, as Karl Marx insisted:

> The battle of competition is fought by cheapening commodities. The cheapness of commodities depends, *ceteris paribus*, on the productivity of labour, and this again on the scale of production. Therefore, the large capitals beat the smaller . . . the credit system becomes a new and formidable weapon in the competitive struggle and finally it transforms itself into an immense social mechanism for the centralization of capitals . . . centralization completes the work of accumulation by enabling the industrial capitalists to expand the scale of their operations.[12]

This accelerated concentration undermined the Keynesian settlement which had made it possible. Speaking of his experience at the Ministry of Technology during the 1966–1970 Wilson administration, Tony Benn described the awful sense of impotence which dawned upon that government: 'We pressed the accelerator and nothing went; we stood on the brake, and nothing stopped'. This uncomfortable situation was a direct result of the rise of the transnational sector, and its evasion of (or, alternatively, exploitation of) national economic policies.

Transnational capital has a whole range of such possible evasions and exploitative strategies open to it, in which its advantage over companies with a purely national base is sometimes absolute, and always relatively greater.

First, it effectively blunts the impact of domestic monetary policy, since it has privileged access to funds which are independent of such policy. These include internally generated surpluses (undistributed profits and depreciation funds), and the international capital market (Euro-dollar and Euro-bond markets). In both respects, international companies have the advantages of size and of superior credit status over purely national companies. Government policy designed either to restrain or to stimulate economic activity through monetary methods (brake and accelerator) is increasingly ineffective, the more so after all efforts to restrict international capital mobility have been abandoned (by the present Thatcher Government) or rendered dubious in law (by the Treaty of Rome).

Secondly, not only can fiscal policy be more easily evaded by international than national capital; but also, because it still bites the purely national sector more effectively, its effects are directly to weaken the competitive resistance of the smaller national companies. Thus, when government cuts public expenditure, or when it raises taxes and national insurance contributions, or health and other social charges, and when it reduces government subsidy to private industry (as for example in the most recent evolution of regional policy), it is the smaller national firms which are most seriously affected – either by direct addition to their costs, or through the concomitant decline in demand for their products in the domestic market. The rest of the adjustment is required from the public sector. These two sectors carry the whole burden of adjustment while international companies practice that supreme form of evasion, transfer pricing.

Thirdly, for similar reasons, national government policies aimed at creating optimum balances of payments run up against the quite autonomous trading plans of the international firms.

Fourthly, international currency movements have reached such proportions that the present government has sworn off any attempt to define and pursue an exchange rate policy. Most of this speculation is carried out by international companies shifting their cash balances in pursuit of capital gain, or of the avoidance of losses; it is their rational response to that instability of which they are themselves collectively the root cause.

Responses to controlled devaluation or to uncontrolled exchange rate collapses alike are no longer within the realm of predictable benefit to the nation state because:

1 International firms often operate in oligopolistic markets where prices are sticky; the exporting firm may derive no profit by lowering final prices by the amount of currency devaluation.
2 International firms allocate national markets to different sources of the firm's supply.
3 Markets may be allocated by an international oligopoly agreement.
4 The assembly of parts into final product often comprises contributions from many separate national subsidiaries of the company; in Britain, the sterling component of the final product may be too small to make a difference to total cost, and in such cases it will fail to justify a price change of the final product.[13]

Finally, the ability of international firms to exploit national policy can be underlined by a single example from among so many; the spectacle of Nissan cars winning massive government aid in 1985 to induce it to establish a plant in the North East of England, an area threatened with yet further devastation stemming from national, internal policies, in the shape of an impending cutback in the regional coal industry.

Robin Murray was able to demonstrate, long before monetarism was engraved on tablets of stone as a new Mosaic code, that:

> It has been as if government policy was actually charged with weakening national capital prior to its incorporation in larger international capital units, or indeed with weakening the national economy prior to its incorporation into a larger political identity . . . from British experience at least it is the corporate rather than the national division of labour that dominates and determines the features of the international economy.[14]

Out of this bitter experience, Stuart Holland identified the transnational sector as a 'meso-economic' block between the macro and micro sectors of the economy.

> This new big business sector is entirely different in size and character from the model of conventional macro-economics and micro-economic policies. Between the small national firm of the micro-economic model, and the aggregates of macro-economic policy, there now is a new intermediate

meso-economic sector (Greek: *micros*, small; *macros*, large; *mesos*, intermediate).[15]

By 1983, Holland had reached the view that the appropriate scale for a response to meso-economic power was itself international.[16] By that time 140 companies accounted for one-third of the gross domestic product of the EEC. These companies could exercise a powerful influence on pricing policies. Their responses or non-responses to state policies of demand management could make or break individual governments. Subsidies designed for aiding small enterprises could divert kings' ransoms to those who were already in the major league, while taxes which fell heavily on the small or medium sized companies could be largely avoided by the firms in the meso-sector. The changeover from trade between different companies to trade between different giant international outposts of the same colossal company could reduce exchange rate policies to nonsense. Taken altogether, these shifts of power destroyed the post-war consensus. Only if multinational corporate power could be brought under control would it be possible to recapture some space in which to recover public control of economic policy. Naturally, such control implied a convergence of action between several important governments at the same time. It did not necessarily imply an attempt to revive corporate institutions, or other parts of the Keynesian settlement. If we were able to learn, it should be possible to combine an international and convergent recovery programme with measures of industrial democracy which could open up new possibilities in production.[17] But this would imply two revolutions in the outlook of labour organizations. For trade unions, it needed priority to be given to political over industrial action, and the integration of industrial responses within an overall political strategy. For labour and socialist parties, it required a totally new commitment to the priority of joint international coordination of policy and action.

How the Base of Corporatism has Consequences at the Top

Middlemas, as we have seen, more than adequately demonstrates the existence throughout twentieth century industrial history of a 'corporate bias' in state–trade union–employer relationships. He shows that, since neither unions nor industry in Britain are organized into tightly authoritarian central, confederal bodies, their entry into corporate relationships is always voluntary, conditional and subject to a 'recall' process if their constituents revolt against corporate constraints on the pursuit of sectional goals.

A similar analysis is offered by Crouch,[18] who takes the story further than Middlemas into the post-war years, applying the model to the experience of Labour Governments of the 1960s, to Edward Heath's administration of 1970–4, and in part to Labour's period in office during the 1970s. Under the conditions identified by both authors, Crouch demonstrates that corporatism has been inherently 'unstable', the instability being located in conflicting pressures on trade union leaderships and their memberships. From their vantage point at the top, leaders come to believe that the uncomplicated pursuit of the primary trade union role of collective bargaining may destabilize an economy which they believe might otherwise be rehabilitated through favourable economic policies pursued in collaboration with governments. As a quid pro quo, governments can in turn be led into granting legislation favourable to trade unions.

This kind of relationship is a 'positive sum game' whenever trade unions are strong. Crouch calls it 'bargained corporatism'. It found its best expression in the period from 1974 to 1976. Yet the gains made by trade unions in these years were heavily concentrated in the two main areas of trade union legal status (the restoration and extension of union powers following the repeal of Heath's Industrial Relations Act), and in the extension of individual workers' rights in such fields as employment protection, equal pay and equal opportunities. On the wider issues of trade union control or participation in economic planning at macro-level, and the extension of industrial democracy through trade unionism in the company, the gains made were minimal or non-existent. No worthwhile planning agreements were made, and there was no Industrial Democracy Act. There was a single useful concession in the establishment of trade union safety representatives in the Health and Safety at Work Act. This, of course, proved entirely inadequate as a means of engaging trade union members in power bargaining around the social contract; consequently they remained locked to sectional objectives, especially in the struggle about wages. So sectionalism brought them into head-on collision with the corporate design which itself because increasingly restrictive, and was eventually made quite subordinate to the IMF-imposed deflation of 1976–9.

Leo Panitch[19] has advanced a third, Marxist, version of these experiences, in which the impulse behind corporatism and consensus politics is seen as the Labour Party's 'integrative' philosophy. He cites with approval R. H. Tawney, reflecting on the collapse of Labour in 1931: 'Until the Labour Party recognizes that it is not Socialist, it is not likely to become Socialist'. On this view, the Labour Left (and its allies in the Communist Party) conduct a largely rhetorical struggle to retain Labour's links with socialist goals, but have failed to retard the Party's tendency, when in office, to pursue corporatism and the 'integration' of the trade unions in a species of managed capitalism. Crouch, from a less committed perspective, finds the politics of the trade union leadership to be equally rhetorical when enunciating the goals of industrial and economic power-sharing. While devoting great industry to the elaboration of economic planning models involving trade union participation, most TUC leaders do not really take such issues all that seriously.

Leo Panitch is responsible for another insight which is important. Corporatism is not evenly diffused throughout capitalism.

> Were monopoly capitalism itself a sufficient condition for explaining the emergence of corporatist structures, one would have expected to find such structures most highly developed precisely in that society which has been the world centre of monopoly capitalism in the modern era – the United States. Instead corporatist structures in the United States are comparatively *least* developed. Conventional interest group lobbying *vis-à-vis* the legislature still plays a major role, and labour representation *vis-à-vis* bureaucratic policy making is largely confined to the Department of Labor, a site which occupies a lowly place in the hierarchy of state apparatuses. However great the incidence of class collaboration in America, its practice is little elaborated in the institutional field of the central administrative apparatus of the state, where trade unions are largely excluded from participation in policy making. Similarly, were the incidence of state intervention in the economy itself the determining variable, one would have expected France, with its extensive state economic planning, or Italy, with its extensive public ownership, to exhibit highly developed corporatist state structures. Instead, these societies are precisely marked by the comparative distance of the trade union movement from the state apparatus.[20]

There can be little doubt that corporatism in Britain has been encouraged by the exceptional powers of patronage in the British political system. This stems from the constitutional position (by no means a fiction) which situates authority in 'the Queen in Parliament'. Notable among the critics of the royal prerogative has been Tony Benn, who has identified the resultant personal patronage as a most corrosive solvent of democratic accountability. Reviewing Harold Wilson's book on the *Government of Britain*, Benn gave a list of some of the personal appointments for which Sir Harold had been responsible.[21]

> A hundred Cabinet Ministers, 403 non-Cabinet Ministers, 243 Peers, 24 Chairmen of nationalized industries controlling 20 per cent of the nation's gross production, and 16 Chairmen of Royal Commissions.

The Prime Minister also 'controlled all top line appointments within the Civil Service, and of course, the Honours List'.

Yet for not one of these appointments is a Prime Minister constitutionally required to consult Cabinet, Parliament, public or party.
Patronage may issue from one fountain in Downing Street, but there
are a myriad of lesser fonts. In 1975 Maurice Edelman identified seven
Cabinet ministers as controlling 4,223 jobs worth £4.3 million in
salaries.[22] In his *Arguments for Democracy*, published in 1981, Tony
Benn returned to his indictment: he identified 2,564 major appointments
which had been made by seven Prime Ministers during a period of 31
years.

> The scale of the patronage is breathtaking, and no medieval monarch could
> compare with it, either in numbers or in importance. Nor could an
> American President approach this level of personal patronage. But there
> is more to come, since Prime Ministers also appoint permanent secretaries;
> ambassadors; chiefs of staff; the heads of the security services, MI5 and
> MI6. And obviously they can have an influence, if they choose to use it,
> over the names of all those put forward for the 31 public boards listed in
> 1977 or the 252 fringe bodies, which themselves employ 184,000 people
> and spend 2,367 million a year.[23]

When we tried to track down the extent of this patronage within the
trade union movement, we encountered many difficulties. In 1979 we
found[24] that the TUC maintained a list of the General Council's
appointments to government committees and outside bodies, which
named 67 major and subsidiary bodies, 10 of which were in the
educational field. Such appointments ranged from membership of the
Royal Commission on the Distribution of Income and Wealth, to
involvement in the White Fish Authority. We consulted *Whitaker's
Almanac* and *Who's Who* in order to follow through these commitments.
Sometimes members of the General Council proved to be excessively
modest about the number of public bodies in which they were engaged.
Even so, we identified 107 committee appointments involving members
of the General Council.

Tony Benn believes that this giant web of patronage plays a significant
role in restricting Labour governments and preventing them from
carrying through their more radical policies. There is some evidence
that this is true. However, it is by no means a sufficient explanation
for the behaviour of such governments. If corporatism has been driven
harder and faster in Britain because British institutions ride so
comfortably on a litter of patronage, certainly it will be harder to impose
democratic accountability. But Panitch is right to observe that other
capitalisms are no less capitalist because they lack a House of Lords.
The French socialist government of President Mitterrand has described
a trajectory which is not at all dissimilar from that of the Wilson–
Callaghan administrations between 1974 and 1979. It was the powerful

obstacles to social reform in one country, and the pressures of adverse balances of payments, which pushed French socialists along the same path previously traversed by British Labourites. Their differing allegiances to Fabianism and Marxism made much less difference than socialist ideologues could comfortably anticipate. We think we may now be beginning to hear the footsteps of other socialist governments following not far behind. In Spain, a socialist party educated in resistance to Franco, full of idealistic, radical, and clever young people, administers the highest unemployment in Western Europe in a context which appears dismal to any outsider who identifies with the cause of Spanish democracy.

If there is to be scope for effective economic action by different national governments, they will need to recover it in joint action, against a hostile environment. Trade unions live in the same bleak world and need to build the same linkages if their proposals are to take serious effect. To create and develop international links is at least as important as to face up to the anachronisms of a semi-feudal inheritance.

All of which takes us only to the frontier of the actual politics of corporatism, for this politics undoubtedly does engage a very serious input of time and energy on the part of the trade union leaders, even while it produces only a substitute for the transformation of the real relations between labour and capital. For, while it withholds most real accretions of power or even influence to trade unionists, as delegates or representatives in planning, and the machinery of controls in economy and company, corporatism has held out ever-extended roles for trade union leaders in the apparatus of quasi-autonomous non-governmental organizations – quangos.

For a realistic view of what corporatism means at the top of the trade union movement, therefore, we might perhaps try to envisage the actual working life of a trade union leader. While we are not privy to the detail of their diaries, it is quite possible from published sources and by inference to suggest something of what it is like to be a typical member of the TUC General Council. All but a handful of general councillors have, as their primary salaried function, the leading executive role as general secretary (or president) of their own trade union, which, in a major union, is a highly demanding full-time post in itself. They have ultimate responsibility for policy implementation, for the administrative machine of the union at head office and for overseeing its regional machinery, a role in major negotiations with large companies and in the public sector, care of the union's finances and for its role in international federations and secretariats, and for its own internal government, its educational, legal, and political functions. Even if much of this work may be devolved upon specialist officers, the general secretary cannot divorce himself (or very rarely, herself) from what is going on in all these fields; at the least he must read, conduct and listen to endless briefings, and digest a mass of communications and minutes generated in the union. He must be sufficiently master of this material to service the union's executive committee, which meets regularly on a weekly, monthly, or quarterly basis, and apply all its policy decisions through the union, sustaining a constant and time-consuming correspondence and telephone contact with his specialist and regional officers. And he must, annually or biennially, hold in his hands the whole complex of union business through the processes of the union's policy-making conference. He will also have a big part to play in the Annual Congress of the TUC (one week), of the Scottish TUC (one week), and the Labour Party Conference (one week).

On the General Council of the TUC, he must attend its formal monthly sessions, appraising himself beforehand with a working knowledge of a truly formidable mass of reports and committee minutes which form the basis of General Council proceedings. But much of the council's work is conducted through these committees – each general councillor sits on three or four of them; they also meet monthly. Our inexhaustible leader must therefore find time not only for the committee meetings, but to digest the background papers produced with considerable assiduity by the TUC backroom staff in specialist departments. In the hey-day of corporatism and its 1970s expression through the TUC–Labour Party Liaison Committee, he may well have been engaged in its production of agreed policy statements which appeared at least once a year; more recently, Trade Unions for a Labour Victory (TULV) may have had a claim on his time too. Beyond the principal committees of the General Council, the TUC runs a further 18 specialist committees concerned with the business of particular industries and sectors of the economy or trade union movement. Our man will be on one or more of these, and he will have to take his share of adjudicating on inter-union disputes through the TUC's internal judicial machinery. The ICFTU, the ETUC and other international bodies all require participation from TUC members.

But it is when we move beyond Congress House that we see the real burdens carried by many. All these activities are confined to work with other union representatives. But in addition, at the height of the quango era in 1979 (to take two examples only), Lord Allen of Fallowfield, General Secretary of USDAW and a TUC general councillor, was a BBC Governor, a Crown Estate Commissioner, a member of the Equal Opportunities Commission, of the National Economic Development Council, of ACAS, of the British Airports Authority, of the Committee to Review the Functioning of the Financial Institutions, of the Central Lancashire Development Corporation, a director of the Industrial Training Service, and the chairman of the Economic Development

Committee for the Chemicals Industry. Harry Urwin (admittedly with only an assistant general secretary's role in his union, the TGWU), was a member of the Manpower Services Commission, the Machine Tools Economic Development Committee, the Industrial Development Advisory Board, the National Enterprise Board, the Committee on Finance for Investment, of the Energy Commission, of the Industrial Tribunals Panel, of the Central Arbitration Committee, and of the board of the National Freight Corporation.

Finally, while much of this activity takes place in the metropolis, we must pencil into those diaries large chunks of travelling time, both around Britain, and on international journeyings – some deeply serious, some perhaps less important; all of which make further inroads into our general secretary's time.

The judgements we make about corporatism when we try to think our way into a trade union leader's diary should not be over-simple. Some real and indispensable business is undoubtedly transacted in all this to-ing and fro-ing. But clearly, for the truly conscientious office holder, such a role is impossibly demanding; most importantly it absorbs far too much attention, making it beyond the physical capacity of all but the most resilient occupants to engage in serious sustained discussion with the membership, either to explore their reactions to events or to learn from their initiatives. Quangos, in their season, promote an upwards meshing with the machinery of governments and industry, rather than democratic involvement from below. For the more complacent, such a life, full of honours and status, the chauffeur driven car from home to office, to meeting, to airport, to hotel, to conference centre, must to some extent dull the responses of some people who began their trade union lives as militants. It may also sometimes be materially rewarding. But this is only the most superficial of the problems raised by this spectacle. The deeply perplexing question which arises from the quango state is – what kind of politics does it generate? Some years ago, we felt bound to ask: 'Who briefs these representatives? More important perhaps, who de-briefs them?'[25]

Beyond doubt some significant trade union purposes have been served through the best of the quango mechanisms – for example, in Health and Safety, in ACAS and (more ambiguously) in Manpower Services. Yet even in these best cases it is equally clear that all that vast input of time and commitment has not produced an alternative politics of health and safety, or of manpower planning, or of conciliation, in all of which the trade union role remains subordinate. And the gulf separating the world of quangos from the majority of shop floor members of trade unions is truly rather wide: so that where there is consequent neglect of the interrelationship between leaders and members this may itself be a disruptive influence. This problem must clearly impinge upon the consciousness, and the conscience, of those leaders who do perceive that there is a problem of report back and accountability. Yet within this maze of committees, power appears to depend upon the capturing of seats and positions, and in the making of alliances within them; for a reforming and democratically inclined leader the danger of goal displacement is acute. The expression of policy at this top level is identified with control of delegations, the placing of resolutions, the votes for office, at the expense of the politics of persuasion and of communication with and involvement of members. Moreover, the model produces its reflections and imitations down the ladder of trade unionism to regional and local corporatist counterparts.

In dismantling some, though by no means all, of the quangos, the Thatcher Government has exposed some of the hollowness, above all the dependence on patronage, which the model always involved, and which can now be seen as a surrogate trade union politics. The trade union leadership, immersed in that model for so long, was entirely unprepared for the rupture of its political habits produced by the reversal of corporate bias. It was even less prepared for the aggressive and skilful populism of the government, addressed over the heads of trade union leaders to a membership whose political involvement and education had been neglected for so long. In response, a majority of the General Council thought it best to appeal for clemency.

Early in 1984, the TUC produced an internal paper, 'TUC Strategy'. It represents the considered expression of the school of 'new realism' and, unusually for such a paper, carries the initials of the then General Secretary Len Murray (now Lord Murray), and the TUC education officer, Roy Jackson. It acknowledges very frankly the extent of the setbacks which trade unionism had experienced from four sources: the growth of unemployment, the anti-union policies and legislation of the government, the sustained media scrutiny of the unions' internal machinery, and the electoral swing from Labour, in which trade union members participated strongly.

There is a note of apprehension about the effects of all these circumstances upon members' loyalty to their unions:

> The constant barrage of propaganda could, in the longer term, change the attitude of workers to their unions, in particular young people and those returning to the labour market after some absence. Indeed there is already evidence that members do not identify with some union policies.
>
> Some polls have indicated that there was lack of support from trade unionists for some policies that in part mirrored the TUC position. This suggests that unions have not yet sufficiently involved members in policy development and have failed to inform members of, and win their support for, union policies.

The paper advances a strong claim for the political role of the unions.

It is not surprising that the trade union Movement should have become the foremost voluntary organisation engaged in exercising political influence. It could lay claim to that role on the size of its constituency alone. But it represents far more. The Movement always took very seriously its responsibilities in the political processes of the country. The persistent use of constitutional political pressure by the TUC and unions has helped to shape social policies for the better, particularly over the last 50 years. Through membership of and evidence to Government Committees, through campaigning, by union influence in the Labour Party, sometimes by working with other organisations the trade union Movement has played a major part in shaping the welfare state. The social security system, the Health Service and the nation's school system owes much to the efforts of the trade union Movement. It is on issues such as these that relationships between Government and unions have to be built.

It continues by listing the range of agency involvement which exemplify its responsible role in government.

Equally, since 1909 and the establishment of Labour Exchanges, unions have been directly involved in supporting the work of a range of Government agencies and authorities. That work still goes on – at national level the work of the National Economic Development Council and a range of working parties dealing with different industrial sectors; in the Health and Safety Commission; the Advisory, Conciliation and Arbitration Service; the Manpower Services Commission, supported by 50 Area Manpower Boards on which local trade unionists play a key role; in the Regional and Area Health Authorities; Governing Bodies of schools and colleges; and industrial tribunals. The contribution made by trade unions has been wide-ranging, and Britain is a better place to live in and to work in for their efforts. Trade unions are part of our democratic tradition.

While the paper properly enters a lengthy indictment of the present government's anti-union measures, it insists on the continuity of the trade union participation in tripartite arrangements even today.

But even while reducing its direct relationships with the trade unions the Government has found that trade unions cannot be removed entirely from playing a role in the affairs of the State. In the areas of manpower, and training, and occupational health and safety the Government still relies heavily on Commissions in which the TUC plays a major role. The MSC's responsibilities for instance, have in many respects widened under this Government. The central policies of the MSC – the New Training Initiative – will depend heavily upon unions for their success. Similarly, the Government continues to meet the TUC and CBI monthly in the National Economic Development Council, where recently the

Government has accepted a major role for the Council in identifying where it is possible to generate new jobs in the economy. Trade unionists still also work alongside employers and representatives of Government departments in all the NEDC bodies that continue to examine the constraints and opportunities for development in different industrial sectors. Trade unions also still play a significant role in the bodies concerned with overseeing the administration of different Government and public agencies at regional and local level.

The TUC, in this passage, appears set upon clinging to, and defending, the shadow of corporate benefits, even when their substance has departed.

But the authors of the paper are conscious of the criticism to which that commitment has been subjected, and respond with their own defence.

The process of Government in democratic society cannot be carried on in the isolation of the Cabinet office and Whitehall. Nor can the need to broaden Government by effective responsible and open consultation in which both sides of industry participate be contemptuously rejected as a form of corporatism, to be compared with the fascist corporate state where Government used industry and 'workers' organisations to achieve its totalitarian aims. The trade union Movement seeks involvement, in order to strengthen our Parliamentary democracy, not to weaken it. But that objective has been misrepresented and the Movement has to win back support for Governments broadening the basis of discussion, consultation and involvement always with the purpose of enhancing and complementing Parliamentary democracy.

This response overlooks the distinction drawn by Middlemas between fascist corporatism and 'corporate bias', in which continued participation in, and consent for, corporatist practice is voluntary and may be withdrawn. It also overlooks Middlemas' description of the erosion of Parliamentary initiative in precisely this pluralist evolution. And it further ignores Crouch's concept of 'bargained corporatism', a condition dependent on strong trade unionism and governments that are ready with concessions for the unions' representations. The new realists in the TUC seem determined to hang on to past practices, even when these conditions no longer apply, and when, at shop floor level, much of the ground won in better days is being lost. For example, while the TUC representatives continue to occupy their seats on the Health and Safety Commission, the workplace trade union safety representatives and that network of supporting advice centres which mushroomed across the country in the seventies, now lead a much less secure existence, their teeth drawn in the context of mass unemployment and legal constraints on industrial action.

Also the new realists clearly seek to assert the corporatist role in the political process, impartially of party ties.

The growing involvement of trade unions in government – particularly since the first world war – has been matched by the development of the Labour Party as a major political force. But while the role of Labour Governments has been a major factor in the achievement of trade union economic and social objectives, the basis of current TUC involvement in Government owes much to Churchill's war-time coalition Government and to the Conservative Governments that established the National Economic Development Council and the Manpower Services Commission.

Many unions, of course, have chosen to exercise their right, enshrined in law, to give considerable direct support to the Labour Party. About half the TUC unions affiliate to the Labour Party. Trade union support and involvement in political parties is found wherever democratic Parliamentary systems exist, providing an alternative to political parties supported by capital and similar employer interests. This is true of almost all countries in the European Community and of longer established Parliamentary systems in the Commonwealth. In the United States, Democratic Party organisation is often dependent on trade union support organised through the American Federation of Labor/Congress of Industrial Organizations.

Significantly, the American political model, with its politically neutral trade unions, is a model very much closer to Mrs Thatcher's heart than that of British practice.

The most extensive and serious attempt by the unions and the TUC to reach down in communication with its constituents during the years of bargained corporatism of the 1970s, has been, in fact, the elaborate and professionalized pattern of the trade union (particularly TUC-sponsored) shop steward training schemes. While this training has been technically very competent, two features stand out in the context of our present concerns.

First, training facilities have been concentrated on the active minority – almost exclusively on the shop stewards. Secondly, the curriculum has for the most part been studiously non-political. It was originally designed to promote shop stewards as effective micro-level bargainers and grievance handlers, and to encourage their acquisition of status in the company, the enhancement of the facilities at their disposal and what Batstone and his colleagues[26] have called 'strong' bargaining relations with their employers. Such a curriculum and purpose gave little or no assistance to shop stewards in critically interpreting their leaders' corporate roles, which might have helped to develop accountability in discharging those tasks. Neither did it help in constructively encouraging them to interpret and express the political significance of their members' alienation from the corporate processes, going on 'up there'. Of course, the shop steward activists express their members' pressures willy-nilly, and this expression, in the form of a kind of non-political militancy, can easily be misinterpreted in political terms as a kind of nascent syndicalism.

In their preoccupation with corporate life at the top, union leaders, particularly those with genuinely socialist aspirations, could make the fatal assumption that 'the activist minority . . . were simply co-terminous with the membership at large'.[27] For union leaders are heavily reliant, for their rudimentary communications with their members, upon that active minority. The habits of mind engendered in corporatist planning schemes produce a flow of literature in the form of TUC Economic Reviews, schemes for macro-economic planning and for the Alternative Economic Strategy, whose abstract, arcane language is the reverse of populist, and which serves in some ways to further widen the gulf of which we are speaking. The art of popular communication, designed to stimulate thought and responsive action, does not flourish in this climate and this structure.

The activist minority, therefore, had an impossible role under corporatism. It was caught between its loyalty to a leadership pursuing remote objectives at the top, and its own members' disaffection with failures in successive 'social contracts'. In the last of these projects, the only one which was actually called a 'social contract', narrowing differentials of the skilled workers in the private sector promoted a substantial defection to the new Toryism in 1979. In a savagely paradoxical parallel, the struggles of the low paid workers in the public sector led to mass strikes which precipitated still further electoral support for Mrs Thatcher. This view of the reasons for the 1979 General Election result has been widely echoed in many commentaries. Here we simply urge an appreciation of the extent to which the state of trade union politics contributed to this result. The more this is understood, the easier it may be to prepare an alternative. It is one thing to understand the practice of corporatism at the top. Equally important is to understand its impact at the bottom, where, we may safely assert that, while it provoked a sharp defensive revolt against wage restraint, it did not at all generate the kind of radicalism (still less revolutionism) to prepare the working people for direct combat when Mrs Thatcher pulled the rug from under the old corporate system.

So far, we have reviewed the impact of mass unemployment on trade union strength, and sought to demonstrate the limits of the policy of bargained corporatism which featured large in trade union strategy before the great slump of the 1980s. In its latest essay, the TUC–Labour Party Liaison Committee harks back, partially, to the corporatist mode. But both the legacy of corporatism and the current phase of mass unemployment have combined to expose some deep organizational problems within British trade unionism. While these have been exacerbated by the present government's Employment and Trade Union Acts, as we shall see, they would have emerged even without this additional source of disruption to established trade union norms.

A renewed trade unionism, capable of popular and democratic political initiative, now needs to tackle its organizational problems as never before. This realization is beginning to grow, as unions examine more critically their recent experience. For example, the TGWU discovered in the miners' strike that it was unable even to identify its own membership in road haulage in order to organize effective measures of support. Indeed, the miners themselves suffered from this problem, while the Coal Board intervened strenuously with letters to NUM members and regular polls of opinion. Perhaps in response to these lessons, the TGWU is now moving rapidly ahead to computerize its rosters.

The 1984 Trade Union Act has shown that the problem of keeping registers of members' addresses, a rudimentary necessity indeed, is not confined to lorry drivers. These are the tip of an iceberg of organizational deficiencies, which require urgent attention.[28]

Many British trade unions have forgotten how to organize independently. In post-war Britain they have become heavily dependent upon management and the state for organizational supports, and many of these supports are being withdrawn. Employers have only ever recognized and encouraged trade unions when it has been in their interests to do so. This interest is no longer automatically evident, in an era of mass unemployment, and when the state's hostility to trade unionism leads to the withdrawal of its legal protection from, and encouragement of, them. In the United States trade unionists have been permanently accustomed to such conditions; when they observe the British scene, they are highly critical of what appears to them careless and amateurish organization in our unions.

The closed shop and the check-off system, widely regarded in the past as promoting stability and security for trade unions, now appear in a new light. We should add to these devices the effects of the Bridlington Agreement, which sometimes reinforces complacency in organization through its protection of unions from competitive pressure. The combination of all these measures has been, to some extent, to distance the unions from their members, even to the point, as we have seen, when unions may not know who their members are, or where they live! The closed shop has not crumbled at a stroke before the balloting requirements of the recent legislation, but it could be vulnerable to them in future, particularly in the public sector where the closed shop contributed substantially to the expansion of membership during the 1970s.

In general, the areas of decline in British industry are concentrated where trade unionism has been most strong. The growth sectors of the economy are in unorganized spheres, such as personal private services and small business. The government's emphasis on the American model of growth through the small firm sector is only another strand in its general drive to free industry from the presence of strong trade unions. The social geography which has become dominant over the past twenty years has separated home, community and workplace, and led to wider dispersal of the labour force. Regional patterns reinforce this trend; the Northern towns – with trade union traditions deeply embedded – decline, while growth occurs in the Thames valley and the South West, where trade unionism must build on weaker foundations.

Trade union structures reflect the inheritance of the nineteenth century, based on geographical area for the branch, the district, and the region. Yet there is little place today for the time honoured 'district rate' and 'district' negotiations. Such edifices creak under an inappropriate weight of past tradition and method.

Trade union information services to their members are equally often in need of modernization. Information flows are commonly inadequate in scale, so news reaches the shop floor too late, and in poor forms. They compare very badly with the fast, familiar and colloquial messages dispersed daily by the media. Trade union information conveys facts, rather than reasoning or method; *what*, rather than *why* or *how*, and hence induces only passivity. Members are told what to think, not what to do. Above all, since the death of the *Daily Herald*, the unions lack a representative organ of opinion and debate. Given the will, this lack could easily be overcome.

Participation and democratic involvement is too commonly focused on a narrow group of activists, whose separation from the mass membership may lead them to think in terms of 'capturing' seats and votes, not on 'winning' them through argument and debate. Policy is advanced through the passing of formal *resolutions*; hence the emphasis on the importance of the formal *meeting*, which becomes a substitute for wider action and communication. In consequence of these habits, organization is separated from policy; for example, low pay (policy) is pre-eminently a *women*'s issue (organization). Trade union structures emphasize hierarchy, to such an extent that branch secretaries may still be discouraged, sometimes with a heavy hand, from communicating with each other, horizontally. Everything must pass up and down, seldom sideways.

All of this contributes weightily to the separation of trade unions, and trade unionists, from the politics of experience, from the wider community and from society. It fosters exclusivity among the activists. The old 'ten per cent democracy' of the AUEW's former branch balloting methods exemplified this narrow activist base. But postal balloting, whether internally determined or imposed by government, provides no answer. Nor, even, does the workplace, which can no longer be seen as the only place where trade union activism must flourish. While this book is not about organization, it is necessary to our concerns to emphasize the interdependence of organization, democracy and politics.

The expectation among some Marxists that, learning from the corporate encumbrances of past Labour governments, and provoked by the militant anti-unionism of the present government, trade union members might embrace 'class politics'[29] through ever-widening solidarity action, has, in this context, been cruelly disappointed by the responses to the miners' strike of 1984–5. Colin Crouch pours cold water on this kind of expectation:

> If you are a trade union official in contemporary Britain you do not have even the embryo of a revolutionary working class anywhere remotely near you. You do have a good deal of syndicalism in the shape of shop-floor activity entirely uninterested in politics, and you do have the prospect of mass unemployment as a possible political response to union power. That is the context within which union action takes place. To construct an entire theory of trade unionism around a non-existent phenomenon – the revolutionary working class – is to produce something of limited usefulness in understanding the real day-to-day choices of trade unions and their members. But that is what Marxist sociology has chosen to do.[30]

The problem then, if we find corporatist prescriptions unsatisfying and wishful revolutionary models unsatisfactory, is to find a space for a trade union politics which might bring together national and local trade unionism, and which could close ranks against the destabilizing device of trade-union-government-by-referendum which the 1984 Trade Union Act has inserted into the gulf with such disorientating consequences. If they do not want a revolution, British workers certainly do not want mass unemployment: they could find a use for the politics of full employment. In the absence of such politics (which must not merely include, but be hinged around, a vital international dimension) even trade union leaders of the moderate wing are driven to obviously hollow rhetoric. For example, in spring 1985 David Basnett forecast the growth of an 'insurrectionary' trade unionism if the government did not treat the unions better. It seems wiser to see in this an exasperated response to Mrs Thatcher's strident triumphalism after the miners' defeat rather than a considered prediction.

Before she came to office, Mrs Thatcher gave it to be understood that she would cut out vast forests of dead wood among the quangos. In fact, her woodmen have spared many trees. The result is a particularly lethal twist to the government's strategy of neutralizing trade unions. At the top, union leaders are still called away from their members on a wide variety of unproductive assignments, some of which are now truly fool's errands. At the grassroots, governmental legislation produces continuous elections and referenda, in the context of a permanent media hunt for irregularities and sharp practices. There is no way that trade unions can win this contest, as we shall see in the chapters that follow. Voluntary organizations can never impose more meticulous standards than those which are maintained by states, with all their elaborate professional apparatus. Not one single Member of Parliament would find his election beyond reproach if some of the more censorious of recent criticisms of trade union elections were taken seriously on the political stage.

The result is that lay activists in trade unions find themselves under increasing criticism, members are inoculated with wholly unjustifiable doubts, and every effort is made to discredit the intentions of leaders. That this is disruption, no one can doubt. Millions of honest, caring trade unionists, including those at the top no less than all the ordinary members, have only one real defence: to work out plausible alternative political goals, and to pursue them through methods which have been elaborated and understood in common.

A new school of trade union leadership could begin this work by turning their activists towards their members, first to listen, and then to campaign to close the ranks for agreed objectives. A 'listening month' of systematic consultation in the workplaces would at least reduce inappropriate responses. Campaigning years should follow, to win united support for the politics of full employment. Whatever may be thought of the corporatist experience, in the 1980s half a million unionists in Hyde Park would be worth more than a whole flotilla of quangos.

APPENDIX 2.1   THE 'CORPORATE BIAS' THESIS

The establishment and proof of Middlemas' thesis is pursued through the use of historical data beginning with an analysis of the structures of society and politics in the Edwardian era. It is in this period that Middlemas finds that the accepted and simplistic explanations of Britain's political coherence, based on formal constitutional law, the national tradition of Parliamentary reformism and the assumption of 'popular consent to the law of the constitution' were breaking down. Government is in fact a 'complicated machine' and the Edwardians had no critical theory to explain its reality, or to tackle the question of how the country was in fact governed between general elections.

Hobbesian explanations of the state as a coercive force holding together an undifferentiated mass of competing individuals, or the traditional Tory reliance on deference, were becoming inadequate, as was the eighteenth century assumption of contract. They did not make apparent the methods by which consent of the governed was to be achieved and expressed.

Ostensibly, the achievement of the nineteenth century had been the establishment of the supremacy of party government through Parliament. Offsetting this supreme power was a wide range of other institutions which are passed in review by Middlemas. These included the civil service, notably the Treasury, the monarch, the popular press, 'gifted outsiders' among the intellectual establishment, regional and civic powers, the churches, the Law Society and judiciary, and social investigators and statisticians such as Rowntree and Bowley. None of these groupings or institutions was judged adequate to a full explanation of the complexities of sovereignty, since there was emerging a new force – the organized working class, which remained unassimilated into the structural analysis. The Webbs, of course, were pre-eminent among Edwardians in discerning this, but in their version, the organized working class was to be 'guided . . . by unassuming experts' and in that view might be adequately considered alongside churches and other institutions without qualitative distinction. It is the virtue of Middlemas that he affirms from the outset that 'The phenomenon of the organised working class could neither be transmuted into conventional theory of Parliamentary consent, nor resisted with jeremiads about the dangers of democracy derived from J. S. Mill, de Tocqueville and Robert Lowe's opposition to the Suffrage Bill of 1866'.

The Edwardians began to study the working class, its poverty and its institutions, and to evolve the reforms made necessary by its political emergence, in order to retain social stability. Yet while seeking means to 'incorporate working class ambitions', politicians found it difficult to acknowledge collective political and industrial activity outside the established forms and structures. Was this activity a threat to be suppressed, or was it in fact amenable to incorporation? State education had at this stage hardly progressed beyond a dismal minimum standard, although a handful of radicals had participated in the formation of the WEA, while the Labour College movement began its work among the unions. The best that state schools offered was the prospect of individual 'ladder-climbing' for the bright working class pupil. The mass was denied any political or civic education. But the need for incorporation became acute with the outbreak of persistent social and industrial unrest between the years 1910 and 1914.

Among the established political parties, it was the Conservatives who adjusted best to the new phenomenon, consciously overhauling their party organization and appeal in the deliberate search for working class votes. They set aside former assumptions of automatic deference; their new respect for the alliance with the working class was expressed, for example, in their restrained opposition, falling short of impedance, to the Trades Disputes Bill of 1906. The Liberals, in contrast, failed to populize their politics or their structures, while the new Labour Party was torn between trade union pressure politics and the affirmation of socialist goals. On key issues, such as female suffrage, temperance, immigration and the Irish question, populism benefited the Conservatives.

The employers' organizations at this stage expressed a quite non-corporate, often brutal, opposition to trade union growth and recognition. During the 1890s the Shipping Federation and the Engineering Employers' Federation had conducted savage assaults against trade unionism in their industries. Significantly, the engineering employers also strengthened their Parliamentary Committee in 1898 in order the better 'to oppose . . . the influence of the TUC in Parliament'. Both sides, however, retained a deep distrust for the political process, and their political evolution ran on parallel lines. The TUC was gripped by a Victorian fear of state encroachment into the trade union preserves of wage fixing and social insurance, and viewed the still modest Labour Party as 'adequate for the purposes for which it had been founded'.

This treatment of the Edwardians' 'problem' handles the ferments of syndicalism, industrial unionism, guild socialism and mass strike action of the period not as the alternative expression of working class ambitions but as a symptom of that 'problem', calling for an intelligent, self-interested response from the political establishment. The goal is conservative but benevolent: the evolution and adaptation of attitudes and structures to head-off what might become hegemonic working class politics into manageable channels. The working class is certainly acknowledged as an actor, but not an actor–manager, far less as the author of the lines it must speak.

In the First World War, employers at the local level 'actually ran the war effort' while nationally 'the business community reached to the centre of Government . . .' The trade unions on their side underwent a parallel reappraisal of their role in government and the management of the economy. But the symmetry is spoilt, as so often in this total historical portrayal, by radical rank and file responses.

The shop stewards' wartime movement deprived the TUC of much of the authority needed to implement full-blooded corporatism and imposed a more overtly political role, in evolving a joint post-war reconstruction policy with the Labour Party. As the war drew to its close, a potential 'socialist front' ranging across from the Parliamentary Labour leadership, through the ILP, the TUC, to the Shop Stewards' Movement on the left, confronted Lloyd George's centre bloc of mixed Liberals and Conservatives. This centre was thus compelled to offer a version of state capitalism in a bid to hold and expand post-war working class electoral support. As part of that bid, the centre politicians, together with employers' organizations, sought to detach the workshop organization from the Labour–TUC alliance by offering forms of 'worker participation'. Included in this package were Whitleyism, and industrial harmony through the grand but amorphous design of 'industrial parliaments', as well as National Industrial Conference and joint consultative committees. Employers contributed by granting varying degrees of recognition to the shop stewards. The employers discovered a 'collective understanding that a strong TUC was the best defence against rank and file indiscipline'. Yet at the same time, harder heads and counsels were preparing the show-down of 1926, since at the stage of corporatism reached in the early 1920s, the TUC had not yet achieved fully representative status and 'the balance between TUC and employers was not yet so level that trade union leaders could ignore the rudiments of the class struggle'. The whole conception of a centre bloc implementing corporate politics as for this reason premature, and Lloyd George's coalition strategy collapsed.

Middlemas' account moves through the great industrial–political crises of the 1920s and 1930s to trace the ebb and flow of corporate bias, as discovered in the vacillating policies of employers, governments and the TUC.

He thus discerns a trend, which is towards the ripening of corporate methods and practice. Of course, progress in this direction was not crudely linear. Subtle advances and retreats mark the front between the three distinct elements.

Thus, even as the gathering crisis over wage levels and the coal industry approached its crisis, Prime Minister Baldwin was heard disassociating the government from a Tory private member's Bill aimed at weakening the union's political levy system (the MacQuisten Bill) and making a famous 'peace in our time' speech which won the applause of the National Council of Employers' Organizations. The same NCEO, moreover, carefully hedged its bets in the General Strike, at first giving private encouragement to the coal owners, but gingerly distancing itself from them during and after the event. The employers did not wish to risk the political influence of their central organization in public support of the intransigent coal owners. Interestingly, it expected a similar cautious pragmatism from the TUC.

Middlemas himself describes the TUC's support for the strike as 'foolish by their standards'. The NCEO's assessment is understandable: their judgement that the TUC would 'pay the price of wage-cutting without a fight' was based on the palpable evidence of the TUC opposition to the Triple Alliance's militancy of 1921. Middlemas has the benefit of not only hindsight, but also his own initial perception of the impossibility of incorporating the analysis of the organized working class inside conventional constitutional theories. The constraints on the TUC's assumption of uninhibited corporatism are evident at each stage of its evolution – constraints exercised by its democratic constituents, and by their alternative altogether more radical version of trade union politics.

Successive convergences by the TUC on a corporate solution have been followed by partial withdrawals (as in 1984); these look 'foolish' only if the observer forgets the ultimately democratic nature of labour movement institutions, a nature which is not adequately embraced by a nod towards that 'element of representativeness' in the description of 'corporate bias'.

Following his theme through to the 1970s, Middlemas advances the not unfamiliar view that Parliamentary sovereignty has increasingly become a fiction. To this perspective, he adds the extra dimension that corporate bias has risen as political party dominance has declined from its nineteenth century heyday. A genuine two-party system existed before 1915, and again between 1922 and 1931. Between 1915 and 1922, and between 1931 and 1945 there was no two-party system. It is noteworthy that in his later *New Statesman* articles of 1983[31] Middlemas spoke of Thatcherism as the re-affirmation of the supremacy of party over corporate interest group government. More, within his chosen period (1911–45) it was only in 1922 that the ideological element of party contributed much to any important crisis. He ascribes the origin of the deep change in the nature of Government to the First World War and the contribution of Lloyd George to the creation of a centrist, corporate bloc above party.

As a result of this change, any explanation of the real division of power must accord great weight to the industrial institutions, as distinct from the 'dignified' version of the constitution. Already, well before 1940, Parliament, as distinct from government, had lost the power of initiating policy and legislation, while 'electoral competition drives the parties towards the ideological centre'. After 1926, for example, the Tories greatly moderated their anti-union and anti-socialist policies and evolved much more sensitive responses to labour issues. In order to ensure that these new attitudes held up against the right-wing pressures of its own membership, the Tory Party centralized control of its own party machinery. A similar process went on in the Labour Party – the pursuit of Parliamentary 'respectability' under Macdonald and subsequent leaders required top-down control of the Party and a demotion of the extra-Parliamentary socialism of the ILP and its successors. But there is a constraint at work here: 'The Labour Party always needed the unions; the unions did not always need the Labour Party'.[32]

How did the industrial institutions relate to party dominance? Middlemas believes that the employers' bodies had no power during the period of the two-party system. They could only dream of a truly 'national' party. Similarly, the TUC failed to establish its rights to participation in the Labour Government of Macdonald, who resented any union challenge to Parliamentary sovereignty.

Following the crisis of 1931, however, what then evolved was government based on 'crisis avoidance' and on brokerage between government and the institutions, to 'the gradual exclusion of purely party voices'. The techniques of Keynesian management furthered this process into the post-war era of Butksellism. It was in this climate, that the TUC reasserted the centrality of its role, pointing to:

> the manifest reluctance on the part of the late Labour Government to have contact with the General Council. That state of affairs must be righted . . . The primary purpose of the creation of the party should not be forgotten. It was created by the Trade Union Movement to do those things in Parliament which the Trade Union Movement found ineffectively performed by the two-party system.[33]

In November 1931 the TUC declared 'The General Council should be regarded as having an integral right to initiate and participate in any political matter which it deems to be of direct concern to its constituents'.[34] It is interesting to juxtapose this statement against the distancing of the TUC from the Labour Party attempted in the General Council after the 1983 General Election defeat.

Bevin, in the 1930s, regarded the Labour Party as under TUC tutelage: he spoke of the 1920s as the days of advocacy, and of the 1930s as the period of administration. At the 1937 TUC he claimed that 'The trade union movement has become an integral part of the state'. (But we should note that this claim and this argument was to be repeated in later generations: thus Woodcock in polemic with Cousins in the 1960s, and Murray versus his TUC critics in the 1980s. The debate is not over; the role of the TUC remains not a little ambiguous.)

In the 1930s, the Tory radicals developed a middle way between Parliamentary rule and corporatism, as may be seen in Harold MacMillan's contribution for example. After 1940 the most significant attack on party supremacy derives from the Liberal contributions to welfare and economic management associated with Beveridge and Keynes. Class politics becomes more and more confined to internal exchanges within the parties as the system moves towards the Butskellism of the 1950s.

At the end of his chapter on the Parliamentary illusion, Middlemas acknowledges the collapse of Butskellism:

For forty years after 1926 Parliament ceased to give sufficient space to ideological divisions in society, and for a time it appeared as if the divisions themselves had disappeared. Those who welcomed an 'end of ideology' however, either ignored or discounted the sheer good fortune which sustained the remarkable (indeed by historical standards, unnatural) prosperity of the 1950s, just as they overestimated the capacity of governments, civil servants, and institutions to achieve compromise once profound economic disparities reappeared. So long as prosperity lasted, the illusion held good that the mass of people acquiesced in the politics of institutional collaboration. But Britain's post-war recovery produced vast changes in the balance between manufacturing and service industry, with repercussions on union and management organisation which put an intolerable strain on their arrangements with government even before multiple forms of breakdown emerged in the mid-1960s. By then the parties had become so debilitated that they proved incapable of giving a lead and had instead to respond hastily and ineffectively *in defence* of the triangular system – in the greatest possible contrast to the ideals of the 'true party men' of 1922.[35]

Between 1911 and 1945, Middlemas claims, a new order was definitely established: not in precise, legal or constitutional forms, but as an understood 'code' or trend. In the long crisis of government, manpower and economic management between 1900 and 1920, 'governments stimulated institutional growth among bodies representing business and labour interests, in order to maintain public consent'. Subsequently, these institutions continued the evolution of a 'complicated ritual' of actual governing institutions; but they were always exposed to popular discontent and their members' right of recall, hence their tendency to develop 'secretive' patterns of behaviour. Even so, governments could not continuously rely on them as if they had been real 'estates of the realm'. The tripartite method was tentative and fragile. 'Progress towards institutional collaboration and the avoidance of economic competition and class conflict is a tendency, not an irreversible trend'. And, Middlemas claims:

> In direct contrast to the rigid links laid down – though not necessarily implemented – in the Fascist constitutions of Italy or Portugal, or the totalitarian systems of Hitler's Germany and Stalin's Russia, the British system in the half-century after 1916 depended on a multiple bargaining process at all levels . . . even though its aims of social harmony, economic well-being and the avoidance of crisis were not dissimilar.[36]

But Butskellism had its day: class tension reappeared in the period between 1964 and 1975. The TUC had to respond to the political requirements of its members – expressed in the role of Jack Jones and Hugh Scanlon. Weakened in its corporate role by these pressures, the

TUC entered a phase of greater direct political involvement, through its central role in the TUC–Labour Party Liaison Committee, and in its direct influence on Labour's legislative programme of 1974-6.[37] Class responses were not missing either, on the employers' side, for example in the CBI response to the Bullock Report and to the idea of compulsory planning agreements.[38]

None the less, Middlemas clings (in the face of evidence already existing in 1979, the date of his book) affectionately to his main argument:

> This thesis depends on a study of the totality of the system, not of its component parts according to prior definitions of each one's functions; I do not deny that, in terms of those individual, non-political, functions, the behaviour of governing institutions and the balance of forces between them – say between management and unions in the purely industrial field – might look different. Nor do I deny the existence of distinctive class interests in those spheres, rising in times of general political crisis to colour, and perhaps determine temporarily the workings of the political system. But *normally* the system has worked otherwise, according to the harmonising activity of government and the governing institutions and political parties, each in their own way mediating between state and nation.[39]

APPENDIX 2.2   THE TUC–LABOUR LIAISON COMMITTEE

The TUC–Labour Party Liaison Committee was established, without public flourishes, in January 1972, 'to discuss policies in the field of industrial relations and the management of the economy'[40] The committee has no formal constitution, but comprises by agreement six members of the TUC General Council, six from the Party's National Executive Committee and six from the Parliamentary Labour Party. Throughout its existence, all three bodies have nominated their senior members as their representatives. The General Secretaries of the TUC itself and of the largest unions have always been members, as have the Labour Party's leaders (who were, of course, Prime Ministers between 1974 and 1979). We may follow the formal summaries of discussions and decisions, though not its inner workings, through the Annual Reports.

The political climate on its inception was dominated by the Heath Government's Industrial Relations Act (1971) and by the evolution of a Labour counter-strategy in industrial relations and economic policy. The Industrial Relations Act pushed the trade unions into closer relations with the Labour Party than they had enjoyed for many years, as they realized the inescapable need to place Labour in power at the earliest opportunity in order to remove that Act from the statute book before it had emasculated them. In origin therefore, the Liaison Committee (LC) symbolized a large swing of the pendulum in favour of political action. But in its later developments through the years of Labour government in the seventies, its deliberations lapsed into the corporate spirit more and more, as Labour in office strove to hold together the incompatible objectives of social and economic reform while bending under heavy external pressures from the IMF which were pushing it towards monetarism and a resumption of restraint on trade union bargaining powers.

But in 1972 the LC silently abandoned the earlier controversy between Harold Wilson and the TUC caused by Labour's proposed curbs on union independence contained in the White Paper 'In Place of Strife' of 1969. These unilateral government initiatives would, if continued, have sundered Labour's relations with the unions. In their place was created, through the LC, a comprehensive process of policy-making for what amounted to a new industrial constitution, giving trade unions unprecedented status and working people a wide range of new individual employment rights. Although the rhetoric of this programme resounded with appeals to industrial and social democracy, it nevertheless seemed entirely adequate and appropriate to its authors that the whole process was directed by an ad hoc committee at the apex of the movement – the TUC, PLP and NEC. The ultimate downfall of its high hopes, in 1979, can be at least in part attributed to this centralized mode of operation.

The first meetings of the LC were concerned with the Industrial Relations Act, which it totally opposed, and which it declared would be repealed by an incoming Labour government. In its place, Labour would legislate for the renewal and extension of trade union protection from legal liabilities in industrial action, and for an independent non-governmental conciliation and arbitration service – the concept subsequently embodied in ACAS. It is significant that, parallel with the LC discussion of this idea, the TUC and the CBI held separate meetings in 1972 which reached a wide measure of agreement on the need for such a service. It was agreed in both forums that the service should be run by a tripartite council – a key example of the type of quango-style institutions on which Labour relied in its 1974–9 legislation. The whole approach of the LC to industrial relations reform harked back to the pragmatic, institutional mode of the Donovan Commission of 1968, and away from legalistic intervention. In the field of employment rights, however, the TUC showed a new willingness to use the law for protective purposes, beyond the limited scope of the Factories Acts, Wages Councils law, and similar devices handed down by Victorian and Edwardian governments.

Beyond these two themes, the LC's third concern was with economic and industrial strategy for growth and full employment, based on a combined Keynesian and interventionist programme. To this was added a new element in the sustained attention given to manpower planning and industrial training. This, deriving from the much-admired Swedish model, constituted a recognition that future employment patterns were threatened with major upheaval through economic and technological change. The management of this change was to be placed in the hands of another tripartite quango, a National Manpower Board, which materialized in Labour's legislation as the Manpower Services Commission. The final item on early LC agendas was an agreement on the need for government action to promote industrial democracy through disclosure of company information and reform of the Companies Acts.

In 1973, on the eve of the convulsions which precipitated Labour into office, the LC published the first of its series of policy statements – *Economic Policy and the Cost of Living* – which foreshadowed the major planks of Labour's election policy, often described in retrospect as its most radical since 1945. Thus, Labour would impose price controls, reform housing and rent policy, extend public transport, redistribute income and wealth, phase out social charges (prescription charges would be the first to go), increase pensions, generate economic growth, investment and full employment, dynamize regional policy and extend the scope of collective bargaining to raise industrial efficiency. The multinational companies would be subject to planning agreements in which the trade unions would have a role. Industrial democracy measures would include provision for 'joint control over investment and closure decisions'. Yet the institutional bases of these policies would be tripartite and change would be through agreement, not compulsion. Above all, the 'first task' of a Labour government would be to agree policy with the TUC.

On pay policy, this major document was silent, although its commitments were soon to be evoked as the Labour Government's side of the Social Contract, fulfilment of which was expected to lead to trade union cooperation in restraining wage increases. However, the fact that the TUC had participated in so intimate and direct a manner in framing a policy statement, subsequently published by the Labour Party, and forming the basis of a government's legislative programme, was without precedent.

For two years after Labour's return to office, the TUC's annual summaries of the LC's proceedings shrank to brief paragraphs, no doubt reflecting the fact that the 1973 document had an impetus carrying the partners through the first phase of government legislation without the need for major reappraisal. However, the LC continued to meet regularly, discussing pending legislation, industrial democracy, the EEC, collective bargaining and the Social Contract. In 1976 the LC once again issued a major public declaration with its second statement, *The Next Three Years and the Problem of Priorities*. In the drafting of this, it was proudly asserted, there had been 'major ministerial involvement'. In its tone, the document reflects the change in economic and political climate which had brought the IMF to Whitehall, and changed the high expectations of all the partners on the LC – the beginning of a progressive sense of frustration and disappointment is evident.

The document begins with the assertion that the committee's earlier publication had exercised a big influence in shaping Labour's 1974–5 programme. It was during this period that the popular press ascribed more political power to Jack Jones than to the Prime Minister, and it was widely noised in the press that the trade unions were 'running the government'. Although this was always a misrepresentation of the real balance of forces, the document's celebration of the close cooperation achieved between unions and government during the £6-a-week flat rate phase of Social Contract wages policy does reflect the momentary position of high influence which Jack Jones and his colleagues achieved. The document ascribed the willingness of foreign Central Banks to come to government's aid with a loan to the evidence of solidarity prevailing between the partners of the LC.

But the document's main concern was with Britain's twin debits, on international payments and on the government's budget. The partners still clung to an embattled Keynesian orthodoxy – it 'made sense' to run a budget deficit at a time of high unemployment. But it was now time to 'level-off' public spending. This gave rise to the discussion of 'priorities', amongst which featured such items as the Temporary Employment Subsidy and the expansion of MSC training programmes, especially for the young unemployed – what we would all later learn to call 'supply-side' measures. The NEDC sector plans for manufacturing investment were also crucial; the increasing tendency for top companies to direct their investments abroad was lamented. The raising of the NEB's disposable funds to £1 billion a year, the enforcement of planning agreements with the top 100 companies, legislation for industrial democracy and the creation of a counter-cyclical Investment Reserve Fund financed from company profits, were all urged as vital next steps.

These demands recur annually thereafter until Labour's defeat in 1979, without ever coming near to being met. Similar frustration is experienced whenever the LC discusses, through those years, the Wealth Tax, social equality, the opening up of government to public scrutiny and accountability, the reform of the Official Secrets Act and the abolition of the House of Lords. The irony in both the contents and the tone of this and later documents of the LC is that, while they reflect the growing anxieties of the trade union wing of the partnership (and no doubt of some members from the NEC), the appearance of solidarity is preserved by their being presented always with the endorsement of the Prime Minister and ministerial wing, who were themselves of course directly responsible for the procrastination under criticism.

In 1977 came another publication from the LC, *The Next Three Years and Into the Eighties*. For the first time, it conceded grounds to the critics of Keynes: 'traditional policies . . . [are] not sufficient to accomplish the goals of full employment, economic growth, and stable prices'.

Let us look at the situation in detail. The world is now reeling from the collapse of the post-war monetary system, the oil price crisis, enhanced inflation and economic recession. The LC again repeats, 'as a matter of urgency, we must reach planning agreements with at least the majority of the top 100 companies'. On industrial democracy and the proposals of the Bullock Committee 'we re-affirm that this policy is an important priority for enactment'. The NEB should have its £1 billion fund 'as early as possible', says the LC. The implementation of the industrial strategy and the negotiation of planning agreements are 'major problems' but the hostility of the CBI 'will not stand in the way of these vital reforms'.

In place of the full employment goal, it is now clear that the MSC's programmes of training and Youth Opportunities are assuming the shape of their contemporary role of mitigators of the permanent unemployment which is becoming entrenched in the economy.

The blight of the inner cities also received its recognition as a permanent problem in a White Paper to be followed by the Inner Areas Act of 1978. Under the constraints imposed upon the government by the IMF and the result of its minority position in Parliament, these are the kinds of measures that succeed in reaching the statute book, at the expense of the radical redistribution of wealth and power promised in 1974 and to which the LC makes increasingly nostalgic references.

The list of the government's unfulfilled obligations in income and wealth redistribution becomes extensive, and the LC's tone is increasingly exhortative: the government 'should' press on with the wealth tax, it 'should' amend the capital gains tax, on pensions 'more must be achieved', price controls 'must be used', etc. Also there 'must' be more open government, the Common Agricultural Policy 'should be reformed'. Even more serious for government are the complaints about the low level of appreciation shown for the role of trade unions in sustaining social consensus, and the first calls for the return of free collective bargaining. A new industrial democracy demand is raised: for the joint control of company pensions schemes. It is clearly the TUC side which is responsible for the exhortation; on the government side there is less and less regard for both the commitments and the aspirations. Moreover, because of the top level, closed nature of the LC's proceedings, together with the TUC's role as moderator of wage pressures, Congress House is unable to mobilize constructive popular participation as a counter pressure to the dominant forces of IMF and City. The unions are caught up in a process no longer expressive of political, party sovereignty but of an unproductive, and always subordinate corporatist relationship with 'its' government.

In 1978 there is more of the same. A new statement, *Into the Eighties: An Agreement*, continues to reflect the partnership's decline. Although it remains 'essential to conclude . . . planning agreements with all the major companies', and the government will legislate to this end, they should be pursued only 'where possible'. [A reminder may be necessary: only one planning agreement was concluded with a private company – the multinational Chrysler car company – during Labour's term of office. It was so loosely binding that it was readily disregarded by the firm. In the public sector, for which such proposals were not designed, the ill-fated *Plan for Coal* may also be classified as a planning agreement. As we have seen to our cost it too has since been overridden by managerial and government power in the 1980s.]

The 1978 statement gives a welcome to the highly diluted form of industrial democracy through company reform promised in a White Paper which emasculated the Bullock Report's proposals on worker representation on company boards, even though Bullock itself was a compromise on the original TUC demand for 50 per cent trade union seats on such boards. The LC asserts forlornly that 'the government does not exclude parity as an ultimate outcome . . . this is clearly still our objective'. The White Paper proposal (for one-third of board places to be occupied by trade unionists) would, says the LC, be fully operative 'in the next Parliament'. In the event, after five years of procrastination, the 'next Parliament' passed into the hands of Mrs Thatcher. Yet even to the last, in the 1978 General Council report, the TUC recorded again the importance which it attached to an industrial democracy act, and to planning agreements, and that 'the Prime Minister accepted this and also that the enactment of the government's proposals should be given a high priority'.

On pay, the 1978 document juxtaposes the incompatible assertions of the unions, that collective bargaining is vital to the trade unions' functions, and of the government, that as the employer it must have a strong influence on public sector pay levels; this contradiction foreshadows the Winter of Discontent and the electoral defeat of 1979. But there was a last effort to preserve the government–trade union consensus in the teeth of the strike wave against pay restraint in the public sector. Omitting the Labour Party NEC element, the TUC and government issued a bilateral statement, *The Economy, The Government and Trade Union Responsibilities*, (14 February 1979). This statement endorsed the TUC's guides *Negotiating Procedures, Conduct of Disputes*, and *Union Organization* (published simultaneously), which were intended to reverse the hostile picture emerging in the media of 'irresponsible', strike-prone public sector and road haulage unions.

In departing from the LC forum in this crisis, and reverting to the older summitry of direct meetings between Prime Minister and TUC General Council, the partners signalled the end of the unique *political* relationship which characterized the LC in its hey-day. The TUC 'guides' urged strikers to maintain supplies and services 'essential to the health and safety of the community', to maintain plant and equipment and to sustain livestock during industrial disputes. [TV pictures of dead poultry, allegedly victims of the disruption of feedstuff supplies, played their part, along with interruptions to funeral services, in preparing the way for Labour's defeat.]

Offering their advice on picketing and strike ballots, the TUC went as far as to concede the case of the Conservative Party (and the press) on the conduct of the strikes, and gave damagingly defensive rulings on the operation of the closed shop, another target of the rising tide of anti-union propaganda. It also conceded that 'there are problems in sectional collective bargaining between competitive groups' and in the traditional concept of 'the going rate'. Clutching at straws, the TUC joined the government in coining a new phrase, an 'Agreed Economic Assessment' aimed at 'a broader national consensus on the overall distribution of income'. The February statement's conclusion even pointed the way towards the priority of the new Toryism, which was waiting a few more months to take over: 'central to the achievement of all this, is the need to defeat inflation. A target of getting inflation below five per cent within three years is a bold one, but we must take it as our aim'. It has since taken the Thatcher Government five years to reach the target bequeathed by the TUC and Labour's departing Prime Minister at a cost which is now legendary.

Following the general election, the LC resumed its work in July 1979, with the briefest (single page) statement in its history, *Planning for Cooperation*. It regretted the slow progress of legislation between 1974 and 1979, but singled out the work of the NEB as 'the hallmark' of Labour's distinct approach to economic regeneration. Back into the habits of opposition, the LC resumed denunciation of the new phase of Tory anti-union law, coupled with promises of future repeal. There followed new policy statements, on *Trade and Industry: A Policy for Expansion* (1980), and *Economic Planning and Industrial Democracy* (1982). The later paper embodies some of the new experience and thinking emerging from local authority economic planning and job creation through enterprise boards and community participation, but its one-sided adherence to the NEB's centralist structures and to conventional tripartism generated criticism from the 'popular planning' school on the left,[41] while the model cannot be said to have been understood, let alone endorsed, by the electorate in 1983. We shall return to this discussion when we examine the arguments for planning agreements and workers' corporate plans.

After the 1983 election defeat there was a period during which conservative spokesmen in the TUC General Council had the upper hand. This was the brief span of the 'new realism', which we discuss in chapter 5. The main text of this was leaked to the Sunday newspapers and the television networks without having been published to, still less discussed by, ordinary members. Among other thoughts, this document gave us this rather ambiguous estimate:

> While workers support for the Movement's policies cannot be measured by the numbers of votes cast for the Labour Party at the General Election, neither can the rejection of Labour's policies be dismissed out of hand: some polls indeed indicated that there was a lack of support from trade unionists for some policies that in part mirrored the TUC position. This suggests that unions have not yet sufficiently involved members in policy development and have failed to inform members of and win their support for union policies. This can only undermine the strength of trade unions in terms of their broader political influence.

After the miners' strike, and the resignation of Len Murray, the work of the Liaison Committee resumed. In March 1985 *Labour Weekly* revealed that a new document on workers' participation in investment decisions and planning had been drafted, for publication in the summer. The restricted information contained in this report seemed to indicate a very cautious statement, which would not 'overemphasize' the 'potential role of public spending'. The policy of the LC on social ownership had not yet been agreed.

In April 1985, the LC was at work on the draft of a joint statement which was to be submitted to the annual TUC Congress and Labour Party Conference. The polls and election results at that time encouraged renewed expectations for a Labour recovery at the next general election. This text placed heavy emphasis on a return to consensual methods for economic recovery, elaborating on an earlier statement entitled *Partners in Rebuilding Britain*, and on another document on social justice (*Building a Fairer Society*).

The draft returns to the language and concepts of bargained corporatism: 'This Statement shows how a Labour government in partnership with the trade unions can stop the waste.' It contrasts Mrs Thatcher's policy of abrasive confrontation with its own advocacy of 'change by agreement'. Labour's policy will 'give workers through their unions the opportunity to tackle [these] issues . . . to influence crucial decisions on investment, training, on product development, on employment patterns . . .' It repeats well-rehearsed criticisms of British industrial relations in which workers are excluded from information and influence to a degree unknown in Western Europe. Given extended rights trade unions are expected to enter into a partnership which will build 'a new consensus on the production of wealth and its distribution'. 'Unemployment, trade, inflation and the distribution of income and wealth will be tackled on the basis of this partnership' and '. . . the first task of the Labour Government on taking office will be to hold early discussions with trade unions and employers – in effect a National Economic Summit – to draw up a wide-ranging agreement on the priorities for fulfilling our policies.'

In resurrecting tripartism, the LC is doing no more than reverting to the tone of its 1973 pronouncements. But in that year, the 'first task' was agreement with the TUC; now it is summitry with the employers and unions. Of course the language of these Statements always defers to public relations needs, but the change of content on this point has its significance. It reflects a general timidity and an absence of specific commitments, notably to the goal of full employment. In this it retreats from the tone which characterized the programme making of 1973. Of course, the draft may prove to be an interim step to firmer commitments. As things are, it shows the movement poised uneasily between 'new realism' and party commitment. To the extent that unions are enfeebled at the level of the workshop, corporate bargaining at the top will also be weaker. To redress the gap, political intervention will be essential.

Notes

1 The phrase is that of George Woodcock, former General Secretary of the TUC. It was coined in a speech rebuking oppositional protest movements: 'We have left Trafalgar Square' was the complementary thought.
2 Published by Andre Deutsch, 1979.
3 Ibid., p. 383.
4 See Michael Hatfield, *The House the Left Built*, Gollancz, 1978.
5 John Elliot, *Conflict or Co-operation*, Kogan Page, 1978, chapter 16, pp. 241 et seq. Bullock's report 'Was attacked with one of the most vitriolic and damning campaigns ever mounted by British industrialists'.
6 Clive Ponting, *The Right to Know*, Sphere, 1985, p. 190.
7 *The Future of British Socialism*, Cape, 1956.
8 'What the Worker Wants', *Encounter*, February 1959, p. 17.
9 So that R. H. Tawney's last major political essay, (reprinted in *The Radical Tradition*, Penguin, 1966) appealed, in vain, for 'a systematic attempt to democratize the practical routine of industrial life' (p. 186). All those social democrats who lionized him strode purposefully in the opposite direction.

10 See our account in *The New Unionism*, Penguin, 1974.
11 Cf. John Elliot, *Conflict or Co-operation*.
12 Karl Marx, *Capital*, vol. 1, chapter 25, section 2.
13 Robin Murray, *Multinational Companies and Nation States*, Spokesman, 1970, p. 40.
14 Ibid., p. 45.
15 Stuart Holland, *Strategy for Socialism*, Spokesman, 1975, p. 13. This analysis is extended in the same author's *The Socialist Challenge*, Quartet, 1975, p. 44 et seq.
16 *Out of Crisis*, Spokesman, 1983.
17 Cf. Coventry, Liverpool, Newcastle and North Tyneside Trades Councils, *A Workers' Enquiry: State Intervention in Industry*, Spokesman, 1983.
18 Colin Crouch, in *The Politics of Industrial Relations*, Fontana, 1979.
19 Leo Panitch, *Social Democracy and Industrial Militancy*, Cambridge University Press, 1976.
20 'Trade Unions and the Capitalist State', *New Left Review*, 125, pp. 21 et seq.
21 Ken Coates, *Democracy in the Labour Party*, Spokesman, 1977, p. 49.
22 Ibid., p. 51.
23 Tony Benn, *Arguments for Democracy*, Cape, 1981, pp. 26 et seq.
24 Ken Coates and Tony Topham, *Trade Unions in Britain*, Spokesman, 1980, pp. 124–133. In all, 38 members of the General Council held 107 quango appointments from the government.
25 Ibid., p. 133.
26 Eric Batstone, Ian Boraston and Stephen Frenkel, *Shop Stewards in Action*, Blackwell, 1977, p. 168 et seq.
27 Bob Fryer, 'Trade Unionism in Crisis: The Miners' Strike and the Challenge to Union Democracy', in *Digging Deeper, Issues in the Miners' Strike*, Verso, 1985.
28 Bob Fryer has made a major contribution to the development of this argument. We have found very relevant a seminar which he conducted at the Northern College on 9 March 1985.
29 Cf. Ben Fine, Laurence Harris, Marjorie Mayo, Angela Weir and Elizabeth Wilson, *Class Politics, an Answer to its Critics*, Central Books, 1984.
30 Colin Crouch, *Trade Unions: The Logic of Collective Action*, Fontana, 1982, pp. 219–20.
31 *New Statesman*, 1983.
32 Ross McGibbin, *The Evolution of the Labour Party 1910–24*, Oxford University Press, 1974.
33 Quoted in Middlemas, *Politics in Industrial Society*, p. 321.
34 Ibid.
35 Ibid., pp. 335–6.
36 Ibid., p. 373.
37 Ross Martin, *TUC: The Growth of a Pressure Group*, Oxford, Clarendon Press, 1980, pp. 304 et seq. Also Michael Hatfield, *The House the Left Built*, Gollancz, 1978, pp. 134–43.
38 The government was bluntly warned off any attempt to implement the Bullock Report.

39 Middlemas, *Politics in Industrial Society*, p. 461.
40 TUC Annual Report 1972.
41 See *What Went Wrong*, Spokesman, 1979; *How to Win*, Spokesman, 1981; *Planning the Planners*, Spokesman, 1983; *Popular Planning for Social Need*, Forum of Combine Committees, 1981; *Economic Planning through Industrial Democracy*, Forum of Combine Committees, 1982.

3 The Trade Union Act of 1984

During 1984 the Secretary of State for Employment, Mr Tom King, saw his Trade Union Bill passed through both Houses of Parliament without fundamental alteration.

Few measures have been more noisily introduced, and none have had a more propagandist significance. Most of the initial proposals of the Bill were canvassed while Mr Norman Tebbit was Secretary of State for Employment, in a pre-election Green Paper. Immediately after the June 1983 landslide, this Paper was re-issued, having undergone a colour change. Now the White Paper differed in one crucial respect from its predecessor: where it had been proposed to legislate to compel trade unionists to 'contract in' to political funds of their unions, now, in a stroke of genius, it was proposed to subject the very existence of political funds to the repeated ordeal of recurrent ballots. This ingenious measure would mean that trade union political expenditure could be completely terminated, if ballots fell during a period where Labour support was going through a bad patch. Therefore the new Act has considerable political significance. Indeed, it will impose a constitutional change of great magnitude, since it is calculated to disable the main opposition party, without in any way subjecting company law to similar reforms controlling the very disbursements by industrial and commercial concerns to the Conservative Party. Overall, the new measure is a good example of the way in which the Thatcher administration uses the rhetoric of 'democracy' as a means for disabling democratic institutions. 'Democracy' in industry can mean many things: from general ballots on the membership of the board of directors down to a more adequate flow of information to employees. Neither on the larger nor the smaller scale is Mrs Thatcher willing to advance so much as one millimetre into democratizing the boardroom, but the trade unions are a different matter. Nothing short of the most comprehensive restrictions on their freedom of manoeuvre will do.

In sum, the Trade Union Act imposes regulations over three distinct areas of trade union government. First, it will regulate elections of trade union executive committees; secondly, it provides for the institution of strike ballots, subject to a penalty which involves the removal of immunities where strikes are called without ballots; thirdly, it seeks to regulate political funds.

The new Act has established two categories of membership of trade union executives. Non-voting members may remain appointed 'civil servants', but all voting members of these committees will henceforth be subjected to five yearly elections. All the voting executive members must be directly elected: co-option or indirect election via sectional committees of the union are disallowed. After such elections, defeated members will not be able to stay in office for longer than six months before their replacements succeed them. Where existing executive members are permanent staff members, their contracts of employment will be overruled, as indeed will union rule books which specify anything contrary to the new law. Voting rights will be extended to all full members of the union in question, leaving out only those who are normally disqualified from voting by rule, such as unemployed members, apprentices or trainees, members who are behind with their subscriptions, or new members who have not completed their probationary period. It will be permitted to establish constituencies on trade, regional or sectional lines, if the union rules so determine. But voters may not be disenfranchised from any of the elections in which they belong to the appropriate constituency. Voting must be by the marking of a ballot paper, at a time and place convenient to the voter, secret, and it must not involve the voter in any direct expenditure. All union members will have the right to stand as candidates, and it will be illegal to require them to belong to a particular political party. But a union may exclude a class of members if all of them are barred from seeking office by union rule.

Breaches of the new law may be contested by any union member. Any person belonging to the union at the time of the election may apply to the courts for enforcement. If the election has yet to take place, then any person who is a member at the time of application may apply to the courts. If the court accepts such an application, it will issue a declaration which must specify the union's infringement of the law. It may also issue an enforcement order, which will be binding on the union. The court will be able to instruct the union to hold the election, or to rectify the declared breach of procedure, and it will be able to compel the union to conform to its declarations in the future. Such declarations will be subject to a time scale, within which they must be enforced. Normally, obedience will be enforced within a period of six months, but any union member can repair again to the courts for enforcement, if this is delayed.

The sanction against strikes which are agreed without prior ballots will be the removal of trade union immunity from prosecution for damages arising from the inducement of breaches of contract. As the Act takes effect, unless a trade union has balloted its members, it will find itself in the same position as the Railway Servants were in the famous Taff Vale case at the beginning of the century. Not only employers, but also aggrieved third parties will have the right to sue for damages in all such cases. The Act provides that each ballot must be held not more than four weeks before the commencement of strike. All those who are deemed likely to be called out must be given the right to vote, which must not be given to people who are not directly involved. But if a member is denied the right to vote, and then becomes involved in the industrial action, the trade union will be deemed to have failed to meet the obligations of the new law. Ballots must pose the question of whether the member wishes to be involved in industrial action in breach of contract (or to continue to be so involved), and the question must be so phrased as to require a straightforward yes or no in answer. Failure to conform to this stipulation will mean that even where a ballot has taken place, the union will remain unprotected against civil actions. The procedures for voting in strike ballots will be the same as those for voting in the election of trade union executive committees.

When we come to the question of political funds, we arrive at a unique legal institution. In most parts of the world, the disposition of trade union funds is not subject to the kinds of impediment established in the British Trade Union Act of 1913, which required unions to establish a special political fund if they wished to be involved in the activities of a political party. Other voluntary bodies are not regulated in this way, and it is quite remarkable that British trade unions have accepted this interference with their right to dispose of their own funds so uncomplainingly, for so long.

The new law provides that any resolution to establish a political fund will cease to be effective after a lapse of ten years. (In the event of a subsequent ballot within a shorter time, it will of course be possible to annul a political fund more quickly.) The new Act provides that any resolution establishing a political fund which was passed more than nine years before it takes effect, 'will be deemed to have been carried' nine years ago. If two unions with political funds have amalgamated, the date of their amalgamation vote will not be counted as a 'resolution'. The oldest political fund involved in the merger will serve as the point from which dating takes place. The Certification Officer must approve the rules of ballots.

Political funds consist of contributions by members, donations from others, and any interest which such assets may earn. Unions will not be able to transfer other union monies into the political fund. If a political fund survives the expiration of its 'resolution' nothing may be added to it except the interest which it earns. It will be illegal to require contributions to it by rule, and all or any of it can be transferred to any other fund, whatever the union rules have hitherto stipulated. It will be illegal to meet the liabilities of political events from any other fund after the Act has been passed. Where a ballot goes against a fund, payments out of it may be made for political purposes for a period of as much as six months or less. Where a resolution ceases to have effect, the union must discontinue collecting political contributions as soon as practicable, and if any contributions are in fact paid over after the cessation of the resolution, they can be paid into any other fund, whatever union rules might previously have said. If a member requests the refund of any contributions made to a political fund after the expiration of a resolution, then such refunds must be made.

All union rules on political funds will cease to be valid six months after a ballot rejects the continuation of a fund, or immediately a resolution expires without a new ballot having revalidated it. After a resolution has expired, however, the rules for administering the assets of a fund may be continued. At the same time, members will continue to have the right to complain to the Certification Officer if they object to the manner in which it has been administered. The enforcement of these provisions will be open to any member of the union concerned. He or she may complain to the High Court, or to the Court of Session in Scotland, if a union does not stop collecting contributions to a political fund once that fund has become outdated or been overturned. The court may then order the union to comply, and this order is enforceable at the request of any member of the union. Supposing there is a gap between the expiration of a resolution and an affirmative ballot establishing a new one, then contributions received in the interim may not be paid into the new fund.

A major change in the idea of the political fund is imposed in the provisions which define what 'political objects' may be. They are now redefined not only to cover any financial contribution to a political party and any provision of services or property to a political party. They also cover the registration of electors, the support for candidatures or the selection of candidates, the maintenance of political office holders, the subsidising of conferences or meetings of political parties and, a disturbing new departure, 'the production, publication or distribution of any literature, document, film, sound recording or advertisement which, taken as a whole' seeks to influence voting for a political party or candidate. No doubt this new control is a result of the very effective advertising campaign undertaken by the National Association of Local Government Officers in the run up to the June 1983 Election. NALGO's campaign did not offer support to a particular party, but it did seek to exert pressure on the governing party. Unless NALGO established a political fund, it would probably not be able to repeat this initiative in subsequent elections. The new Act will define 'candidates for political office' as persons seeking election to Parliament, the European Assembly, local councils, or office within any political party.

Obviously this is a radical, even revolutionary programme of deep structural change. Were it to succeed, trade union behaviour would be fundamentally transformed, and the structure of the political opposition might easily be laid in ruins. For this reason, we must now examine in detail the politics of intervention in these three chosen areas covered by the Trade Union Act: ballots for union elections, strikes and political funds.

The Politics of Union Election Ballots

As we have just seen, the 1984 legislation requires that, from October 1985, all elections for voting members of trade union national executive committees must be conducted by direct individual secret ballot of all members entitled to vote. Such elections must subsequently be held at intervals of not more than five years. Leading officials, such as general secretaries and presidents, who have votes on their national executive committees, come under the same requirements. The High Court will be empowered to enforce these requirements on receipt of any complaint from a member of the union against which complaint is made. These provisions override anything to the contrary which may formerly have been contained in a trade union's rule book. Defiance of this law could quite normally lead to contempt of court proceedings, followed by imprisonment or fines for any offenders. Postal balloting is given priority in the Act (section 2, sub-section 7), but a union may substitute workplace balloting if it is satisfied that secrecy, accessibility and convenience would not be impaired. We do not yet know how judges will assess workplace ballots if and when they are challenged. But on any default, they will be able to order a fresh election, which would normally have to be held by post, even if the original election was held at the workplace. Block branch voting is not allowed: only individual votes may be counted. Ballots at branch meetings away from the workplace will not meet the Act's requirements. A new legal duty is placed on a union to compile and maintain an accurate and up-to-date register of the names and proper addresses of its members (section 4 of the Act).

A sustained and principled criticism of the discriminatory nature of the legislation was provided in the House of Lords debates on the Bill by Lords McCarthy and Wedderburn. Lord McCarthy proposed that the Bill be amended to allow for indirect, as well as direct elections, to union executives. The exclusive adherence to the enforcement of direct election was defended by the government on the grounds of securing undiluted accountability of the leadership to the members. Lord McCarthy pointed to the common practice, in clubs, professional associations, companies, and above all in the government of the realm, of the delegation of powers of appointment and co-option (as distinct from direct election). The majority party in the Commons, having been of course subject to direct election, elect their Prime Minister by indirect election, and that supremely powerful individual then appoints by personal fiat the whole of the Cabinet, to say nothing of the thousands of other executive personnel or government, over which the electorate has no control through ballots.

The government of course argued throughout the debates that trade unions are not like clubs and associations; they have a peculiarly formidable influence in society and the economy. It is reasonable, to say the least, to ask, as did Lords Wedderburn and McCarthy, why unions should be singled out in this way, when government itself, and the great centres of economic power in company boardrooms, are excluded. Lord Wedderburn's judgment on the government's rejection of the amendments is inescapable and indeed restrained: 'Government are insistent that their comprehensive method for direct election to the principal executive committee is the only method of democracy which shall be permitted to trade unions. It is part of a new campaign to control the autonomy of trade unions . . .'[1]

A further opposition amendment sought to limit the compulsion on direct election to 51 per cent of executive seats, leaving 49 per cent to be filled by any method chosen autonomously by the unions' own rule-making procedures. This proposal tested the government's dogmatism to the limit, and was again supported by reference to the law and the practice in all other social and political institutions, and to the relevant ILO Conventions requiring legal abstention in the rule-making of trade unions. Would the government, having insisted on a trespass into this territory, bend even just a little, and limit its intrusion, leaving at least a minority control of its rules to the union? Lord Wedderburn deployed his great knowledge of union rules in support of this plea; relatively innocuous unions, in which supposed baronial power was nowhere evident, such as the Health Visitors Association and the National League of the Blind and Disabled, provided for co-option in filling some seats on their executives. It was a nice point to add to this list the British Airline Pilots' Association, of which the recent Secretary of State for Employment, Norman Tebbitt, was once a member. Lord Wedderburn summoned also, in evidence, the conclusion of the Donovan Commission in 1968 'that it is not practicable to prescribe a set of model rules which would be suitable for every trade union'. The government, he argued, by insisting on 100 per cent direct election were promoting a politicization, a 'party system', in union elections. After his amendment was rejected by the government spokesman, he concluded: 'The Government will not hand back the constitution of the unions to the members . . . the Government will not even hand back 49 per cent of the constitution to the members. That is now clearly established.'

Lord Wedderburn also foresaw endless judicial interventions over the application of the straitjacket of obligatory electoral law which was being laced around trade unions, and he sought to mitigate their impact with a further amendment. This would have provided that a union was not guilty of negligence or default or breach of duty 'by reason of an unintended mistake, by those conducting a ballot, which it is reasonable to excuse'. In support, he cited section 448 of the Companies Act of 1948, which grants exemption from liability to an officer of a company wherever he acts 'reasonably and honestly'. (The same principle is acknowledged in the Health and Safety at Work Act, which requires employers to fulfil its standards only to an extent which is 'reasonable and practicable'.) Unions needed particular protection in relation to the requirement in the Bill that all eligible members must have the right and the opportunity to vote. He said:

> Unions, we say, faced with all the tripwires in . . . this measure, are bound to make mistakes. Already people are lining up to bring actions. We all know who they are. We know too, that available registers of members in some unions are not, with the best will in the world, easy to maintain, especially where the work force is mobile, as in the construction industry. Even in a union like the AUEW, there is the recent famous statement of Sir John Boyd in which he said: 'We rely on 2,558 branch secretaries to advise the executive council in their fortnightly reports of deaths, transfers, resignations and expulsions. If they fail, then certain inadequacies are inevitable. Twice a year all secretaries are provided with an up-dated voting register, and attention is drawn to the names and addresses of members whose ballot papers are returned undelivered. To have a register of 805,350 voters out of a membership of one million is a wonderful achievement.'

Sir John Boyd's eloquent statement had previously been cited in evidence in the Committee stage of the Bill in the House of Commons, by Derek Fatchett. It evoked no warmer response from Mr Gummer than it did from his colleagues in the upper House.

The rigid formulae imposed in the Act had emerged after a long process of debate, proposal and counter-proposal among (particularly) conservative critics of trade union rules and organizational practice, spread over the past two decades. It was sparked off by the rise in trade union negotiating power in the full employment era which climaxed in the 1960s. The effect of a full employment economy on trade union membership, activism and in some cases militancy, was a source of anxiety among dedicated pluralists and of hostility among conservatives and the counter-union wing of employers' organizations. The Donovan Royal Commission of 1968[2], a classic of pluralist analysis and prescription, confined its immediate recommendations to the institutional reform of collective bargaining, hoping thereby to avoid more drastic remedies to the perceived 'problems' of strikes, and the accumulation of new pragmatic powers at the shop floor level of trade unionism. The Commission was reluctant to use the law, particularly when this pointed towards state intervention in trade union rule-making and administration. More robust critics, with no such inhibition, in the Conservative Party and a number of employers' organizations, did seek remedies in the legal reform of unions. Their prescriptions ranged widely, only most recently homing in, via restrictions on the legality of industrial action, on the closed shop and picketing to the direct promotion of what they styled democratic internal reform of trade union decision-making processes.

It is difficult to overemphasize the inconsistency of the concern for trade union democracy among the genuinely hostile critics of trade unionism. Since the Second World War such opponents have been consistent neither in their methods, nor in the intensity of their campaigning. Their prescriptions have varied quite fundamentally between one phase of post-war development and another. The present phase, embodied in the 1984 Act, emphasizes the supposedly un-accountable and unrepresentative powers of trade union leaders, to initiate industrial action, to engage in political activity and to occupy their offices. In contrast, the voice of their members is said to be ineffective and unheard. Conservative opinion on the role of leadership in trade unions, however, was once quite different. An admiration for the role of national leaders was highly fashionable in the 1940s and 1950s, when those oligarchs held sway over a generation of workers who were only slowly recovering their self-confidence after the depredations of the pre-war slump. The powers of the titans of the General Council to 'control their members' were then applauded by the press and fostered by the Establishment. If, in those days, there was no concern about how such leaders actually came to hold power, nor was there much worry about how they exercized such power. Malcontents believed that the flowering of knighthoods and peerages among them was in inverse proportion to the degree of their responsiveness to shop floor pressures.[3]

When this authoritarian elite began to lose its grip, as it did in the late 1950s and 1960s, the first concern of the establishment was how to reinforce it against the growing evils of shop floor autonomy and unofficial strikes. Union leaders who resisted these evils were admired, while those who fostered them were regarded with alarm. As the 1970s witnessed a further shift towards democratic responsiveness by official union bodies, to the point where the number of official strikes increased, and political commitment turned leftwards, the new trend towards examination and criticism of union rule books became a dominant preoccupation. Although the 1980s have seen a diminution of rank and file pressure, as mass unemployment has eroded militancy, not all trade union leaderships have been reclaimed for 'moderation'. Moreover, the prevailing neo-liberal doctrines of market economics have not found a niche in their model for corporate-inclined trade union leaders; it has therefore become necessary, while turning them out of the corridors of power, to restrain them, by whatever devices can be invented, from exercizing their instrumental and political roles in hindrance of the operation of the market model. The 'popular bossdoms' of Bevin, Deakin and others once functioned as a stabilizing factor in the old consensus, corporate model. They played in concert, if sometimes in descant, with the state and the employers. The present government rejects this music and seeks instead a legalistic and apparently constitutional method by which to control the somewhat bemused successors of the old union hierarchs. Ready to hand, it is thought, is a 'silent majority' of members who might be enlisted to perform this restraining role by extending trade union democracy through the single device of balloting – applied to strikes, political action and union elections.

This silent majority, in this reading of the trade union situation, has been persuaded, by stringent labour market conditions, as well as by the impact of conservative populism, to revert to the pursuit of individualistic and quietist private solutions for most of its problems. Such a force must be mobilized in a distinctly limited way if it is not to be overmobilized. On the one hand it must acquire, via the ballot box, and the courts, the power to clip the wings of union leaders at both national and local levels. On the other hand, for this formula to produce the desired result the quiescent voters must be permanently kept in their present condition; that is, they must always know the fear of the dole, and never be encouraged to venture beyond the role of inhibiting those responses which they dislike. It is not at all the government's intention to encourage them to participate actively and collectively in the positive work of decision-making and opinion-forming within the constitutional structures of their unions. Only if people can be permanently prevented from developing an appetite for involvement, discussion and activism can the device of representational democracy be abused safely for this special purpose, which is the prevention of participative democracy – the chosen method of trade unionism from its infancy. Balloting for trade union executive bodies is therefore quite cynically seen as one option, among many, for inhibiting unions from the achievement of collective, group and class purposes. Not for the first time we see how institutions only make sense within their overall social context. Ballots would almost certainly radicalize the unions during times of full employment, self-confident shop floor organization and rising trade union membership. If the move to neutralize union action succeeds, this will not be because it is a mistake to hold thoroughly representative elections, but because the scope for conventional trade union action has been painfully reduced in economic adversity.

Policy has run through a number of stages to arrive at the provisions of the 1984 Act. In their election manifesto of February 1974, the Conservatives called for postal ballots in union elections to be made mandatory. In October 1974 they offered public funds to finance voluntary ballots for the same purpose. In January 1979 Mrs Thatcher called for subsidized secret postal ballots for both union elections and to sanction major strikes. At this stage postal ballots were favoured, an opinion no doubt strengthened by the apparent evidence from the EETPU and the AUEW(E) that they produced compliant leaderships, in elections in which the conservative-minded popular newspapers could intervene effectively. But opinion amongst the Tory Party's industrial backers was more pragmatic and divided. The most doctrinaire of their formal organizations, the Institute of Directors, even feared that postal balloting might be subject to abuse. Industrialists, however, did tend to argue that all public subsidy for balloting costs should be accompanied by public (i.e. legislative) control over the balloting rules.

The government took its first step in the 1980 Employment Act, part 1 of which provided for public funding of trade union ballots for a range of purposes, while leaving the trade union rules under which ballots were held untouched. The argument for postal ballots has not been advanced by the result. Now that the Certification Officer, who administers the subsidy in question, has reported on the earliest claims, we can see how restricted has been postal participation. All the trade unions that claimed reimbursement before 1985 were not affiliated to the TUC, which had resolved to ignore the legislation that made refunds of postal expenses possible. (In 1985, after a ballot of members, the AUEW broke ranks with the TUC policy, as did the EETPU.) Many returned very low polls indeed (table 3.1). Only one of the recipients of subsidy achieved the levels of electoral participation attained by the mineworkers' union, which ballots at the pithead in an orthodox election conducted in exactly the same way as national and local government ballots in Parliamentary and municipal elections. This beneficiary had less than 9,000 members, a much easier constituency to poll than a mass industrial union. What prevents other unions from adopting the sane and expedient procedure of the mineworkers is mainly their anachronistic branch organization, often not based upon workplaces, and, as we argued in chapter 2, commonly tangential to the real

Table 3.1 Percentage polls among unions claiming reimbursement of postal ballot expenses, 1982–4

Trade union	Poll reported 1982 (%)	Poll reported 1983 (%)	Poll reported 1984 (%)
Assistant Masters and Mistresses Association	73	75	41[a]
Association of Education Officers	62	68 ⎫ 49 ⎭	60[b]
Association of Management and Professional Staffs	31	—	
Association of Public Service Finance Officers	29	35	31
Association of Public Service Professional Engineers	27	—	
Association of Optical Practitioners	24 ⎫ 37 ⎭	—	22[c]
Barclays Group Staff Union	45	—	56
British Association of Occupational Therapists	24	74	28
British Orthoptic Society	—	53	—
Chartered Society of Physiotherapy	17	14	—
Immigration Service Union	—	70	72[d]
Institute of Journalists	29	16 ⎫ 33 ⎭	32
National Association of Fire Officers	—	72	
National Association of Head Teachers	55 ⎫ 57 ⎭	52 ⎫ 17 ⎬ 39 ⎭	
Professional Association of Teachers	34	20	15[e]
Retail Book Stationery and Allied Trades Employees		76 ⎫ 90 ⎭	70[f]
Royal College of Nursing of the United Kingdom	11	48	19
Society of Chiropodists	22	24	23
Society of Radiographers	—	23	23

[a]One application, two ballots; [b]three ballots; [c]two ballots; [d]two ballots; [e]three ballots; [f]five ballots.
Also in 1984, the Ministry of Defence Staff Association made three separate applications. Its highest poll involved 51 per cent, and its lowest, 21 per cent.
Source: Reports of the Certification Officer.

work of workshop union representation. Since the government is so anxious on this score, however, it might be noted that employers have by no means always been willing to co-operate in offering facilities for general union elections.

In 1982, a second Employment Act laid down particularly stringent conditions for the legalization of Closed Shops by ballot among the workers involved. Finally, the 1984 Act is, as we have seen, *all* about balloting, and removes any shred of voluntarism from balloting over strikes, or union executive elections, or concerning political activity in trade unions. It therefore intervenes directly in the process of trade union rule-making, a step towards state control of unions which careful commentators find disquieting 'because of the uncertain effects of ballots on union behaviour, and the threat to pluralist democracy posed by government intervention in union affairs, the overall long term consequences may not be justified by short term gains'.[5]

This step-by-step encroachment reveals quite evidently a growing confidence among the interventionist wing of conservative and business opinion, that balloting as a method will generate the desired results. Such confidence is directly related to the rise in the government's electoral fortunes among trade union voters between the 1979 and 1983 general elections, and to the success of its populist appeal to parts of working class opinion. But also it is connected with the effects of the regime of mass unemployment on trade union behaviour. What is manifestly not the case is that the development of this legislation has followed careful, disinterested inquiry into the actual, detailed and infinitely various practices of union democracy as embodied in rule books and custom. For such work we have to turn to independent sources, notably and most recently the comprehensive study by Undy and Martin.[6]

These authors distinguish two types of trade union office, the 'professional', normally including general secretaries and other full-time officials; and 'representative' officers such as presidents, executive committees and their equivalent. The former are mostly appointed after examination and/or interview, the latter are almost exclusively subject to election and re-election by the membership. There have hitherto been three further distinct electoral methods used in trade union balloting; voting may be arranged by post, in the branch and at the workplace. The rules and practices of unions using each of these methods were subjected, in this study, to detailed scrutiny. It is instructive to examine some of these.

The AUEW(E) adopted postal balloting in 1972, for all full time officials, after a long history of branch balloting based on rules reaching back to the nineteenth century. The national president, general secretary, assistant general secretaries, a full time national executive committee, the final appeal court, and full time officials at division and district levels are all subject to this procedure. All of these (with the exception of the appeal court, which is composed of lay, part time members), are subject to re-election after three initial years in office, and subsequently every five years up to the age of 60. The union's system of government is consciously based on the principle of separation of powers, with a full time national executive running the day-to-day affairs, a lay national committee meeting once a year providing the legislature and the lay final appeals court, the judiciary.

The union has been familiar with a developed form of party conflict since the 1940s, when The Group, a right-wing anti-communist organization, established a formal structure with membership and officers. The broad left within the union also organizes faction meetings and promotes candidates, and both sides use their own journals for communication and electioneering.[7] The Group dominated the National Executive and full time officer posts during the 1950s and 1960s, following which a swing in the voting (held then at branch meetings) gave the left wing control of the presidency, three-sevenths of the executive, two assistant general secretaryships and the majority of full time posts. Disillusion with the Labour Government's wage control policies (with which the right wing was associated) and effective organization of the left's electoral machinery are suggested as the causes of this turnaround.

As participants in this story, we would augment Undy and Martin's explanation: it was the Campaign for Nuclear Disarmament, and its supporters in the unions, which gave the impetus for launching the newspaper *Voice of the Unions* in the early sixties, upon which a non-communist left wing could base itself. The 'Broad Left' which emerged in this process was not like previous front organizations under communist hegemony. Hugh Scanlon was a genuine independent, as were many of the officers associated with him. All were committed to an extension of democratic accountability, and were able to fault the Carron leadership (of The Group) for numerous infringements of the union's constitution.

Difficult though wage control was for all unions, it was the Labour Government's White Paper 'In Place of Strife', and the confrontation this provoked, which cemented the left in place during its ascendancy in the AUEW during the early seventies. While it was in opposition The Group opted for postal balloting, and won a rule change to establish this when it held a majority on the National Committee. Since the institution of the postal ballot, the right has recaptured and held most of the posts, including those at head office. The final appeal court came under right-wing control only in the 1980s, after it, too, had been included in the system of postal ballot. Early in 1985, the union obtained a twelve to one majority in a membership ballot to authorize it to claim government funding for the costs of this postal balloting. This placed it in a position of clear defiance of TUC policy, which, as we have already said, has been to refuse to apply for such finance, made available under the 1980 Employment Act. The thought of conflict between the engineers' union and the TUC was too much for the union's national committee, which, when it met in April 1985 called for a re-ballot with an adverse recommendation that might enable the members to close ranks with other trade unionists.

The effects of the introduction of postal balloting into this union can be summed up thus:

1 The right clearly gained ascendancy in internal elections to office.
2 The number of contested elections rose.
3 The number of candidates did not rise.
4 The dominance of section 1 (craft-qualified) members among full time posts was not reduced (section 1 represents 25 per cent of members, but 86 per cent of all successful candidates for office).
5 After the switch to postal balloting, electoral turnout rose from its average of 7 per cent in the last decade of branch balloting, to 27.4 per cent between 1972 and 1980. This percentage relates to the numbers on the union's electoral roll, which excludes 23 per cent of those entitled to vote. This deficit is the result of relying upon the union's 2,500 branches to maintain a register of eligible members, a difficult task in any union, and particularly so in one relying on geographically defined branches, part time branch secretaries and ill-attended branch meetings. The real average of voting over the 1970s was only 21 per cent. In 1973, the polls represented 38 per cent of the electoral roll; by 1982 this had fallen to 23.7 per cent, or only 18.6 per cent of total membership.

This situation was graphically illustrated in 1978, when a group of activists in the Bury, Lancashire, AUEW district surveyed voting behaviour in one small branch with 513 members. Only 384 of these turned out to have been on the electoral roll. The branch secretary, upon whom, as is customary, was devolved the task of maintaining an up-to-date register, was regarded as 'hardworking and efficient', but 129 members were disfranchised. This amounted to 25 per cent of those entitled to vote. Often, of course, these people had failed to report changes of address. More disconcerting still, 87 of the householders visited, among the 384 to whom votes were in fact allocated, claimed that there was no AUEW member in the house. This amounted to some 23 per cent of those actually registered. Sixty-two of those wrongly receiving votes had returned them to the Post Office; 15 had thrown the package away; 12 had handed it over to the branch official of the AUEW; 6 could not remember what they had done with it. By contrast, 7 per cent of those correctly on the register did not receive papers. If these numbers were more generally replicated, they would give serious grounds for doubt in narrowly divided contests. In 1982, for instance, the margin between Gavin Laird and Ken Brett in the election for general secretary was 1,000 votes. Had these discrepancies in Bury been nationally applicable, 180,000 people would have been sent votes in error, and 63,000 registered voters would not have received their papers.[8]

The other major union to use postal balloting on an extensive scale is the EEPTU. The Communist Party's control of the union and of its former branch balloting system was discredited in the High Court judgment on ballot rigging in 1961. The union's rule book had closely followed that of the AUEW; and full time officials had been elected by branch ballots. Following the trial, the union switched to postal balloting, and by stages, to the appointment of all full time officers except the general secretary and the full time national executive committee. Full time officer appointments are tightly controlled; a panel of candidates is maintained from members who have attended a special course at the union's own college. Students for these courses are selected by a team from the executive and full time officials, and the executive appoints officials from the course 'graduates'. The Communist Party's members are barred from holding office, although the union's Broad Left still retains two executive seats. As with the AUEW, turnout under postal balloting rose, in this case, from 10 per cent under branch ballots, to over 30 per cent. Despite the superficial evidence, the Left probably did not lose control of the union as a *result* of postal balloting; it would have lost anyway, as a result of the ballot rigging scandal.[9] But the tough, even repressive attitude of the present leadership towards any sign of organized dissent undoubtedly helps to sustain the right in power.

Three other unions with postal balloting for officers and executives, the Furniture, Timber and Allied Trades, the bakers union and the seamen all show evidence of left-wing control or leftwards drift in recent polls. This would suggest that the apparent correlation between postal balloting and right-wing control often deduced from the cases of the AUEW and EETPU does not constitute a 'law' of postal ballots. The relationships are more complex; for example in the National Union of Seamen, malpractice in electoral procedures by the former right-wing leadership was punished, when exposed, in future ballots, and the left, which had exposed it, benefited.

We turn now to branch balloting, the most favoured method for choosing executives in most trade unions. This can be broken down into two types: the recording of individual votes at branch meetings, or the casting of a branch's total membership for the candidate who wins its support in a branch meeting vote – the branch block voting system. Two types of branch may also be distinguished: that based on a geographical area (this predominates in, for example, the GMBATU), and that based on the workplace (this predominates in among others, the TWGU).

The largest union of all, the TGWU, elected Moss Evans to its general secretaryship in 1977 with a turnout of 39 per cent of the members, a return surpassing the results obtained by postal balloting in the main TUC affiliates. In the subsequent election, which was marred by some irregularities, the turnout was higher. But on an appeal from the winning candidate, Ron Todd, the election was run again, in order to eliminate any doubt about the result. All other full time officer posts are, in this union, chosen by executive committee appointment. The national executive council however, with more than 50 members, is a lay body chosen by branch balloting in regions and by indirect election from trade groups. Turnout for these elections varies between 10 per cent and 40 per cent. Political factionalism is not obtrusive in the elections, although the broad left organizes and agitates on general policy issues among the active membership. The union is remarkable for having made the transition from a position on the right wing of the labour movement under Arthur Deakin in the 1950s, to a consistent stance left of centre under Frank Cousins, Jack Jones and Moss Evans, without any change in its constitution or voting method. In recent years, the lay National Executive Council has assumed a more decisive role too, particularly since the retirement of Jack Jones.

The union is also unique in ensuring that lay members, from the executive, are regularly nominated for seats on the TUC General Council. Despite the heterogeneous membership of the TGWU, it has been able to mobilize a relatively high degree of membership participation in the general secretary's election, and in day-to-day government of the union at all levels, through its frequent use of large workplace branch structures and its trade group structure of committees.

The GMBATU uses a system of block branch voting based on geographically defined branches, and it lacks the trade group devolution of power found in the TGWU. The union's regional secretaries and regional committees, however, enjoy a large measure of power. Its national executive committee contains ten full time regional secretaries ex officio, together with two lay members from each region, who are elected indirectly by the regional councils. Of all the large unions, the GMBATU will have most changes to make in its EC electoral system in order to conform with the requirements of the 1984 Trade Union Act. Even the general secretary's election is at present governed by the block branch voting system, which was disallowed in the Act. Moves are now afoot to end the general secretary's vote in the executive, and thus exempt his office from the provisions of the Act. There are no formal political groupings at work, although the union has been well known for its loyalist tradition in TUC and Labour Party affairs. It also has a long tradition of nepotism, sons and nephews of former full time officials emerging through lower offices to fill several of the top posts over the years.[10]

The NUR uses a system of transferable branch block voting to elect its general secretary, its executive and its full time officials. This system produces an apparent high turnout since branches vote according to their total membership. Thus, in the election of Sidney Weighell as general secretary, a 90 per cent vote was recorded, but it is most likely that about 10 per cent actually attended the branches to determine this vote.

While the general secretary, as in most unions, wields power and commands loyalty, this did not prevent Weighell's preferred candidate from being defeated after his resignation, following his dubious use of the union's block vote at the Labour Party Conference in 1982. The left-wing candidate, Jimmy Knapp, won decisively.

Workplace ballots are used in, among others, the Civil and Public Services Association and most notably in the NUM. The CPSA membership enjoys the right to time off work for its balloting, but uses a subsidiary system of postal ballots for those in widely dispersed job locations. The result is a 30–40 per cent turnout, and a very high degree of political factionalism and volatility. There is a high proportion of young and female members.

The NUM is a federal union comprising 14 areas which enjoy substantial autonomy. All full time officials at area level, together with the national president and general secretary, have been until now elected for life in pithead ballots. Recent rule changes will introduce quinquennial elections. The vice-president is elected at the annual delegate conference. A poll of 80 per cent gave Arthur Scargill a 70 per cent majority in the presidential election of 1981. This represented a particularly remarkable result given that the popular press was universally hostile to his political beliefs, which were afforded wide coverage.

The NUM's National Executive Committee will fall foul of the 1984 Act, since it is at present elected indirectly by area councils. As has already happened in GMBATU, the NUM is also discussing a rule change to deprive its president of an executive vote, thus removing him from the need to contest regular elections.

It is possible on the basis of this and other evidence to make certain general statements about the politics of union ballots for their governing bodies. First, it is clear that there has been a very wide variety of rules and practices operating up to the moment of the 1984 Act's introduction. Union rule books are the product of history, and comprise a remarkable 'laboratory of democracy'. The 1984 Act may have only marginal effects in forcing rule changes, since over 90 per cent of unions already elect their national executives (which are mostly composed of lay members) for periods of three years or less. A few unions, however, may need to make substantial rule changes to conform with the new law. This is true using branch block voting such as the GMBATU and the NUR, and for those – notably the NUM – which have elected voting presidents or other national officials for life under their recent rules.

There are some potentially more disturbing and disruptive elements in the Act, the effects of which are difficult to predict with any precision. These include the obligation to maintain an accurate and up-to-date register of members entitled to vote, and the attention given to greater supervision of the secrecy, convenience and integrity of the voting, and of the count of votes. We have already noticed, for example, that the AUEW(E) has great difficulty in registering more than 70 per cent of its members on its electoral roll. There is no reason to suppose that, on average, other unions do better than this. Some, like the seamen's union with a widely dispersed membership, or like USDAW, with a very high annual turnover of members, may well do much worse. Any disaffected or disfranchised member may in future use section 4 subsection (1) of the Act to invalidate an election in such circumstances. The unions' concern to avoid this possibility is leading them at present to place a huge and tiresome extra burden of record keeping on shop stewards and branch secretaries. For decades the check-off system under which employers deduct and remit trade union subscriptions has weakened contact between union offices and their members. Frequently this has ensured that unions have had no means of recording members' addresses. The new law's intrusion into internal trade union government not only in this but other areas (ballots for strikes, closed shops and political funds), may well have the general effect of generating anxieties, stress and extra work for hard-pressed voluntary activists. Those of them who have studied the Act are already aghast at the crippling and diversionary new demands on them, which come at a time of recession in union morale, which may already be drying up the flow of recruits to replace stewards and branch secretaries. If such duties are taken up by full time officers, the unions' administrative costs will increase, and the efficiency with which their main roles are performed will be impaired.

If we compare official expectations (under the 1984 Act) about union voting registers with the actual practice in compiling electoral registers for general and local elections, we have reason for considerable disquiet. There is a growing tendency for the poor, the unemployed and sections of immigrant populations not to register. A recent study in London showed massive abstention from registration, on a scale large enough to eliminate an entire Parliamentary constituency, since boundaries are determined on the strength of registers not on the basis of numbers of people who should have been registered.[11] The unions, it seems, are to be compelled, by voluntary unpaid labour, to uphold very much higher standards than the paid registration officers employed by official bodies. Such is the tribute paid by vice to virtue . . .

Finally, the general threat posed by the Act may be more potential than actual; should the results not be to the liking of this or future governments, a precedent has been set for state intervention in trade union rule making and internal government which has potent and disquieting constitutional implications for union autonomy, and for all the other elements of pluralism in society.

This survey of union rules and experience suggests that there are no simple relationships between voting method and politics, or between extensive or restricted voting and politics. Electoral malpractice has been exposed in unions with both left and right-wing dominance; when exposed it tends to be punished heavily but indifferently. It has also more frequently been alleged on the basis of extremely unconvincing evidence. The Conservatives' favoured method, postal balloting, does not appear to benefit one or other political wing exclusively, and does not result in higher turnouts than workplace voting, although it does surpass branch balloting in this respect.

Workplace ballots as practised in the NUM and CPSA, and partially in the TGWU, consistently result in the highest turnouts. This method clearly combines the best of all worlds: it *can* be secret but – unlike postal balloting (which may not always be secret at all) – it encourages high levels of active, workplace debate and participation; that is, it does not privatize the whole electoral process. While the malpractices which occurred in the TGWU's ballot for the general secretary do reinforce the arguments for careful control and supervision of elections, and emphasize the need for strict enforcement of rules, they do not invalidate the greater access to members which proper workplace ballots afford. We should note that political elections are not conducted through the post, and that there are strict rules to ensure that the arguments involved in them are heard and extensively tested in discussion on radio and television, while all candidates in general elections are afforded free postage for their election addresses.

While we may speculate about why the government no longer insists on postal balloting, trade unions may note that, in many circumstances, the Act allows for, indeed specifies, the use of the workplace for the ballot, 'immediately before, immediately after, or during . . . working hours'. Balloting away from the workplace would have to satisfy the provision that it would be at a place 'more convenient' than work. Most branch meeting places would find it hard to comply with this requirement. The remedy, for those unions which have used branch ballots should be to move the branch into the workplace. This move, accompanied by campaigns to obtain work time for all necessary meetings, would accomplish much to bring together the participative and representational elements in trade union democracy, although neither will be fully effective in a prevailing climate of mass unemployment, which has been deliberately designed among other things to weaken the independence of thought and action of working people, and to discourage active trade unionism. It would until recently have gone without saying that none of these or other procedural reforms should be forced by law.

Perhaps the government drew back from compulsory postal ballots after contemplating the unpredictability of postal balloting. Perhaps they were swayed by arguments such as this:

> There is a mutual conspiracy between union leaders and government – aided and abetted by the media – to convince the public that unions can deliver their side of a national bargain on pay or anything else. It is not so. The pressure from the rank and file can upset even the most complacent and self-righteous of union bosses. At a crunch they lack leverage, the means of coercion to compel acceptance of something the members refuse to stomach. Far from helping the cause of 'moderation', the compulsory existence of postal ballots in all union elections could undermine the full-time activists in their struggle to retain cohesion and stability in the organization.[12]

The author of this view, a national journalist with a sympathetically 'moderate' and corporatist attitude towards his subject, goes on to argue:

> Those who want unions to be more democratic than they already are would be upset if those fragile, defensive organizations faced too many buffetings at the hands of the fickle rank and file, whose mood can change drastically from day to day.

We might reasonably expect that the government found more inspiration in the author's next sentence:

> Too much union democracy could wreck the attempt to establish an alliance between the TUC and the government of the day on a more permanent basis.

From a government which positively dislikes such alliances, is it unreasonable to suggest that compelling 'democracy' by Act of Parliament is part of a subtle design to destabilize them, and all such tendencies? A trade union movement now held at arm's length from what was formerly a governmental embrace needs some substitute controls perhaps? Most importantly, the government's intent must include the separation of rank and file activists (the hated 'small minority of extremists') who function at branch and workshop levels, from the national and full time leadership, and at the same time, from their own memberships. Bypassing the activists, by subjecting national leaders to the largely passive, anonymous control of the ballot box, is clearly seen by the present administration as a form of demobilization, of neutralization. For it is, in truth, in the reciprocal relations between the three elements, national and local leaders and rank and file, that the quality and nature of union democracy shows itself.

In representational democracy, trade unions can and should embark on their own reforms, even though they may already, in their best practice in workplace balloting and workplace branch life, sometimes surpass the proportionate 'majorities' that have given national governments their 'mandate' to rule the land through Parliament. In participative democracy, again as measured best in workplace meetings, informal debate and spontaneous pressure, they are already in no way inferior to Parliament. The degree of intercourse between an MP and his constitutents rarely betters that between workers, shop stewards and their full time officials, much though we favour improvement in both fields of action. And if these tests may be applied to unions and Parliament, we could with even greater justice point the contrasts between unions and commercial companies and public corporations, where it is clear that a highly autocratic and non-voting, non-participative form of government prevails. Constant pleas to government to legislate to amend this state of affairs, for example to conform with the European Community's extremely modest Directives on industrial democracy, meet with a consistent reply from ministers: 'Voluntary methods of reform are preferable to legislative compulsion'. Double standards could not conceivably be more evident than they are in this case.

The Politics of Strike Ballots

As we have seen, the 1984 Trade Union Act makes it a condition of trade unions' legal immunity for organizing and endorsing industrial action that they first hold a secret ballot in which all those due to take part in the action are entitled to vote. A simple majority of those voting must say 'yes' in order to legitimate the union's subsequent endorsement of the action. The ballot must be held not more than four weeks before the commencement of the action. The government's official guide to the Act further states:

the Act's provisions do not apply when industrial action is organized without the authority of the trade union since it would be unreasonable to put a trade union under threat of legal penalties for industrial action over which it might have no control (or indeed might know nothing about).[13]

In a cross-reference to section 15 of the 1982 Employment Act, the guide goes on to clarify the circumstances in which a trade union will be held responsible for authorizing industrial action. A union is to be held responsible where an action is authorized by its executive committee, its general secretary or president, or by any other person given power to do so under its rules. It will also be held responsible where authorization comes from any full time official or any committee to which an official regularly reports *unless* they are forbidden to give authorization by the union's rules, or unless their call is repudiated by the executive, president, or general secretary. The repudiation must be prompt, and in writing, and the subsequent behaviour of the repudiators must be consistent with their repudiation. Individual organizers of an action may also be joined with the trade union, in any legal action, where immunity does not apply.

Failure to comply with these provisions means that a trade union will be open to legal proceedings brought by either the employer concerned, or by customers or suppliers who can demonstrate that their contracts have been interfered with. Proceedings may take the form of an appeal for an injunction to call the action off (defiance of injunctions leading to heavy fines or imprisonment for the contempt of court), or may even result in an action for damages for amounts up to £250,000 (depending on the size of the union) in respect of each action. The guide concludes:

> It should be noted that the right to claim damages does not depend on having previously applied for an injunction to have the industrial action called off. Moreover, actions for damages may be started after the industrial action has ended. Any trade union which organizes industrial action without first holding a ballot must therefore be prepared to face quite unpredictable and possibly very severe financial penalties for doing so.[14]

The present law differs in one important respect from previous attempts to legislate to compel balloting before strike action. On this occasion, the statute gives no direct powers to the state to initiate legal enforcement of a ballot; instead it gives this power to employers and customers or suppliers. They may proceed against the union, confident that the 1906 immunities against civil actions no longer cover the non-balloted strike, or other industrial action such as an overtime ban, which falls short of a strike. This shift apparently removes the state from involvement in the contention which ensues when the law is involved in industrial relations, an effect which is now judged by most commentators to have invalidated past intervention in this field.

The Labour Government in 1969 was involved in a major controversy with its own trade union supporters over the provisions of its White Paper, 'In Place of Strife'. One of its proposals was that the Employment Secretary should have the authority to require a union ballot before calling a strike which, in the view of government, was detrimental to 'the national interest'. Sustained pressure from the TUC persuaded the government to withdraw the White Paper. The Heath Government's legislation, the 1971 Industrial Relations Act stepped in where Harold Wilson had held back, providing for precisely the powers which had been proposed and then withdrawn by Labour. This facility was used on only one famous occasion. In 1972, the government claimed that a work to rule and overtime ban by the railway unions was 'gravely injurious to the national economy' and succeeded in obtaining an order from the National Industrial Relations Court to force a postal ballot of railway workers, which was conducted by the Commission on Industrial Relations. The vote favoured the continuation of the action by more than five to one. The outcome was an improved pay offer from the British Railways Board, and the calling off of the action by the unions. The government never again resorted to use of its powers, and the whole Act was repealed by the next Labour government in 1974.

This experience confirmed the findings of the Donovan Royal Commission on the question of compulsory strike ballots.

426 Compulsory strike ballots. A number of witnesses have suggested to us that a secret ballot should be required before a strike can lawfully take place. This proposal is based on the belief that workers are likely to be less militant than their leaders and that, given the opportunity of such a ballot, they would often be likely to vote against strike action.

427 It is clear that the scope of any legislation to this end, if it were to be effective, would have to be confined to major official strikes. A law forbidding strike action before the holding of a secret ballot could not be enforced in the case of small-scale unofficial stoppages, which make up the overwhelming majority of the total number of strikes.

428 There is little justification in the available evidence for the view that workers are less likely to vote for strike action than their leaders; and findings from our workshop relations survey, already cited, confirm this. Experience in the USA has been that strike ballots are overwhelmingly likely to go in favour of strike action. This is also the experience of Canada, where strike ballots are compulsory in the provinces of Alberta and British Columbia. Two instances of ballots held in recent years in this country where the vote went against strike action are sometimes quoted in support of the case for compulsory secret ballots. One was held in connection with

an industry-wide wage claim in engineering in 1962, and one in connection with action to secure the reinstatement of certain employees dismissed by the Ford Motor Company in 1963. *But these ballots were held on the initiative of the unions concerned.* They do not provide reliable evidence of what the outcome would be if ballots were held in quite different circumstances, and under the compulsion of the law.

429 There are other objections to such ballots. Once a vote has been taken and has gone in favour of strike action, the resulting stoppage may delay a settlement by restricting union leaders' freedom of action. Moreover, how is the question on which the vote is to be taken to be framed? If the vote is, for instance, about whether to accept the employer's latest offer, its result can be stultified if the employer subsequently makes a slightly improved offer.

430 We do not recommend that it should be compulsory by law, either generally or in certain defined cases, to hold a ballot of the employees affected upon the question whether strike action should be taken. We think it preferable that trade union leaders should bear, and be seen to bear, the responsibility of deciding when to call a strike and when to call it off. Occasions may of course arise when union leaders would themselves wish to hold such a ballot or are required to do so by their rules. The decision on such a matter should continue to rest with the unions.[15]

Until yesterday, very few informal commentators would have dissented from this conclusion, or from the more recent findings of Undy and Martin, who offer this evaluation: 'Ballots are treated as one form of decision making and consultation with union members in the process of collective bargaining, not as a universal panacea, or as a *sine qua non* for union democracy.'[16] To withdraw legal protection from all but ballot-authorized strikes is in fact to outlaw a rich variety of forms of industrial action and disputes. Strikes may be variously official and unofficial, constitutional and unconstitutional (according to union rules), short and long, local and national, large and small, partial and complete, defensive and offensive, sectional and general. Accordingly, we should expect to find, and do indeed find, great variations in their treatment in union rule books, or in custom and practice.

The 1984 law, not by chance, confines its insistence upon ballots to the authentication of strikes and industrial action. In the practice of collective bargaining, however, there are a number of other serious occasions on which unions need to consult their members before embarking on a course of action or reaching a decision. Real concern with democracy would examine these at least as closely as strikes. This is notably true of the making of collective agreements with employers. In this field, unions may make use of a variety of methods, including the reference back of provisional agreements for approval to branch meetings, mass workplace meetings, special delegate conferences of representatives of members in the bargaining 'unit', and, of course, ballots or referenda. Where ballots are used, again we find a marked variety of methods, again including polling in branches, postal voting and ballots at the workplace. The past two decades have witnessed a substantial development of internal democratic mechanisms in this field. The TGWU, under Jack Jones' initial insistence, evolved from an authoritarian bargaining machine dominated by full time officers, to one upholding the general practice of direct involvement of lay shop stewards in plant-based bargaining. Within this framework developed the habit of referring back draft agreements for membership approval. Almost all unions have made greater or lesser moves in the same direction. So it has been that the Department of Employment, in a recent study, has found that a large majority of unions have practised some form of consultation over bargained agreements. This finding is confirmed by the CBI's databank.[17] A large measure of this healthy evolution has been achieved without formality; union rule changes have not been necessary, since this has been a matter for experiment and discretion, rather than a rigid constitutional ritual.

The authority to call and endorse strike action is, in most unions, vested in the national executive committee. In most cases, this authority is hedged by rules that are much more specific than they are in the matter of consultation over bargaining agreements. The need to keep this power at national level has been learned from an experience which has sometimes been bitter, because early forms of decentralized organization in which the industrial initiative was more generally dispersed, or undefined, sometimes led to the dissipation of union funds. This commonly happened when executives were compelled by rule or by moral obligation to finance all strikes called in their name, by widely dispersed and inadequately coordinated branches and regions.

This concentration of responsibility does not mean that strike ballots have not been used; on the contrary they have often been a recognized part of that complex process of consultation through which union head offices measure the opinion of their members before deciding whether to embark on official strike action. In this sense they are devices to enable leaders to read members' opinions and dissatisfactions accurately, and to decide how far to go on a particular issue. The usual rule provides for the discretionary use of ballots in such decisions. A mandatory requirement for pre-strike ballots is more often associated with big unions with centralized bargaining traditions (such as have grown up in recent decades in the case of the NUM). The TGWU is so conscious of the industrial weight of its whole membership that it requires, by a special belt-and-braces rule, that when a national strike, or one involving more than one of its trade groups, is contemplated, this must be endorsed by *both* a re-called biennial delegate conference *and* a national ballot.

In contrast to this actual variety of procedures, hostile media stereotypes of strike decision making have at successive times presented two incompatible myths. Both are distinguished by touching simplicity. In the 1960s, we heard a great deal about 'irresponsible' strikers who decided – apparently on mere whim – to strike without regard to the supposed 'authority' of national leaderships. These leaders, in all other respects sober and exemplary, were therefore said to have 'lost control' of their members, and over the influence of locally based malcontents and 'militants', who were once engagingly described by Lord Carron as 'werewolves'. As official strikes multiplied in scale, number and significance in the 1970s, we heard less about these earlier offenders and much more about the 'unrepresentative' nature of national official leaderships themselves. Their organizations were now increasingly represented as being insufficiently democratic to allow the silent majority of the members an adequate voice. It is this second myth which has formed the climate during the framing and passage of the 1984 Act. Yet even before it came into force, the evidence that a ballot could act to restrain leaders intent upon strike action was to some degree contradictory.

Thus, in the NUM, whose own constitution is clear on the point, national ballots for strike action, or for rejection of NCB wage offers, went against the recommendation of the national executive committee on a number of occasions.

With turnouts of over 80 per cent on each occasion, the membership rejected the NUM executive's recommendation to strike in 1979 and 1982. But in 1970, 1971, 1972 and 1974, the NUM members had voted in favour of strikes following NEC recommendations that they should so choose. Before the 1984 strike, therefore, the evidence suggested that there was no uniform one-way correlation between balloting and 'moderation' in the union, up to that time most fully committed to balloting over national strikes. A more plausible connection was that between voting behaviour and the state of the overall labour market, to which question we shall return.

In 1984, of course, the union executive changed its behaviour to endorse area-by-area strike action, thus jigsawing together a national response, and by refusing to apply the rule that had required a national ballot before launching a national strike. Such a response was endorsed by the national executive committee with the support of leaders and members of all political tendencies within the union, partly because the immediate past-president had sanctioned area-by-area agreements on productivity incentives in spite of adverse votes at his annual conference and in a national ballot. When his ruling had been challenged in the courts, it was upheld. This precedent was taken as a justification for the subsequent 1984 decision. But of course, the coal fields were not unanimous in following the reasoning of their leaders. This complex story requires more extended treatment.

The Miners' Strike of 1984–5: To Ballot or Not?

The most outspoken of all the critics of the leadership of the NUM during the 1984–5 strike was Jimmy Reid, the former leader of the Upper Clyde Shipbuilders during their 1971 work-in. In a succession of articles in the Scottish press, and then in a Channel 4 TV broadcast at the beginning of 1985, Reid maintained a constant, and, it must be said, acrimonious, fire of criticism against Arthur Scargill and the other NUM leaders.

Essentially Reid's complaint was that the NUM rules were disregarded when the ['rolling'] strike was approved under Rule 41, which licenses area action under national sanction, rather than Rule 43, which governs national action. 'The absence of a national ballot' says Reid, 'is the rock on which the Union is floundering'.[18] We shall examine this argument in a moment.

To its detriment, Reid further alleges that in the absence of a ballot 'Scargill chose to separate the strike area by area, using flying pickets to coerce brother miners. Picketing became a means of coercion, a substitute for winning minds . . . In the absence of a ballot, the only way of spreading the strike was by muscling men out. When you use muscle to get men out on strike, then you need to apply muscle to keep them out.' Through this junction, Reid's argument takes him to the point where he denounces 'people being beaten up in their homes by thugs masquerading as trade unionists'.

Let us try to look at these issues carefully, without such hyperbole. Certainly the NUM's decision not to call for a national ballot cost the union some support. A proportion, we do not know how large, of the Nottinghamshire miners might have joined a national strike after a ballot, if that ballot had voted accordingly. The evidence of some contemporary pollsters was that a majority of mineworkers in the country would indeed have done so. Peter Kellner reports[19] that other (then secret) NCB polls pointed in the opposite direction. If Kellner is right, and if the polls about which he writes were also right, there would not have been a strike. Another well-informed source shares this view. Arthur Scargill was reported, after the strike, as believing that a ballot would have voted against a strike. But if these witnesses were wrong, a strike without internal divisions in the NUM, might have found a proportion, we do not know how large, of the other workers to whom the NUM appealed for support more willing to respond. Yet it must surely remain doubtful whether the Trades Union Congress could have delivered any substantially greater industrial support than was in fact forthcoming, whatever percentage of the mineworkers had agreed to involve themselves in the strike. A significant but small minority of activists apart, the trade union movement as a whole was not at all ready to go for direct and general industrial action on behalf of the miners. Even though trade unionists often identified with the miners, and activists usually did so, levying themselves in order to support miners' families, attending meetings and demonstrations and offering moral support, they did not for the most part envisage any possibility of more general industrial action. When Tony Benn and Dennis Skinner went so far as to call for a general strike, they did not receive support from even one factory, office or workshop, however small, in spite of the respect and indeed affection which they aroused among many trade union militants. The more intelligent socialist journals immediately distanced themselves from what they regarded as a completely unrealistic proposal.[20]

In spite of the restraint of British trade unionists, which surely reflects the experience of mass unemployment, great and continuous sacrifices were made to sustain the miners in their strike. A very large campaign was developed, involving union members from an even wider spread of trades and industries than came to the support of the Glasgow shipbuilders during the 1971 work-in. Jimmy Reid, even when his polemic hit his target, showed himself strangely insensitive to the feelings of these people, just as it is unusual to encounter a former strike leader who is so apparently willing to pass over the incredible suffering of those who directly participated in the longest mass strike in British industrial history.

Quite clearly, Reid's remarks were not intended to censure the mineworkers, but were concerned to criticize the miners' leaders, and, as he was at pains to point out, Arthur Scargill in particular. But the strike was not the personal property of these leaders, and the dedication of the mineworkers and their wives and families is truly one of the most extraordinary episodes in trade union history, showing a courage and resilience which is quite staggering. By no democratic test can the readiness of the miners of Yorkshire, Scotland, Wales and the lesser striking areas to endure so many months of struggle and hardship be seen as an unimportant indicator of support for the action, even when it had been unconventionally sanctioned, region by region.

Reid's complaints about violence are also too one-sided. In spite of a ferocious propaganda campaign, many of the more sensational charges of intimidation alleged against striking miners had already been proved false before the end of the stoppage. One person from Yorkshire who appeared on television as having been sprayed with ammonia by pickets, and was subsequently widely interviewed, was, later still, charged with 'wasting police time'. The famous case of the burning of a house belonging to a miner who had returned to work turned out to have nothing to do with pickets or, as far as is now known, intimidatory behaviour. The area within which violence erupted with most tragic results was South Wales which is the area in which, normally, the strike had been highly disciplined, and conducted in the closest conformity to Reid's own guidelines. Certainly this was the area most completely committed in the strike, and most dubious about giving pickets priority above all other responses. Within the solid strike bound areas, in general, Reid's criticisms do not seem to carry the weight which he seeks to load upon them. The overwhelming majority of picketing was peaceful and relatively good humoured. Often it only turned sour with the intervention of the metropolitan or other outside police forces.[21]

In the crucial matter of Nottinghamshire, however, it is quite clear that the attempts made by flying pickets to influence the Nottinghamshire miners were unsuccessful, and indeed counter-productive. Of course, Reid is right to point out that an area-by-area sanction for the strike, as opposed to a national decision, left the Nottinghamshire miners in a radically distinct constitutional position when their own area balloted against strike action. From this point on only a national ballot could constitutionally engage them, whatever situation applied in the other regions of the union, which is jealous of its federal constitution. Undoubtedly this division of attitudes harmed the interests of mineworkers, both in Nottinghamshire itself and in the rest of the country. Even so, it is arguing well outside the established facts to attribute the early invasion of pickets to an organized national design. While they endorsed the Yorkshire action in flooding across the county borders, it seems that the national leaders were supporting a largely spontaneous reaction. Yorkshire and Nottinghamshire miners share a county boundary, and often live in the same villages. Indeed had the NUM leaders stood aside, the results could have been very much worse than they were in the event. Of course, the NUM's Nottinghamshire leaders who remained loyal to their national executive, and later paid a heavy price for so doing, did call upon their colleagues outside the coal field to allow their ballot to continue unhindered by external pickets, and they were ignored. By contrast, when the strike ended, Kent miners who had been picketing in Yorkshire to prevent a return to work before the granting of an amnesty for those miners dismissed during the dispute, called off the action once the Yorkshire Area had resolved that such pickets were unauthorized.

The argument which has been generally used to validate this distinction has been that a national ballot would have involved persons not affected by closures in voting, in effect, to impose them on those who *were* directly threatened. This, it was held, would justify picketing Nottinghamshire against their expressed wishes, while subsequently withdrawing from Yorkshire in accordance with their later decision and request. But this view is not evidently consistent. Refusal to order a general vote means that people are asked to take action regardless of the cost to themselves, in order, it is true, to prevent injury to others. But there were many possible forms of action which could have been taken against this threat of injury, and only one of these involved national strike action. Only if all were considered, and found equally inadequate would it have been seen to be reasonable to insist upon a national strike as the sole remaining option. Even then it remains plain that national rules could not both be overridden by area-based procedures and at the same time enforced in despite of them. When Mick McGahey argued that the NUM 'would not be constitutionalised' out of a strike, even though he meant to appeal to the spirit, not the letter, of the rule book, he hardly appreciated the social and political costs of this fundamentally inconsistent, indeed contradictory, reading of the union's rules. The elemental force of the strike, once it had erupted, overrode this constitutional problem, and would doubtless have overridden the 1984 Act's provisions, had they at the time been in force. But once the momentum relaxed, the riddles posed by the rule book resumed their importance, because the rule book was, in truth, no external imposition, but the most profound expression of the miners' own democratic aspirations.

Within strict trade union principles, this conflict involved a conflict of rights – right against right, posing the imperatives of solidarity against those of the union's own democracy. Such conflicts are deeply destructive, and undoubtedly this one played right into the hands of the government. Had the conflict been simply between the NUM on the one side and the government (and its battery of legislative measures) on the other, then the outcome could have been different, especially if the central thrust had been transformed into political persuasion from purely industrial action.

For this reason, it is necessary to explore the meaning of this division. On the one side, the miners were acting well within the traditions of their union in taking industrial action against the unilateral abrogation of a key agreement governing the procedure for pit closures. The fact that the 'moderate' leaders of the NUM were, at the beginning of the strike, completely in accord with the more militant members of their executive, indicates that they saw no choice in this matter. This was true of Nottinghamshire and other non-striking area leaders no less than the others. The closure of Cortonwood and the associated threats to other pits were a deliberate challenge, not only to the employment of those on the relevant colliery books, but also to the whole post-war industrial relations settlement in the mining industry.

However, given the industrial weakness of a trade union movement harassed by mass unemployment, while certain types of elementary trade union solidarity were possible, external aid for the mineworkers would depend mainly on moral support, and the generation of public sympathy. Most trade unions made themselves responsible for raising money and publicizing the miners' cause. Some tried to deliver sustained industrial action, but, with the notable exception of the seamen and the railwaymen, this proved difficult to mobilize, and transitory once it had actually come about. Two dock strikes not only ended quickly but brought the docks section of the TGWU into acute internal difficulties. Contrary to certain myths, union leaders were often far more keen to help than were rank-and-file members. Harassed by hecklers holding to these myths, Ron Todd, who had throughout the dispute conducted himself in a manner totally supportive of the NUM, exploded in anger, 'You cannot make a backbone out of a wishbone!' He was right.

Because 1984 was not 1972, there would be no triumph at Saltley Gate. Solidarity by industrial force was not an available option for the miners, and its attempted use became self-destructive. The only resource that could have won for the miners was that of public opinion and, first of all, mass trade union opinion. Prime targets for sympathy were the six million pensioners and the families of four million unemployed people, living on the edge of fuel poverty, many of them in one or another of the six million damp houses which make life so dangerous for the poor, the old and the very young. The NUM tried to answer the (quite absurd) claim that coal had been overproduced by an appeal for appropriate export subsidies. But the politically apposite answer was, surely, was it not, that fuel poverty produces the 'surplus' by forcing poor people to freeze? For a fraction of the cost of the miners' strike, Britain could have abolished hypothermia and surplus coal stocks at the same time, by instituting free or cheap electricity and energy supplies to claimants and pensioners. Too late, the Labour Party embraced this demand, which was never adequately expressed. Leading bishops were quicker to take it up. Had the NUM systematically campaigned upon it, while the strike focused public attention on the grievances in the industry, the pickets could have ignored Orgreave and concentrated in small but entirely persuasive numbers around supplementary benefit offices, local authority Social Services departments and employment exchanges. They had a constituency of millions to win, and once won, it could have burnt Mrs Thatcher's tents behind her lines.

Instead of persuasion, though, the predominant industrial logic was that of the set-piece shunt. For this the miners were cast in the role of victims, and, ultimately, that of losers.

The massive deployment of a coordinated police force introduced a new dimension to the dispute, and involved violent clashes going far beyond previous experiences at Grunwick and Warrington. While many trade unionists were worried about confrontations between massed pickets and police, and concerned to diminish their likelihood, this in no way led them to support police actions which can only be described as repressive. After all, the police were often taking the responsibility for 'enforcing' their own peculiar interpretations of a civil law which employers themselves had been careful not to invoke.

But because of the divisions inside the NUM, almost none of the apparatus of trade union law brought in by the Conservative administrations after 1979 was actually applied during the dispute (see appendix 3.1). Indeed, there were strong allegations that the government had intervened to prevent the British Steel Corporation from having recourse to law, since it was felt that such recourse would be politically disadvantageous. An early injunction obtained by the National Coal Board was left marooned in splendid isolation and no attempt was made to enforce it. Most of the legal restraints imposed upon the NUM resulted from civil actions by dissidents within the union calculated to enforce particular readings of the rule book. The most 'creative' legal initiative during the dispute was the decision, arising out of one of these actions, to impose a Receiver on the union. The very possibility of this had been specifically excluded in the 1871 Trade Union Act and it was only by an oversight that this prohibition was not reinforced in the 1970s, during the repeal of the ill-fated Industrial Relations Act of 1971. The short truth is, that the very idea of such receivership seemed, at the time, ridiculous. After lying fallow for more than a century, however, the idea took fertile root in the brain of Mr Justice Mervyn Davies as his own special response to the miners' strike. This development, and the entire surrounding fog of legal actions and counter-actions, offered a dreadful warning to trade unionists about the possible shaping of industrial relations in the future, and we shall return to it later.

It seems to us that these are the real issues involved in the tragic decision of the NUM to avoid a national ballot. They are far more serious than the pursuit of scapegoats, from which the trade unions will learn little or nothing. But it is not too late to learn that, when one's industrial strength is weakened, political responses become far more, not less, important.

Pointers for the Future of Strike Action and Ballots

In general terms, arrived at from data assembled before these dramatic events, Undy and Martin find that balloting before strikes can from a union's viewpoint be a useful and necessary form of member consultation where it is convenient, or where the nature of the constituency requires it, in order to reconcile different sectional interests or to reach a membership dispersed by, for example, shift working practices. But, quite unsurprisingly, they also find that balloting can reduce the flexibility often thought desirable in industrial negotiations and that it may also unduly lengthen and formalize bargaining and disputes. For a government that has consciously rejected the pluralist model of collective bargaining in favour of an individualistic philosophy of industrial relations and the labour market, such deficiencies may not count for much.

It has often been argued that the objective of British industrial relations law has been to redress the balance in which work people have been individually powerless in the face of the greater strength of their employer. This objective, we have been told, the law has sought to achieve by recognizing the need to allow collective restraints, by workers acting as a group, on arbitrary behaviour by their bosses. Within such a framework there could be different kinds of regulation of the right to strike, but there remained a strong presumption that it was a 'right'. Now, with the government removing legal immunities wholesale, we are left with no such unqualified 'right'. On the contrary, under the 1984 Act, and its forerunners of 1980 and 1982 only a narrow residual category of possible disputes will be protected from the risk of civil actions of one kind or another. But even these relatively few protected members of the genus must be seen as an endangered species, if it is accepted that slump and mass unemployment will inhibit the willingness of many workers to vote for industrial action. Sensing this, employers will drive harder bargains in the hope that the necessary strike vote may not materialize. To the extent that this prediction is found to be true, if we could imagine an even-handed administration, it would seek alternative methods to buttress trade unions through the period of their maximum difficulty in discharging their duties. Far from even-handed, the 1984 Act is merely the latest in a series of measures to disaggregate, restrict and roll back the influence of organized labour. If it 'succeeds', and the adverse climate of mass unemployment may for the foreseeable future ensure that it commonly does, then to that extent unions will become industrially toothless. In this condition, unless union strategies change, those of their members who do not abandon them altogether will become more and more discontented with their achievements, and the new rules governing union leadership elections will thus come into maximum (and most disruptive?) play. All this adds up to a ruthless implementation of tough prescriptions based upon a forensic diagnosis of union weakness. This is aimed not at reinforcing democracy, but at abusing the mechanisms of democracy in order to enfeeble still further, and even possibly actually to destroy, the ailing subject. A precise analogy would be to consider what might happen to capitalist corporations if some future government were to legislate to curtail the privilege of limited liability, by rendering it contingent upon a regular ballot of all employees to determine whether conditions of employment were in all respects satisfactory. But then their motive is not to make unions more representative or efficient, but something different.

To see how this might work, we may turn to the (limited) evidence so far available on the impact of compulsory balloting in 1984–5. Two cases stand out: the Austin–Rover strike of November 1984 and the teachers' strikes of 1985. In both cases, the employers invoked the appropriate sections of the 1984 Act to combat strike actions which had been sanctioned by unions without prior recourse to a ballot.

In the Austin–Rover case a pay strike involving 28,000 workers, spread across nine different trade unions, commenced on 2 November 1984. The largest membership was in the TGWU, which also dominates the joint union negotiating machinery in the company. Austin–Rover (a state-owned company), immediately sought and obtained a High Court Order that the unions should instruct their members to return to work until a ballot had been held in compliance with the 1984 Act. The TGWU refused to hold such a ballot since it held strongly to the TUC policy of non-compliance with the new law; it preferred to continue its normal method of mass meetings as the means whereby it measured members' wishes. Six unions in all failed to meet a six-hour deadline set by the Court on 7 November for calling off the strike. The EETPU, however, emphasizing its willingness to cooperate with the Court, ordered its members back to work and balloted them on the pay offer. It also pursued the company for repayment of its legal costs, since the company dropped its action in respect of that union.

Austin–Rover then unsuccessfully challenged a subsequent ruling by the court, that the AUEW, by declaring the strike unofficial, had removed itself from the scope of the injunction to order a return to work. Four other unions succeeded in avoiding contempt proceedings by distancing themselves in similar fashion from the strike. Eventually, against the background of a collapsing strike, the TGWU stood alone in its defiance of the court and the company. On 26 November, when the strike had been totally abandoned, the High Court heard from the company that the TGWU had refused either to hold a strike ballot or to order a return to work. At this stage, the court fined the union £200,000 for contempt. Mr Justice Hodgson said that the union's conduct was 'one of the worse cases of disobedience of orders of this court that there can ever have been . . . If orders of courts of law in this country are not obeyed then the only result is an approach to anarchy'.

It was widely expected that, if the union continued its defiance, then its £50 million of assets would be sequestrated. In fact, the union did sustain its position, and the court contented itself with collecting the fine. It is probable that behind-the-scenes counsel determined that it would be unwise to take on, through sequestration, the whole weight of the TGWU while the government was concentrating its main attentions on the task of defeating the miners. In other respects, the circumstances of the strike seemed unpropitious for a trial of union opposition to the ballot law. The level of the strikers' commitment to their cause was uncertain – witness the drift back to work, which was complete within three weeks of the commencement of the action. There was also some pressure from sections of the trade union outside the company for the strikers and the local union officers to maintain a hard line in order to link the strike with the wider cause of the miners' struggle, a tactic upon which the majority of the membership was probably less than keen.

Throughout this dispute, the company, following tough management doctrines it has developed over recent years, maintained stiff legal pressures on the unions, and particularly on the TGWU, despite the evident confusion and weaknesses which were visible among the workers themselves. Even without legal pressure, it is entirely possible that the strike would have collapsed anyway. The company, however, insisted that the new law had assisted them to break the strike, a view enthusiastically endorsed *pour encourager les autres*, by Employment Secretary Tom King. In this new climate, the traditional concern of a large company like British Leyland to retain the goodwill of national union officials in the face of unstable plant-level relationships was completely discarded by Austin–Rover's management. Whistling to keep up their courage on their way to court, union officers tried to convince employers that dire consequences might result from the use of the balloting requirements of the Act.

Here is the view of a senior AUEW official, ruefully put in the light of the Austin–Rover action:

> If my members vote in a ballot for a strike how can I negotiate to arrange a compromise – to negotiate a settlement? Austin–Rover has unleashed something that it might be unable to control by introducing the law into industrial relations. I am not sure what the future will hold for the company.[22]

The government and the more confrontational employers are of course assuming that unemployment may well persuade his members that tomorrow is the wrong day for a strike, so that his real problem is more likely to be, 'what possible sanctions are open to me when argument fails to convince, and how can I bargain without them?'

The TGWU's position, although involving defiance of the new law, in conformity with TUC policy, was in industrial relations terms entirely in line with the formerly unquestioned orthodoxies of post-war negotiating procedures. Moss Evans, the general secretary, declared:

> All TGWU members should be aware that negotiating procedures had been exhausted before action was taken. The company had paid for two delegate conferences to take place and afforded facilities for mass meetings. Having used these facilities, considered the Austin Rover offer and rejected it, our members observed and exhausted all the established agreed procedures. After all this, it was impossible for the TGWU to repudiate the lay officials and full-time officers of the union. It seems that those workers amongst the nine unions who accepted the offer were considered all right by the company. T&G members observed to the letter the agreements we have with the company. With negotiations at Fords Motor Company going on simultaneously, the use of similar procedures resulted in a settlement. Are we now to go to Court at every disagreement or are we to follow agreed procedures?[23]

Clearly this decision is not in the hands of the unions, and will not be restored to them until the law is changed. Without a new framework of law, or the prior restoration of full employment, unions have lost the initiative in every case save those in which rebellion has risen to the point of open mutiny. That is why there is no choice about it now: unions will either turn to new forms of political activity, or be very largely neutered.

While the courts and government were content with a limited punishment of the TGWU in this case, the special circumstances of the miners' concurrent conflict may well mean that such 'clemency' will not always be forthcoming. Moreover, the company has felt no inhibitions about subsequently pursuing the union through the courts for the losses it claims to have sustained in the strike.

The policy of non-compliance was not followed by the teachers' unions in the next major case involving the balloting provisions of the 1984 Act. In February and March of 1985 two unions, the National Union of Teachers and the National Association of Schoolmasters and Women Teachers were involved in separate campaigns of industrial action to press their wage claim against the education authorities, behind which stood the government which had withheld funds necessary to satisfy that claim. The NUT favoured a tactic of 'withdrawing goodwill', which meant that their members refused to carry out many activities outside class teaching hours or to cover for absent colleagues in class. The union also embarked upon selective three-day strikes, region by region, town by town. The Conservative-controlled Solihull Borough Council obtained a High Court order requiring the NUT to call off its campaign of sanctions because it had not held a ballot. The union responded by compliance with the ballot requirements of the Act, and obtained an 80 per cent vote in favour of its industrial action. An area of legal dubiety remained in this case, since the court's ruling failed to settle the question of whether the sanctions constituted a breach of contract or not. The employers claimed that they did; the union argued that duties undertaken voluntarily were not contractual. The NUT intends to test this question after the end of the pay campaign, by calling on all its 235,000 members to refuse lunch-time supervision of children until all LEAs have distanced themselves from the Solihull position, which defines such duties as a supplemental contract.

As the NUT moved on to the calling of three day strikes, it continued in compliance with the law by organizing ballots in the affected areas. In Humberside for example, it won its ballot for the strikes by a majority of 80 per cent. The other union, the NAS/UWT, also responded to the Solihull injunction by holding a ballot, and won the vote for strike action by 83 per cent. It went ahead with a national members' ballot to establish its right to call, not only for half-day strikes, but also for the withdrawal of its members from administrative work, including preparation for and invigilation of external examinations. Both trade unions were careful to take legal advice about the wording of their ballot papers, in order to stay in line with the 1984 Act.

In a third case, members of the National Graphical Association voted by 154 to 33 to continue strike action at the Wolverhampton Express and Star newspaper over the introduction of new technology. On this occasion too the ballot had been forced by the newspaper's owners through a High Court injunction.

These last two cases suggest that the ballot Act has not marked the end of legality in strike actions, and that where members feel a sense of outrage, or when a union is pursuing a popular policy it may still be able to win very large majorities. This of course, was the response predicted by the Donovan Commission, which made reference to experience in the United States; and it was reinforced by the railway case of 1972. But the 1984 Austin–Rover case will be read as a more disturbing indicator by many trade unionists. Whatever the pattern which emerges, it is difficult to see how unions will be able to avoid a significant transfer of energy from the industrial to the political sphere if they are not to be reduced to impotence in a number of key areas of their work.

The third major area covered by the 1984 Act has been precisely designed in order to render such political reactions as difficult as possible.

The Politics of Political Fund Ballots

As we have already insisted, by legislating to inhibit trade union political action, the government has moved beyond control of trade union behaviour into the sphere of major constitutional change. Were the opposition to be disabled by this measure, qualitatively new political relationships would emerge. For this reason, we shall examine the development of political fund ballots in a good deal more detail in chapter 4.

Mrs Thatcher's success at the General Election of 9 June 1983 obviously placed the trade unions in a great predicament, because only slightly less than 39 per cent of their members voted for the Labour Party. The remainder divided almost equally between the Conservatives and the Alliance. Whether or not this weakening of the traditional political allegiances of trade union members proved to be temporary, the continuous slump in the labour market which has eroded the Labour Movement's industrial strength, has had certain other entirely predictable effects upon morale. In these circumstances an old theory offered many years ago by G. D. H. Cole suggests that, pendulum-fashion, as trade unions' industrial strength ebbs, so they will turn to political action. Whatever the state of historical evidence for this theory, few will doubt that the movement's response to its current crisis should indeed be political. In this crisis, there are profound threats, but also opportunities and imperatives for new developments in Labour politics. It was precisely against these that Mr Tebbitt took up his legal blunderbuss, which was subsequently handed over to Mr King.

They clearly perceived that mass industrial action as a resistance to government policies stood little chance of evoking a response among a demoralized and fearful trade union membership. This was evidenced for example by the repeated reluctance of the mineworkers, both nationally and locally where particular pits were threatened with closure, to employ the method of overall industrial action. The miners' caution was not the result of diffident leadership. On the contrary, miners' leaders had constantly made plain their view that direct action should be authorized, in a succession of ballots which had withheld such authorization. When such action took place without the sanction of a ballot, it was bound to be seen as a major test. Had the miners won, even if some of their supporters were prone to exaggerate the meaning of victory, few can doubt that the government's industrial policies would have been badly shaken. Since they lost, it is equally difficult to overestimate the impact on trade unionism.

Trade unions in a number of other industries have also had serious reverses, albeit on a much more modest scale, over the past few years. The need to find responses to stimulate realistic and effective forms of counterattack is therefore urgent. Many of these involve campaigning for law reform, and the unions would be wise to consider every proposal for practicable action on this plane.

But this is the very moment which the government has chosen to launch a crippling attack upon the political connections and traditions of the trade unions. Because the Labour Party derives up to 80 per cent of its national funds from union subscriptions, the government needed a judicious approach to its objectives. Having ensured the necessary legislation to compel political ballots on whether or not to continue the institution of political funds, it then pretended to keep a low profile on the outcome of the ballots themselves. It fell to the Parties of the Alliance to make most noise about how people should actually cast their votes. Of course, the newspapers projected this, together with their own opinions, fortissimo. For the government, the main expectation was that the reduction of the proportion of trade unionists normally voting Labour could be maintained by the maintenance of a high level of overall aggravation for which unions would get the blame. It was in this context that the miners' strike was managed in order to produce maximum confrontation and maximum levels of fear and apprehension among ordinary trade union members. We shall return to this question later in our argument, but it is necessary here to point up the very careful management of conflict by a government armed at all times with sophisticated polls accurately reflecting all the movements of trade union opinion. Just as the National Coal Board anonymously polled the mineworkers themselves, repeatedly throughout the length of the strike, and to lethal effect, so it seems inconceivable that the government were not monitoring the impact of such set-piece battles as that at Orgreave on wider trade union opinion.

If we consider for a moment what happened: some 10,000 pickets were allowed to mass repeatedly in the same place, where their action would be taken by all but the most committed union supporters as a threat to the jobs of another group of workers, in the steelworks. True, from the trade union point of view, Orgreave was an entirely legitimate target. Quite specific agreements were being unilaterally abrogated by management and the mineworkers were understandably deeply resentful. But the question which is bound to present itself is: how could so many pickets mass in this place, when police techniques of control were sufficiently sensitive to detect even one car passing under the Dartford tunnel in the direction of pickets more than 120 miles further north?

Mr George Bolton, the Vice-President of the Scottish Area of the NUM, gave it as his opinion that the police had set a trap for the men at Orgreave in order to mete out physical punishment on them. It seems quite reasonable to argue that a trap had indeed been set, even if not for that reason. The trap was intended to inoculate rank-and-file trade unionists with fear of trade union intransigence, and at the same time it was intended to reinforce the distance between ordinary trade unionists and the Labour Party, with more than half an eye on the upcoming political fund ballots. In short, the major industrial battles, the climate of mass unemployment and economic uncertainty, and the thrust of legislation must all be seen in their intricate interrelationship. When an effort is made to do this, it seems absolutely plain that the attacks on union political funds are intended to neuter trade union action in the one area in which it could be both resolute, widespread and effective.

Mr Tebbitt's original proposals, as we have seen, were modified to impose amendments to the 1913 Trade Union Act which had, up to 1984, regulated trade union political activity. Under this Act, trade unions were required to hold an affirmative ballot of their members in order to authorize the setting up of a political fund. In the case of most unions, these ballots were held once only, many years previously. It was an ingenious move to subject the continued operation of such a political fund to the recurrent test of an additional ballot of the whole membership of each union (in accordance with the procedure laid down in 1913, which requires a simple majority of those voting) every ten years.

The second change to which we have already referred was that the definition of 'political objects' in section 3(3) of the 1913 Act must be 'brought up to date' so as to cover expenditure on television, radio and other forms of publicity, on elections to the European Parliament and the printing of political literature.

In the run up to the 1983 General Election, a Green Paper had been published, in which the other main proposals of the Trade Union Act were trailed as a kind of official election manifesto. But there was one intriguing difference between the Green Paper and the subsequent bill. This concerned this very area of political funds. Initially the Green Paper had pledged the government to deal with 'widespread disquiet' about the operation of the system by which trade union members could 'contract out' of making political fund payments. The 1913 Act stipulates that people who have conscientious objections to financing trade union political activities have the right to be exempt from such payments and may not be discriminated against in their other trade union activities, if they do so. After the General Strike, the then Conservative government had legislated to repeal this provision, substituting a much tougher requirement which established that anyone wishing to make a political contribution should actually 'contract in' in order to do so. The result was a sharp decline in the numbers of persons paying political contributions, and a severe reduction in the amounts of money which unions had available to pay to the Labour Party. (We examine this story in chapter 4.) However, this did not prevent Labour from winning the largest number of seats at the subsequent general election, and installing Mr Ramsay MacDonald for his second term of office.

Interference with the law at this level would certainly have been a problem for the unions and the Labour Party, but it was potentially far less lethal than the actual proposal, now implemented, which was published for the first time when the Bill finally emerged after the election. An adverse vote in a political fund ballot would mean that all those persons who wanted to contribute to a political fund would be unable to do so, since it would have been officially annulled. Among the major unions affiliated to the Labour Party, five quite important ones have, for a long time, already had a majority of their members contracting out of the political levy: SOGAT, NGA, ASTMS, COHSE and ACTT. A number of lesser known unions have been in the same position for some time. Unions with large proportions of members contracting out have included: TASS, the Fire Brigades Union, the Furniture, Timber and Allied Trades, NATTKE (the cinema union), Tobacco Workers and UCATT (the building workers' trade union). Since large numbers of people were specifically contracted out of these bodies, it seemed likely that it would be difficult to win a vote to establish a political fund, unless members showed a remarkable degree of political sophistication. This would involve them in accepting that it was reasonable to bring a fund into being, or to maintain an existing one even though their personal intention was to refrain from paying in to it. Even those larger unions in which huge majorities have hitherto cheerfully paid the levy, could not, after 1983, necessarily maintain confidence about the outcome of the ballots. A MORI poll of January 1982 reported that opponents of Labour Party affiliation outnumbered supporters in the TGWU, the AUEW, GMBATU, ASTMS, EETPU, NUR and USDAW. On the findings of this poll, only in the NUM and in NUPE would Labour win an affirmative ballot such as is now scheduled under the 1984 Act.

While we must always approach polls with some caution, we must face up to the calculations now being made by Mrs Thatcher's closest advisers, that by the time of the Party's conference of 1985 or 1986, a large proportion of Labour's historically loyal trade union affiliates might very well be compelled to absent themselves from the deliberations. Subsequent polls tell different stories, and we shall examine these in chapter 5.

The difficulties for a trade union, reliant on the voluntary work of local branch officials and shop stewards to fulfil the role of ballot officers, scrutineers and returning officers, in trade union ballots, have been demonstrated by the problems of the TGWU general secretary's election in 1984–5. Under the 1984 Act, conformity with union rules will become conformity with the law, and a most complex law at that. In applying the Act to the political fund ballots, the Certification Officer has been obliged to publish a 19 page *Guide to Political Fund Ballots* (December 1984), and seven separate documents, amounting in all to 80 pages of text, setting out the model rules which should be adopted by trade unions to cover one or more of the different methods of balloting allowed for under the Act.

The guide lays down a four-stage procedure which a union must go through before holding a ballot. This comprises:

1 Preparation by the trade union of draft ballot rules.
2 Submission of draft ballot rules for preliminary approval by the Certification Officer.
3 Adoption of ballot rules by the union.
4 Submission of ballot rules for formal approval by the Certification Officer.

Only thereafter may a union be sure that, in proceeding with its ballot, it has complied with the law. The model ballot rules cover seven distinct forms of balloting:

1 Fully postal ballots, in which ballot papers are sent out and returned by post.
2 Workplace ballots, where ballot papers are made available and votes are cast at the workplace or at a place more convenient for the voter.
3 Semi-postal ballots, where ballot papers are made available at the workplace or at a place more convenient for the voter, or handed out, and returned by post.
4 Fully postal and workplace voting – a combination of fully postal and workplace voting.
5 Fully postal and semi-postal voting – a combination of these two options.
6 Workplace and semi-postal voting – a combination of these three options.

A union is not obliged to adopt these rules in every word, and may submit for Certification Officer approval other rules, or modifications to the model rules; however, it is clear that the models will have a dominant influence. They amount to a massive state intervention in union rule-making. All the seven models contain some standard features, to ensure secrecy, convenience and accuracy, and to avoid interference with either the balloting or the counting of votes. In at least one respect they go beyond the requirements of Parliamentary balloting in providing for the use of a sealable envelope in which the marked ballot paper is inserted, even in the case of workplace ballots where a sealed ballot box is used to collect the vote. In another, they require that all ballot papers should carry the printed text of the Trade Union 1984 Act's definition of political objects, a 46 line extract resounding with legal jargon.

A further standard requirement is that, 'if the result of the ballot is that the resolution approving the furtherance of political objects as an object of the union is adopted, the executive committee shall, as soon as practicable after the adoption of the resolution, cause a notice in the following form to be given to each member of the union . . .' There then follows a summary of the members' right to contract out of paying into the political fund which has just been approved. This provision highlights the unique nature of this process, enshrined since 1913. It demonstrates very clearly that, after a rigorous ballot, in which a majority has made a decision to operate a political fund, the minority, who voted contrary to that decision, is entitled to refuse to comply with it. Imagine the consequences of applying this to Parliamentary elections. All those who voted against the government party would be entitled to contract-out of paying any taxes made necessary by that party's election programme!

The provision is of course defended on the grounds of the rights of minorities; yet an actual majority frequently votes against the eventual winner in Parliamentary elections. Moreover if the trade union minority may contract out after a positive vote for a fund, why does the 1984 Act require the abolition of a political fund if the majority votes against one? The rights of the minority who voted *for* a political ballot are, in this case, explicitly denied. They may not go through some process of contracting *in*, in order to continue to engage in collective political objectives. It is an extraordinary piece of constitution making by any standards.

All the model rules provide for vote-counting to take place at the union's head office. The executive committee must appoint three persons who are not members of the executive committee to be counting officers. 'No persons shall be present at the count other than the counting officers, those acting under their supervision, and the general secretary and as many members of the executive committee as desire to attend'. This may be thought to be an adequate safe-guard against irregularities at the count, yet an executive with tight control over the loyalty of the appointed counters and clerical staff have opportunities here for interference which are at least as available under a postal as under any other system, since the destination of the ballots in either case is the union head office, whose staff could, if they were so minded, rig the result by tampering with the returned papers or boxes before the counting officers set eyes on them.

The Lessons of an Unprecedented Attack

What would be the consequences of a divorce between the unions and the Labour Party? The Party's finances, precarious to the point of insolvency already, would be devastated. Even after recent major increases in constituency party contributions, three-quarters of the Party's ordinary revenue comes from trade union affiliations, quite apart from the substantial sums which the unions donate to general election funds, and have made available to capital projects such as headquarters' buildings.

Financial losses at regional and local levels would also be severe. Trade union participation in the Party's work at all levels would be decisively reduced as all formal delegate representation from union branches to the constitutional committees of the Party was withdrawn. Already, under present practice, a dangerous tendency has arisen for trade union influence over Labour Party policy-making to become too heavily concentrated in the hands of a few trade union leaders, while rank and file union participation at the local level has been reduced. But a formal severance of trade union links would have its greatest effect at the local level; we can assume that informal discussion and influence at the top level would continue, although not involving direct financial assistance from unions to the Party. Trade union influence at Parliamentary level would be excluded as union-sponsorship of MPs was rendered illegal. Campaigns on single issues, even by 'non-political' unions such as NALGO (for example against privatization) could become illegal.

Quite apart from these formal, constitutional and financial consequences, the ending of the trade union link with the Labour Party would encourage those who seek to further weaken the loyalties of union members to the Labour Movement. We might then expect less principled, more opportunist lobby politics at the apex of the trade union movement. Quite possibly some leaders of the TUC would seek to emerge as the 'neutral' spokesmen of workers' interests, functioning as the expression of just another lobby.

It is clear that the Trade Union Act is the keystone of a legislative process, through the arch of which the government seeks to drive Labour organizations into an altogether more passive, regulated and docile exis-tence. The laws which have restricted picketing rights, rendered the closed shop desperately precarious and removed protection from the weakest and most ill-paid sections of the workforce all gain added signifi-cance if it becomes possible to disconnect trade unions from political objectives. This is a Catch 22: without political objectives, none of the other iniquities can be redressed: it will not be possible to organize the secure repeal of adverse laws, or enactment of beneficial ones. There are therefore very strong reasons for concluding that this Act culminates the most direct and blatant assault on trade union powers in British history.

Royden Harrison has pointed out that from previous legislative attacks, the Labour movement has derived permanent lessons, and embodied them in its institutions. After the 'Sheffield outrages' of 1866, the appointment of the Trades Unions Commissioners and then of the Royal Commission on Trade Unions offered a possible threat to the existence of the unions which brought together the foundation meeting in Manchester, which was, although none of the founders knew it at the time, to be the beginning of the TUC. The employers' offensive of the late 1890s, culminating in the Taff Vale judgment of 1901, gave solidity to the newly established Labour Representation Committee, and directly produced the Labour Party.

What will be the institutional lesson of this latest wave of repression? There are strong reasons to think that, whatever the domestic response may be, unions will need to strengthen their international, and above all, their European links. The economic reasons for this were already present in the development of transnational capital and the creation of the meso-economic sector about which we wrote in chapter 2. The political necessity for such a convergence of trade union forces arises from the overriding need to restore full employment, which is a task for convergent action by several determined governments at once, and not an option for beleaguered national outposts acting in isolation. But we should not overlook the fact that democratic institutions draw support from one another, and that the maintenance of free trade unionism is of profound concern to trade unionists everywhere. The interpenetration of capital in Europe implies that trade unions can exercise power if they are able to co-ordinate effectively on the appropriate scale. It is not fanciful to suggest that British workers now need some of the help which they and their Western European colleagues once gave to unions in Spain, Portugal or Greece during their different, but not irrelevant, sufferings under autocracies. It would be a mistake for British trade unions to seek to respond only on the national plane, necessary though it is for them to remove the present administration and create a new legal framework within which they can operate effectively. More and more it becomes necessary to see the convulsive shifts of British politics as part of a more fundamental and wider crisis, and to seek our remedies in joint action with the victims in other countries.

APPENDIX 3.1   LEGAL INTERVENTIONS IN THE MINERS' STRIKE

In March, soon after the beginning of the miners' strike, the National Coal Board applied for an injunction at the High Court. It sought to prevent the Yorkshire miners from organizing flying pickets. Predictably the injunction was granted, and promptly disregarded by the miners. Faced with this response, the National Coal Board asked the court to adjourn its case against the Yorkshire Area of the union for contempt of court, and the strike accordingly wound its way without any attempt to enforce this judgment.

Legal action began in earnest in May, at the instance of a group of working miners, led by Mr Colin Clarke of the Pye Hill No. 1 Branch of the Nottinghamshire NUM. Mr Clarke and two colleagues secured orders from the court upholding their right to work. The court decided that the strike in Nottinghamshire was unlawful, because there had been no national ballot as required by union rules. Mr Clarke's initiative was followed by similar applications to the courts on behalf of groups of (or individual) working miners in Yorkshire, Derbyshire, Lancashire, North Wales and Staffordshire.

The success of these forays emboldened Mr Clarke to return to the High Court in July. Together with 16 other working miners, he sought a ruling which would invalidate certain disciplinary changes in the rules of the NUM. These changes were accordingly declared illegal. This very successful legal process was to continue. After a series of actions, area by area, Mr Justice Nicholls ruled the strikes in Yorkshire and Derbyshire to be unlawful, in the one case because there had been no recent ballot and in the other case the ballot which had in fact been held had produced a marginal majority against striking. Thus, on 28 September the judge forbade the use of the word 'official' to describe the Yorkshire strike. This order was instantly defied by Arthur Scargill during an interview on television immediately following the judgment. As a result, there followed a tense drama at the Labour Party Conference, which was in progress at the time.

A writ was served on Mr Scargill on 1 October, initiating contempt of court proceedings on him and the union. The union boycotted the subsequent hearing which took place on 4 October. Mr Justice Nicholls thereupon deferred the judgement in order to allow the union time to rethink its position, and avoid contempt. However, the union maintained its original attitude, and was judged to be guilty of contempt. A fine of £200,000 was levied on the union and a further £1,000 fine was imposed upon Mr Scargill personally. This last fine was met by an anonymous donor, who issued a declaration through lawyers to the effect that he feared that the miners' president might otherwise be given the status of a martyr.

The union, however, refused to pay its fine, and its assets were totally sequestrated on 25 October. There followed a bizarre search for the union's funds which had been moved to foreign banks, and which were not easy to locate. It turned out that the union had received prudent financial advice, since its moneys were held in dollar bearer bonds and thus avoided the severe depreciation of the pound which was careering rapidly on a downward helter-skelter towards parity with the dollar. Be that as it may, the sequestrators, Price Waterhouse, tracked £2.7 million of union funds to a Dublin bank and, days later, a further £4.63 million were located in Luxemburg, together with just over £½ million which were on deposit in Zurich. On 9 November Price Waterhouse claimed that they had actually seized £8,174, out of a fund of more than £8 million. By the end of November they returned to the court to explain that they had exaggerated the extent of their success, since they had not in fact got possession of £6,322 of the original £8,000-plus which they had claimed.

At this point Mr Clarke returned to the court with two proposals: that the individuals comprising the NUM executive should be held personally liable to meet the fine: and that the trustees of the union should be replaced by a Receiver. A Receiver was duly appointed: he turned out to be a Conservative Party activist from Ilkeston in Derbyshire. After a frustrating wrangle with the Luxemburg bank, which proved less than enthusiastic to uphold the decisions of British courts, he asked to withdraw from his new responsibilities and was duly replaced.

On 4 December an astonishing report was published in the *Daily Telegraph*. Although Mr Macgregor's first legal actions had been put on ice, now the *Daily Telegraph* sought to show that he had not in fact been absent during the long litigation which had accompanied the dispute throughout its history.

> The long running legal process culminating in the appointment first of squestrators and then of a Receiver to control the funds of the National Union of Mineworkers was masterminded by Mr Ian Macgregor, Chairman of the Coal Board, Government sources disclosed last night . . . While the legal moves were initiated by working miners, Mr Macgregor used his good offices to put them in touch with 'small town' solicitors and with businessmen eager to give financial backing.

The report went on to say that Mr Macgregor had drawn the conclusion that the Coal Board's own legal action would do nothing to divide the union leadership, since it would only deepen the solidarity of the miners and their supporters in the wider trade union movement. 'He took the view that the only challenge which might weaken the miners' leadership and hasten the end of the strike would come from within the Union.'

The next day the newspaper featured a strong denial of this story from Colin Clarke. He made five points. First, he said there had been no contact, direct or indirect, between the working miners' committees and Mr Macgregor, who had 'not masterminded any of the legal actions' under discussion. Secondly, his family lawyers had conducted the cases.

Thirdly, no businessmen had backed the funds of the working miners' committees which had all 'been raised by donations from ordinary members of the public'. Fourthly, the court actions were solely motivated by the desire to return the union 'to the democratic control if its membership'. And fifthly, Mr Clarke could not easily comprehend why 'Government sources' could tell such tales.

If we can believe that the government was, as reported in the *Daily Telegraph*, directly involved in counselling those who carried the NUM into the courts, and secured judgment after judgment against the union, then the governmental strategy for dealing with the miners can be seen to be fairly sophisticated. This process of intervening within the ranks of the unions in order to overcome and nullify trade union action has been a consistent feature of government industrial relations policy.

In total, the recourse to law by a variety of individuals and agencies occasioned by the miners' strike broke all records. Working miners initiated more than a dozen actions against the NUM, all based on the interpretation of the union's rule book, especially Rule 41 (dealing with area strikes and ballots), and Rule 43 (dealing with ballots for national strikes). Interim injunctions flowed continuously from these actions, forbidding official support for the strike, banning disciplinary measures by the union, compelling the holding of meetings and elections, restraining intimidation and besetting, barring the union from implementing rule changes.

Recourse was had to the secondary action and secondary picketing provisions of the 1980 and 1982 Employment Acts by third parties, in one case leading to the fine and sequestration order imposed on the South Wales NUM for contempt. 'Watching and besetting', a criminal offence under the 1875 Conspiracy and Protection of Property Act, thought to be obsolete, was rediscovered and widely applied. Police authority to stop motorway movement was challenged unsuccessfully in court by the strikers. Challenges to bail conditions by striking miners were also unsuccessful.

Unfair dismissal proceedings have followed the wholesale sackings in which the NCB has indulged during and after the strike. The Child Poverty Action Group has supported a miner disputing DHSS deductions from social security because of assumed payment of union strike pay.

Outside the NUM itself, an NUS member successfully challenged the union's levy on seamen in support of the miners' funds.[24]

Notes

1　House of Lords Debates, *Hansard*, vol. 453, 19 June 1984, cols. 188 et seq.

2 Lord Donovan (chairman), *Report of the Royal Commission on Trade Unions and Employers' Associations*, HMSO, Cmnd 3623, 1968.

3 Cf. Vic Allen, 'The ethics of trade union leaders, and the acceptance of State honours', in *Trade Union Leadership*, Longman, 1957, pp. 30 et seq.

4 The term coined by H. A. Turner in *Trade Union Growth, Structure and Policy*, Allen & Unwin, 1962.

5 Roger Undy and Roderick Martin, *Ballots and Trade Union Democracy*, Basil Blackwell, 1984, p. 3.

6 Ibid., especially chapter 2.

7 Cf. J. D. Edelstein and Malcolm Warner, *Comparative Union Democracy*, Allen & Unwin, 1975, pp. 263 et seq.

8 *Tribune*, 21 May 1982.

9 C. H. Rolph, *All those in Favour?* Andre Deutsch, 1962.

10 Cf. Ken Coates and Tony Topham, *The New Unionism*, Penguin, 1974, pp. 183–7.

11 The New Statesman (22 February 1985) reported 'thousands of lost voters' in the London borough of Haringey. In Tottenham, almost 6,000 people were not registered. In Hornsey and Wood Green over 4,000. The borough would have been divided into three seats instead of two, if the missing 10,000 electors had been registered. But the Boundary Commissioners work on the numbers on the register, not on the numbers who should be on it. The extra seat would almost certainly have gone to Labour.

12 Robert Taylor, *The Fifth Estate: Britain's Unions in the Seventies*, Routledge Kegan and Paul, 1978, p. 123.

13 Department of Employment, *A Guide to the Trade Union Act, 1984*, October 1984, p. 14.

14 Ibid., p. 15.

15 Lord Donovan, *Royal Commission on Trade Unions*, pp. 114–15. (Our italics.)

16 Undy and Martin, *Ballots and Trade Union Democracy*, p. 118.

17 Cited in Undy and Martin, *Ballots and Trade Union Democracy*, p. 126.

18 *New Society*, 10 January 1985.

19 Peter Kellner, 'How the Coal Board privatised the strike', *New Statesman*, 8 March, 1985.

20 See, for example, the editorial in *Tribune*, 8 March 1985.

21 Cf. Sheffield Policewatch, *Taking Liberties*, 1985; Susan Miller and Martin Walker, *A State of Siege*, Yorkshire Area NUM, 1984 and following reports in the same series. (Revised and expanded edition, Jim Coulter, Susan Miller, Martin Walker, *State of Seige*, Canary Press, 1984.)

22 *Financial Times*, 22 November 1984.

23 TGWU *Record*, December 1984.

24 Date from Incomes Data Services, Brief, no. 294, February 1985.

4 The Political Fund

Political Action in Trade Union History

> It is a broad and general principle that Companies incorporated by Statute
> for special purposes, and societies, whether incorporated or not, which
> owe their constitution and their status to an Act of Parliament, having
> their objects and powers defined thereby, cannot apply their funds to any
> purposes foreign to the purposes for which they were established, or
> embark on any undertaking in which they were not intended by Parliament
> to be concerned . . . This principle . . . applies . . . in every case where
> a society or association formed for purposes recognised and defined by an
> Act of Parliament places itself under the Act, and by so doing obtains some
> statutory immunity or privilege.[1]

It was with these words that one of the judges in the Osborne case of
1909 declared illegal the pursuit of political objectives by trade unions.
The legal jargon, which purports to give objective judicial weight to the
decision, would imply that company payments to the Conservative Party
were equally illegal. If unions enjoyed a limited degree of immunity from
civil actions preventing them from acting in 'restraint of trade', did not
companies all enjoy the principle of limited liability? But the Osborne
judgment never stopped a penny payment by companies to the
Conservatives. Behind it lay a deep-seated resentment on the part of
an anti-union establishment at the persistent excursion of British trade
unions beyond the limits of collective bargaining into the area of political
action. Yet the history of trade unionism shows very clearly that political
action has been an integral method of the movement from its earliest
days.

Sidney and Beatrice Webb, whose approach involved them in a
compulsion to classify, distinguished three basic trade union methods
of work: these they styled 'mutual insurance', 'collective bargaining'
and 'legal enactment'.[2] Of course it is difficult in practice to draw sharp
demarcation lines between these three processes, which intertwine
throughout industrial history. Each process has its vogues, its general
ascendancies and its moments of disuse. These vary with phases of

113

advance and retreat in the trade union movement as a whole. Nevertheless, the Webbs gave the third of their 'methods' a considerable importance in their analysis.

> We do not need to remind the student of the *History of Trade Unionism* that an Act of Parliament has, at all times, formed one of the means by which British Trade Unionists have sought to attain their ends. The fervour with which they have believed in this particular Method, and the extent to which they have been able to employ it have varied according to the political circumstances of the time. The strong trade clubs of the town handicraftsmen, and the widely extended associations of woollen workers of the eighteenth century, relied mainly upon the law to secure the regulation of their trades. So much was this the case that the most celebrated student of eighteenth century Trade Unionism declares that 'the legal prosecution' of transgressors of the law was the chief object of these combinations, and that, in fact, English Trade Unionism 'originated with the non-observance of' the statutes fixing wages and regulating apprenticeship. Its fundamental purpose, says Professor Brentano, was 'the maintenance of the existing legal and customary regulations of trade. As soon as the State ceased to maintain order, it stepped into its place.'[3]

A brief resume pointing out a few signposts will demonstrate the obvious continuity and persistence of the method of political action in trade union history.

As the Webbs and Professor Brentano insisted, eighteenth century trade unions were often involved in petitioning Parliament to ensure continued enforcement of long-established statutory protection of wages and trade conditions. Such campaigns also developed by appealing on these questions to Quarter Sessions and to the Privy Council. Early unions demanded, in addition, new legislation, organized opposition to new employers' Bills in Parliament, lobbied and demonstrated in support of their petitions and even sought to influence Parliamentary elections through their few enfranchised members.

As Parliament and the judiciary fell under the sway of Adam Smith's doctrines, embracing the idea of *laissez-faire*, the practice of petitioning fell into disuse. It would in any case soon have been driven underground by the advent of the Combination Acts. On reacquiring a degree of legality in the 1820s, the trade unions of the immediately ensuing decades developed the widest possible political interpretation of their role, going far beyond their early supplications to Parliament, to demand not only the reform of that unheeding institution, but the total transformation of industrial society in pursuit of the visions of Robert Owen. These were the earliest years of advocacy of the cooperative commonwealth.

At the same time, unions by no means rejected demands for piecemeal ameliorative measures. Some of these succeeded, such as the early Factory Acts and the statutory limitation of working hours. Moving between reform and revolution, this highly political generation of trade unionists reached out to an ultimate goal in which we can see close affinities with the objectives of early twentieth century syndicalism:

> See into what position this mode of pursuing things resolves itself. Every trade has its internal government in every town; a certain number of towns comprise a district, and delegates from the trades in each town form a quarterly district government; delegates from the district form the Annual Parliament; and the King of England becomes President of the Trade Unions.[4]

All that had changed between the age of Senex and that of Tom Mann was that the role of the monarchy was somewhat differently perceived.

Following the destruction of the Owenite unions, the path of working class betterment led through opposition to the Poor Law and the Corn Laws directly into Chartism, in which the demand for political emancipation was to be found in its most overt state. The specific trade union contribution to Chartism was manifest; many strikes and disputes of the 1840s which began as 'purely' industrial issues spilled over into militant support for the Charter. 'The trades of Great Britain carried the reform bill and the trades of Great Britain shall carry the Charter', declared the delegates to the Charter Association.

In a different way, the predominantly craft unionism of the 1860s was pushed into the political arena by the attentions of both judiciary and government. Encouraged by the Trades Councils, it moved beyond sectional horizons to convene and sustain the first gatherings of the Trades Union Congress, specifically in order to mount political campaigns against the judgement in *Hornby v. Close*, against the Master and Servant laws, and against the threat to its future status which had been implied in the setting up of a Royal Commission on Trade Unions in 1867. The naming of the TUC's embryonic executive body as 'the Parliamentary Committee' (a title it preserved until after the First World War), clearly indicates its intentions. Its permanent remit was to monitor and lobby on all legislative questions affecting trade union rights and interests.[5]

The extension of the male franchise to some of the urban artisans in 1867 was followed in 1874 by the arrival in Parliament of the first (miners) trade union Members of Parliament. In this period both miners and cotton workers organized elaborate structures to permit sectional political initiative, variously showing allegiance to the existing Tory and Liberal parties. Yet already in the 1860s, the cautious English craft union leaders played a prominent part in the International Working Men's Association, which was led by Marx into the declaration: 'The social emancipation of the workmen [sic] is inseparable from their political emancipation'.

The awakening of socialist thought among the new unions of the 1880s, pioneered by the Social Democratic Federation and later carried forward in the Independent Labour Party, led, through an edifying confrontation with old-guard Liberal TUC leaders, to a resolution at its 1899 Congress which instructed that leadership to summon what became the founding conference of the Labour Party in the following year. The Taff Vale judgment of the House of Lords in 1901, rendering all strike action vulnerable to court actions, persuaded many waverers among the unions of the virtues of speedy affiliation to this new Party. At this point, the trade unions had created, by trial and error, that bifurcated form of general allegiance to two distinct bodies whose functions were differentiated: the coordination of political lobbying was to be continued through the TUC, but direct representation in Parliament was hived off to the new Labour Party. (A third national multi-union organization, the General Federation of Trade Unions, was established and given the function of coordinating industrial action.)

The slow achievement of the franchise and the very existence of a Parliamentary form of government meant that this division of function was not only possible, but apparently natural and inevitable. There is nothing unique in this development; almost all Western labour movements have produced, from a common origin in the working class, separate trade union and political party structures. (Exceptions to this generalization are to be found in anarcho-syndicalist forms, and of course in the American case, where a separate working class political party has not yet matured.)

However, the separation of functions into distinct organizational responsibilities has had, and continues to have, the effect of reinforcing an unreal understanding of the nature of working class politics. It can assist in bolstering the prejudice against 'politics' as something extraneous to the basic processes of trade unionism. Industrial and bargaining functions can, in times of relatively full employment, appear 'normal' and legitimate, while the political function may seem to be, at best, an optional extra, at worst, an intrusion by trade unions into an arena properly reserved for an elite professional Parliamentary caste.

This eccentric, if not uncommon view, has damaging consequences. It assisted in creating the judge's view in the Osborne case, and then later, more permanently, in legitimating the restrictions imposed on political affiliation in the 1913 Trade Union Act. To these issues we must now turn. However, we cannot fail to note that the TUC retained its original political role even after the formation of the Labour Party.

Its function as lobbyist and representative of the corporate collective interests of the affiliated unions, evolved from the 1860s, continued unhindered, if somewhat modified, by the emergence of labour as a political party. It never ceased its efforts to mediate workers' interests with government, and with corporate employers' organizations, and indeed these efforts developed in the succeeding years.

The new Labour Party was financed from its infancy by contributions from affiliated trade unions. They paid a compulsory levy to the Parliamentary Representation Fund and an affiliation fee in addition. Some unions paid these contributions from their general funds, but from the beginning others instituted a special Parliamentary fund which they financed by a separate (but compulsory) levy on all their members. Among other purposes, these funds helped to maintain the new Labour Members of Parliament, who did not receive a state salary at that time. Very soon, establishment spokesmen were to be heard expressing the first doubts about the legality of all this. For example, the Chief Registrar of Friendly Societies observed in 1904 that:

> As many trade unions are seeking to include in their objects such extraneous matters as the promotion of Labour Representation in Parliament and in other elected bodies, I have found it necessary to point out that such matters are not within the definition of a trade union contained in Section 16 of the Trade Union Act of 1876.

This very broad hint was soon taken up with enthusiasm in the courts, particularly since the 1906 Trade Disputes Act had resulted from effective pressure by both the TUC and the newly elected Labour Members of Parliament. This Act had reversed the House of Lords ruling on the Taff Vale case, thus restoring and strengthening legal immunity for trade unions in industrial action. Moves to outlaw the unions' support for the Labour Party followed immediately, and developed to the point where Mr Osborne of the Amalgamated Society of Railway Servants brought a legal action to prevent his union from financing the Labour Party. This case went through to the House of Lords, which upheld the judgment in Osborne's favour. (He was enabled to finance this lengthy litigation through financial assistance from capitalist sources, and his own political motives are clear from his membership of the 'Trade Union Political Freedom League'.

There followed a whole series of similar cases brought by disaffected union members against their own unions' political expenditure. Soon more than 25 unions were debarred in this way from further involvement with with Labour Party. The Labour movement faced a crisis which, in the view of contemporaries, was every bit as serious as that engendered by the Taff Vale case. It responded with a major campaign, directed by the TUC and by Labour in Parliament, to restore the previous position. The goal of this campaign was to achieve total legal abstention in the matter of trade union political activity and expenditure. But what was offered by the Liberal government fell far short of this: it was a Trade Union Bill (subsequently the Trade Union Act of 1913) which placed serious and unique restrictions on trade union freedom in the political field.

The Establishment of Political Funds

It is very largely forgotten by trade unionists today that the 1913 Act was regarded by the whole movement at the time of its passage as an unfair and discriminatory piece of law. It is fair to say, however, that this view is now being resurrected by Labour spokesmen in the new climate generated by the debate on the 1984 Trade Union Act. Thus, John Smith, MP, at the time the Labour Party front bench spokesman on employment, during the committee stage of the Act's passage through the Commons, compared the law on company political contributions with that applying to trade unions as follows: 'The only existing restriction on companies is that contributions of more than £200 must be noted in the Annual Report . . . That is pathetic, compared with the massive restrictions imposed on British trade unions for over 70 years'.[6] The 1913 Act was accepted only as an interim measure pending total withdrawal of the law from the issue. The debate was launched at the TUC Congress of 1910, when the president's opening address described the Osborne judgment as 'the most important subject you will have to consider'. He went on to trace the history of trade union struggles to obtain Parliamentary representation and to affirm that, from the 1860s:

> . . . the trade union world had no other idea than the one that it was one of their objects, not only to work for, but to maintain in Parliament, Labour men representing the Trade Union forces of this country and from 1874 onwards the funds of Trade Unions have been applied to the purpose of returning and paying Members to the House of Commons.

The successful motion debated at that year's Congress declared:

> Whilst welcoming any Bill which provides for payment of members (of the House of Commons), this Congress cannot recognize such a measure as a solution of the difficulty created by the Osborne judgement, regarding it as essential that Trade Unions should enjoy *absolute freedom* to engage in political actions.[7]

In the debate on this motion, speakers unanimously demanded 'the right of our members to vote their money for what purposes they liked'. In this, trade unionists received support from some unusual sources. For instance, Winston Churchill defended the unconditional right of trade unions to support political activities:

> I should have no hesitation in saying that it is quite impossible to prevent trade unions from entering the political field. The sphere of industrial and political activity is often indistinguishable, always overlaps, and representation in Parliament is absolutely necessary to trade unions, even if they confine themselves to the most purely industrial forms of action, and the moment you touch representation you reach the very heart and centre of political life, because the disputes as to representation raise every question of general politics and party politics which can be imagined . . . in the great majority of cases workmen do not feel injured even if their very small contributions are taken to support trade union politics with which they do not agree. They do not in the great majority of cases object. Many of them do not think very much about it. Very few workmen, luckily for them, are cursed with logical or theological subtleties of mind. They do not mind, in practice and as a general rule in the great majority of cases, pay for their union politics, which they regard as advancing the interests of their class, then voting for a different political party which they regard as advancing political affairs upon another road at the same time. There is a great deal more sense and deep reason and sagacity in that lack of logical subtlety than might appear upon the surface . . . It is not good for trade unions that they should be brought in contact with the courts, and it is not good for the courts. The courts hold justly a high and, I think, unequalled prominence in the respect of the world in criminal cases, and in civil cases between man and man, no doubt, they deserve and command the respect and admiration of all classes in the community, but where class issues are involved, it is impossible to pretend that the courts command the same degree of general confidence. On the contrary, they do not, and a very large number of our population have been led to the opinion that they are, unconsciously no doubt, biassed. . . . We know perfectly well that the trade union movement ought to develop, ought not to be stereotyped, ought to have power to enter a new field and to make new experiments . . . We wish to set the trade unions free to develop their efforts, to build up in this country a minimum standard of life and labour, and to secure the happiness of the people.[8]

Encouraged by such opinions as Churchill's, unions pressed their case. The 1911 TUC had before it the government's proposals for a new law (embodied in the 'Trade Unions No. 2 Bill') which included the provision for individual contracting-out of the political fund. The Railway Clerks' union moved the following motion:

That inasmuch as the Trade Unions (No. 2) Bill denies them the right
to exercise the elementary principles of self-government, this Congress
regards it with great dissatisfaction, reaffirms previous decisions claiming
liberty of political action, and urges the Parliamentary Committee to give
strenuous opposition to the Bill unless it is so amended as to restore
completely the political freedom enjoyed by Trade Unions for over 40 years
prior to the Osborne Judgement, as demanded in the Bill previously
promoted by the Labour Party.'[9]

In 1912, the Trade Unions (No. 2) Bill was still grinding its way
through Parliament, and the TUC President told Congress, that although
some amendments had been accepted by the government, 'the Bill in
no way concedes the right of Trade Unions to use their own money in
their own way, as may be provided for in their rules and subject to a
majority of their members being in favour'.[10] In the same year, the
government sought to mitigate trade union opposition by instituting
the payment of members of parliament: a salary of £400 a year was
provided. Congress declared that this concession in no way obscured
the issue of trade unions' political freedom, (although some speakers
remarked caustically on the waning of enthusiasm for the subject by
some Labour MPs, following on their receipt of a salary!). The argument
against contracting-out reached its high point in this 1912 debate at
Congress.

Mr T. Shaw (Amalgamated Weavers), for example, said:

They want to prevent us from using our money in our own way and time
in defence of our own interests; and if we speak of the rights and wrongs
of the case, surely a union which has been straightforward in the matter
has the right to say that the majority shall rule. Are we to have this
objection forced upon every other part of our work? ('No.') Well then, a
man has no more right to refuse to pay his Parliamentary levy definitely
voted on by the majority of the members than he has to decline to pay
any other part of his subscriptions. And look at the unfairness of the
proposition, that he should have the right to vote equally with the majority
while refusing to pay his portion of the contributions. Talk about
morality![11]

And Mr G. Barker (Miners' Federation) reinforced this stance:

I look upon the man who refuses to pay his Parliamentary levy and takes
all the benefits from the Labour movement, as a sneak and a blackleg.
The Minimum Wage Act was also got chiefly through the Labour members,
and the reason the Labour Members voted against the third reading of it
was because it did not contain the schedule the men were asking for.
Through that Minimum Wages Act tens of thousands of the miners had
their wages raised 8s., 4s., and 5s. Are those men entitled to refuse to pay

the Parliamentary Levy? We have the right to exact the Parliamentary levy out of every man until they contract themselves out of the benefits which are derived from our Parliamentary action' (Cheers).[12]

By the time of the 1913 Congress, the Trade Union Act had become law. Arthur Henderson, fraternal delegate to Congress from the Labour Party, spoke as follows on the subject:

> . . . our success has been of a qualified nature, as not being all that we have desired in that direction, but the partial success we have achieved imposes upon every Trade Union, and especially upon every Trade Union official, a great responsibility. The ballots that we are about to take under the new Trade Union Act will, in our opinion, determine the measure of our political activity for some time to come . . . those ballots must be carried to a success . . . to defeat the political fund resolution at the forthcoming ballots of the unions will do more than strike a blow at the Labour Party. It will make practically impossible, so far as the unions are concerned, political action in any shape or form.[13]

The 1913 Congress also received and approved a report of a Special Conference convened by the TUC, the General Federation of Trade Unions and the Labour Party, which had been held on the subject (at the Memorial Hall, Farringdon Street, the venue of the 1900 founding conference of the Labour Party) in June. This report, signed by all three organizations, concluded with the following paragraph:

> We cannot but express our deep regret that the Government have made themselves responsible for a Bill which allows men to remain full members of the unions and accept benefits, both industrial and political, without recognising or meeting their full obligations. In view, however, of the fact that the Bill does allow trade unions to engage in political action under conditions which, though unfair, can nevertheless be made immediately operative, the Conference would, in our opinion, be securing the immediate future of the political Labour movement if it accepted the measure under protest, and regarded it as an instalment, and not as a final settlement, of Labour's demands.[14]

However, if Labour was to prove amnesiac about the need for this final settlement, their opponents were less than fully reconciled to the 1913 'instalment'.

The Conservative Party, and Conservative governments, have in fact returned again and again to the business of amending legislation in order to reduce the contribution of the trade unions to the Labour Party. The 1984 Act is thus simply the latest, and perhaps most potent, manifestation of a long tradition. In the Parliamentary debates and proceedings leading to the passage of the 1913 Act itself, the Tory opposition sustained a long campaign to amend the Liberal government's proposals. This included an amendment seeking to exclude the political funds of trade unions from the protection against actions in tort afforded by the 1906 Trade Disputes Act. It went on to an amendment to provide that a majority of a union's members, and not simply a majority of those voting, should be required before a union ballot could authorize the establishment of a political fund. It also included a proposal that contracting-in should be substituted for contracting-out. None of these amendments was successful at the time.

Immediately following the passing of the 1913 Act most unions which today have political funds held their ballots, and almost all were successful. By 1939, over 200 unions had voted on the question and only 13 failed to obtain a majority.[15] Some unions, however, made several attempts to win a ballot, such as the Draughtsmen, who were only successful in 1944 after four previous votes.[16] Since the Second World War, only a handful of new unions have won ballots and there is now of course a considerable weight of supposedly 'non-political' unions affiliated to the TUC.

The Tory opposition to the 1913 settlement resumed their attack in the 1920s. No great issue of political principle is involved in that party's policies despite the rhetoric in which they are presented – as a defence of the individual against intimidation. One Conservative minister was honest enough to record, in a Cabinet Memorandum:

> The real point which we have to decide is this. Do we wish to attack Trade Unions as such or do we not? . . . the major part of the outcry against the political levy is not motivated by a burning indignation for the trade unionist, who is forced to subscribe to the furtherance of political principles which he abhors. It is based on a desire to hit the Socialist party through their pocket . . . What I submit is that at least we should not delude ourselves as to our intentions.[17]

Every effort was made to assemble evidence of trade union obstruction to the operation of contracting-out and zealous resolutions calling for amending legislation were passed regularly at Conservative Party conferences in the early 1920s. These were given expression in back-bench Bills sponsored by Tory MPs but failed to carry during the government of Lloyd George, which was anxious to avoid the appearance of union-bashing which might reinforce left-wing positions in the unions. Some of these back-bench measures went so far as to require a total legal prohibition on trade union political action. Another (entitled *Trade Unionists' (Restoration of Liberty) Bill!*) would have required not only contracting-in, but an annual signed re-affirmation of that process. Baldwin, the Prime Minister at the time of this last attempt, also resisted back-bench pressure. Conciliation remained the order of the day at this stage, and the premier made a famous and effective speech on the question:

> I want my party to make a gesture to the country . . . and to say to them: 'We have our majority; we believe in the justice of this Bill which has been brought in today, but we are going to withdraw our hand, and we are not going to push our political advantage home at a moment like this . . . We, at any rate, are not going to fire the first shot.[18]

The right wing of conservatism was finally given its triumphant opportunity following the defeat of the General Strike. The Trade Disputes and Trade Unions Act of 1927 made political and sympathetic strikes illegal, forbade the closed shop in public services and banned Civil Service unions from affiliation to outside bodies, such as the TUC and the Labour Party. This resulted in the withdrawal from the Labour Party of the unions for Post Office workers, the Inland Revenue and the Civil Service clerical workers. The Act finally substituted contracting-in for contracting-out. The Labour Government of 1929–31, being a minority administration, failed to win Parliament for a return to contracting-out. The consequence of the 1927 Act was to reduce the proportion of trade unionists affiliated to the Labour Party from more than 75 per cent in 1925, to 48 per cent in 1938.[19] The Party's income fell by one-third between 1926 and 1929, but financial disaster was avoided by a series of expedients, including special levies on the unions, and the raising of affiliation fees. While it is true that the Labour Party won its greatest electoral victory in 1945 during the currency of the 1927 Act, it is clear that this was despite the disadvantage in which it had been placed by that law.

Labour and TUC conference resolutions through the 1930s called for the repeal of the 1927 Act with steady regularity, and it was inevitable that the victorious Labour government after the war made this one of its first priorities. The repeal did not at the time arouse great controversy; what is significant about it was that Labour was content merely to restore contracting-out which it had come to accept as a 'reasonable compromise'. The strong arguments of the 1910–13 trade union campaign, for full legal abstention on the issue, had been forgotten.

The Working of Political Funds before the 1984 Act

What, then, is the state of trade union political funds in the 1980s, before the new compulsory ballots have had time to take full effect? To a surprising degree, trade unions have maintained their representation in

Table 4.1 Individual union sponsorships

	Total			Elected		
	1974	*1979*	*1983*	*1974*	*1979*	*1983*
TGWU	23	27	29	22	20	24
AUEW	23	16	17	21	15	12
NUM	20	17	14	18	16	14
NUGMW	13	14	14	13	14	11
ASTMS	13	12	11	12	8	10
NUPE	7	8	10	6	7	4
APEX	6	6	3	6	5	3
NUR	6	11	12	6	10	10
USDAW	5	5	2	5	5	2
TSSA	4	3	1	3	3	—
UPW	4	4	1	2	2	1
UCATT	3	4	2	3	2	1
EETPU	3	4	7	3	4	3
Total, including other unions	141	159	153	129	132	114
Co-operative Party	24	25	17	16	16	14
All sponsored candidates	161	184	170	142	148	128

Parliament in spite of ups and downs. During the 1983 General Election, 120 union-sponsored MPs were returned, out of a total of 153 such candidates who stood and of 209 actual MPs now representing the Labour Party. The largest contingent, of 25, came from the Transport and General Workers Union, while several important trade unions sponsored only one member apiece. The roll call of the most involved unions is featured in table 4.1, which shows how representation has changed during the three most recent general elections, October 1974, 1979 and 1983. The long term position is made clear in table 4.2, which records the progress of sponsored candidates in successive general elections from 1900 onwards.

If we begin with 1900, we find that the embryonic Labour Representation Committee had a capacity to field 15 candidates. Today's Labour Party, of course, is expected to contest all Parliamentary seats. Often these contests are not nowadays directly supported by any one trade union. While in 1906, 35 out of the 50 Labour candidates were directly sponsored, by the time we had entered the 1970s this proportion had fallen significantly: 137 (in 1970), or 159 (in 1979) out of more than 620 candidates does not represent a high involvement of trade union sponsors when we remember that the unions affiliate around six million people to the Party. However, it should be remembered that in 1945, which was Labour's big year, there were only 126 sponsored candidates,

Table 4.2　Success of union sponsored candidates

| Election | Candidates | | MPs | | Union sponsored MPs as % of all Labour Party MPs | Union sponsored MPs as % of all Labour sponsored candidates |
	All Labour Party	All union sponsored	All Labour Party	All union sponsored		
1900	15	?	2	1	50.0	?
1906	50	35	30	21	70.0	60
1910	78	?	40	38	95.0	?
1910	56	?	42	39	92.8	?
1918	361	163	57	49	85.9	31
1922	414	?	142	86	60.6	?
1923	427	?	191	102	53.4	?
1924	514	?	151	88	58.2	?
1929	569	139	287	115	40.1	83
1931	491	132	46	32	69.5	24
1935	552	128	154	79	51.3	62
1945	603	126	393	121	30.8	96
1950	617	140	315	110	34.9	79
1951	617	137	295	105	35.6	77
1955	620	129	277	96	34.6	75
1959	621	129	258	93	36.0	72
1964	628	138	317	120	37.9	86
1966	622	138	364	132	36.3	95
1970	624	137	287	114	39.7	83
1974	627	155	301	127	42.2	82.7
1974	626	141	319	129	40.1	91
1979	622	159	268	132	49.5	83
1983	633	153	209	114	54.5	75

There is occasional disagreement among various authorities for the actual number of candidates supported by the Labour Party or sponsored by a trade union. This problem is especially acute for the years prior to 1929.
Source: W. D. Mullen, *The Kept Men*, Harvester, 1977. For 1979 and thereafter sources are the Labour Party's press releases and the Labour Research Department.

or 30 per cent of the total.[20] Of course, trade unions tend to invest their money in safeish seats: 96 per cent of their 1945 team did in fact secure election. By 1974, their success rate was down to 91 per cent; 1979 was a bad year, and only 83 per cent of the union nominees were returned. But the casualties included not only long established members, but also former Ministers. Worse still, only 75 per cent of the 1983 sponsored candidates secured election. But in these last cases we are dealing with electoral adversity, and not with a conscious decision to support lost causes. Very little union money is put into the deliberate contesting of marginal seats, and even less into hopeless ones.

There are different kinds of sponsorship. Classically, sponsorship is to be found in the slowly declining numbers of safe mining seats, in which the National Union of Mineworkers used to be able to boast that they could weigh the votes necessary to secure their victories. Today, in some places the weighing machine has broken down. The 1977 by-election in Ashfield, solid mining country, produced a Conservative victory, which was replicated in 1983 in the adjacent area of Sherwood, which contains more collieries than any other constituency in Britain. There are at least two contributory causes for this. First, changes in the Labour Party's federal constitution, which we have discussed elsewhere, have opened up the former mining fiefdoms to wider competition. Until the middle 1960s, local trade unions could delegate any of their members who paid to the union's political fund to represent them in their local Party organizations. Now, only persons who pay a separate individual membership contribution are eligible to serve as delegates on Party Management Committees, and thus to arrive as members of the 'selectorate' which chooses Parliamentary candidates. Under the old order, when Morgan Phillips, then General Secretary of the Labour Party, sought nomination for a miner's seat in North-East Derbyshire, NUM delegates came from every village and hamlet to prevent this from happening, and chose instead to support a local miners' spokesman, the redoubtable Tom Swain. But the choice of a non-miner in the constituency of Ashfield in 1977, and again in Sherwood in 1983, has been followed by a number of similar choices in mining country, simply because the NUM has not been able to find enough individual members qualified to represent it on Party Management Committees. A second cause of change, however, is that this internal constitutional shift is of course strongly reinforced by sociological convulsions, resulting both from pit closures and mergers, and the migration of populations.

We have pointed out before that in Labour's heyday there used to be 'mining' constituencies, 'railway' constituencies, or 'engineering' towns.[21] Today, these things are all changing and the more amorphous general unions, with members distributed over a wide area and sometimes across a wide social spectrum, are becoming much more important than they used to be in the sponsorship stakes. However, these changes take effect rather slowly, because there is a time lag in the replacement of Members of Parliament in safe seats. Notwithstanding reforms in the Labour Party's constitution, constituencies are loath to part with their long-standing Parliamentary representatives. Once adopted, in spite of the institution of reselection procedures, MPs still tend to continue until they are either beaten in the polls, or brought to retirement by age or infirmity.

The trade union contribution to the maintenance on sponsored MPs does not, nowadays, involve any payment to the Members themselves.

In 1900 sponsors had to be ready to contribute to the maintenance of any victorious candidates, because state payment of Members had not yet been introduced. After its advent, this practice was considered unnecessary. Normally, under the terms of the 1933 Hastings Agreement, the Constituency Labour Party (CLP) which adopts a sponsored candidate receives grants for the conduct of elections, and towards the maintenance of electoral organization between elections. Sometimes sitting MPs may take on sponsorship after having been elected. Since 1983 there has been a marked increase in such sponsorships, and by the beginning of 1985 132 members in all, or 62 per cent of all Labour Members, had been adopted by one or another affiliated union. This means that 16 Members were sponsored after securing election.[22]

Outside the relationship of sponsorship, some unions without political funds employ Members of Parliament as consultants. In this case, it is usual to pay a fee to the Member of Parliament, or certain agreed expenses, rather than to make payments to the appropriate CLP. This, of course, may well be passed on from Member to Party in a variety of ways.

In the 1983 Parliament, the National Union of Teachers adopts three Labour MPs and the Civil and Public Services Association, the Civil Service Union, the Musicians Union, the Transport Salaried Staffs Association and the Society of Civil and Public Servants employ one member each. Some other unions choose consultants from several parties at the same time, which is the case with NALGO and the Banking, Insurance and Finance Union. Two of the TUC unions have, until recently, employed consultants chosen only from the Conservative or Liberal Parties. These have been the Association of University Teachers, and the Association of First Division Civil Servants. However, in 1984–5 the AUT engaged Jack Straw, the Labour Member for Blackburn as an 'adviser'. During the same period two Social Democratic MPs were engaged as consultants by three different unions.

Unions which maintain political funds have sometimes complained about these arrangements, and the draughtsmen drew attention to them in their evidence to the Donovan Commission.[23]

In addition to the payments involved in direct sponsorship, many unions make generous donations to non-sponsored candidates at election time. Sometimes such payments will involve local or district organizations, and sometimes they will be made by head offices. It is difficult to estimate a figure for this, but there is no doubt that such contributions may be cumulatively substantial, even if they do not equal the costs incurred in becoming a sponsor.

For all this, the main trade union political expenditures are not nowadays restricted to support for particular candidates. It is necessary

Table 4.3 Proportion of members paying the political levy in 1983

Paying levy (%)	No. of unions
91–100	25
81–90	7
71–80	5
61–70	7
51–60	3
41–50	4
31–40	0
21–30	1
11–20	0
1–10	4
	56[a]

[a]There are 57 unions with political funds, but ASTMS has not filed its returns with the Certification Officer. Several of these unions are area organizations already represented in the statistics by their national bodies.
Source: Annual Report of the Certification Officer, 1984, published May 1985.

to look at actual trade union participation in the processes of the Labour Party if we are to see what actually happens to union political fund monies.

Levels of trade union involvement in the Labour Party

The political influence of trade unions in the legislature is obviously important, but their most direct and continuing influence is that which is exerted within the Labour Party itself. Delegates nominated by the unions take their share in determining the policy of the Party and staffing its machinery, at national, regional and local level. At the national level, unions participate in the Labour Party Conference, where they cast block votes in accordance with the number of members on which they have affiliated. In 1985 affiliation involves a standard national rate of 60 pence per member. At regional level, a similar arrangement applies at regional conferences, except that the fee is levied at varying rates, between £2.50 and £5 per thousand affiliated members. Locally, unions may also nominate delegates to management committees in the constituencies, which are responsible for the day to day local organization of the Party, as well as the selection of Parliamentary candidates. The cost of such participation varies between 3 pence and 6 pence per member per annum. Some constituencies impose a minimum fee of £5 per local branch which affiliates.

Table 4.4   Unions with more than 90 per cent of members contributing to political funds

Union	1976	% contributing 1981	1982	1983
Society of Textile Workers		99	*ª	
Textile Workers' Union		94	94	95
AUEW (Foundry Section)		91	(63)	(47)
ASLEF		94	93	93
Ceramic & Allied Trades		97	98	99
COHSE	91	92	92	91
Loom Overlookers		91	92	100
ISTC				91
NACODS				
National		97	97	99
Durham area		100	100	99
Northumberland area		99	99	99
Scottish area		99	100	100
Yorkshire area		99	99	99
NATSOPA		90	90	*
Agricultural Workers		99	*	
Co-operative Insurance		96	*	
Dyers, Bleachers & Textile		99	*	
Footwear, Leather & Allied Trades				97
NUGMW	98	91	(88)	(87)
NUM				
National				96
Durham area				99
Northumberland area				100
North Wales area		100		
Leicester area	99	(50)	99	99
NUPE	99	98	98	97
NUR		97	96	97
Powerloom Carpet Weavers		98	98	98
Boot, Shoe & Slipper Operatives		99	99	98
Scottish Carpet Workers		100	100	100
TGWU	96	98	98	98
Communication Workers	95	95	94	93
USDAW	93	92	92	92
Bakers, Food & Allied Workers		(81)	96	98

Certification Officer's Report for 1976 does not give full returns but shows only those given as having over 90 per cent contributing. The NUM does not appear at all until the latest year.
ªindicates where a union has disappeared through a merger.
Source: Report of the Certification Officer, 1984, published May 1985.

Table 4.5   Unions with under 50 per cent of members contributing to political funds

Union	1976	% contributing 1981	1982	1983
ACTT[a]		9	7	9
ISTC		44	(52)	(91)
NGA	46	44	42	(52)
NUM (Durham)		37	44	(99)
NUM (Northumberland)		36	35	(100)
Scalemakers		1	1	1
ASTMS	37	30[b]	—[c]	—[c]
SOGAT 1975	18	39	44	63[d]
SLADE		41	37	—[e]
Shuttlemakers		5	6	5
Blastfurnacemen		(55)	48	46
Domestic Appliance and General Metalworkers		(72)	28	24
AUEW (TASS)	48			(62)

[a]ACTT held its initial ballot for a political fund in 1943 when contracting-in was the law. It has retained contracting-in to the present day.
[b]1980 figure.
[c]Returns not made.
[d]SOGAT 1975 became SOGAT 1982 on merging.
[e]Merged.
The 1976 figures in the Certification Officer's Report are confined to the unions entered here.
Source: Report of the Certification Officer, 1984 published May 1985.

Affiliation to the Party thus always involves the decision to make a payment to national Labour Party funds of so much per affiliated member per annum. Only parties which have affiliated nationally are entitled to affiliate again at the regional and local levels as well, upon the payment of further per capita or block contributions.

This three-tier system of payments complicates the problem of tracing where political funds actually get spent. A breakdown of the total costs involved for one union helps to explain this. In 1983, the political levy of ASTMS raised £133,000: £66,000 of this was spent upon national affiliation to the Labour Party; £25,000 went on affiliation to local CLPs; £4,000 was spent on sponsorship, and £7,000 on support for the election campaign. Conferences cost a further £7,000, yielding a total outgoing of £109,000.[24]

In ASTMS, about one-third of the members contribute to the political fund. The proportion of members contributing varies from one union to another, and is recorded in table 4.3. Table 4.4 records the unions in which more than 90 per cent are paying to their funds. Table 4.5,

Table 4.6 The rate of political levy in Britain's largest unions

Union	Rate per annum in 1985 (£)
AUEW (Engineering)	1.00
(TASS)	1.56
APEX	1.04
ASTMS	3.00 (some still pay only £1.20 old rate)
COHSE	1.56
EETPU (skilled)	0.70
(unskilled)	0.55 (represents one week's full union sub)
GMBATU	2.40 (represents 3 weeks' full union subs)
NGA	2.60
NUM	2.88 (represents 4 weeks' full union subs)
NUPE	2.00
NUR	2.60
POEU	1.56
SOGAT	1.56
TGWU	1.56
UCW	1.56
UCATT	0.80
USDAW	1.04

by contrast, lists those unions in which less than half the members contribute. It will be noted that three unions moved from less than 50 per cent in 1982 to more than 90 per cent in 1983, which is not easy to understand.

All this data is complex enough. Additionally, the amount of money levied from each member varies considerably between unions, and the efficiency of collection systems is by no means standard. In 1977, for instance, NATSOPA and NATTKE maintained a levy of 20 pence a year.[25] Their political fund contributions had remained static through inflation, and a 20 pence levy, collected at the rate of 5 pence a quarter, did not permit full affiliation to the Labour Party, which in that year involved a levy of 21 pence per member. As a result, these unions maintained affiliation levels which were considerably lower than the numbers of their members paying into the levy. Obviously they could only pay the Labour Party's standard charges if they did this, since they were not allowed to transfer monies across from the general to the political funds. In the late 1970s political levies varied between this lowest level of 20 pence per member and the £1.56 charged by the ACTT. The largest union, the TGWU, was collecting 32 pence for each member, the AUEW Engineering Section 40 pence per member, and the Municipal Workers 60 pence.

By 1985 these levels had been adjusted somewhat. The lowest fixed contribution was now to be found in the EETPU, at 55 pence for an unskilled worker or 70 pence for a skilled one. Most other unions fixed a levy of more than £1.50, while the highest contribution was levied at the rate of £3 per annum, in ASTMS. Table 4.6 gives the rate of levy in the largest unions, and reflects the influence over successive years of increases in the standard affiliation fee charged by the Labour Party itself. More and more trade unions seek to allocate a particular week's contributions to the political fund, or choose a different device by which to standardize (and inflation proof) political fund payments.

But not all of these monies are successfully gathered in. In general, the lower the political contribution, the easier it has always been to collect. The NUR in 1977 collected an average of 60 pence out of the prescribed £1 levy. The rules of the NUGMW required a 60 pence levy in 1977 but the total yield produced only 35 pence per member.

All these complications follow from the fact that trade unions are voluntary organizations, inspiring different degrees of commitment among different sections of their membership.[26] And these are not the only problems which are involved in arriving at a clear picture of the state of trade union political involvement.

The fact is that the numbers of members upon which national affiliation to the Labour Party is decided are often chosen completely arbitrarily. Thus, the TGWU had a peak membership of 2¼ million in 1979, but it has never affiliated to the Labour Party on more than 1¼ million, its present level. During its most successful years, the TGWU had only a handful of members refusing to pay the levy. From those members who were eligible to pay, approximately 90 per cent of the levy which fell due was actually collected. But the proportion of members affiliated to the Labour Party in 1977 was 55.7 per cent of the total. Today it is very much higher, but sadly this is because of the serious contraction of union membership during the slump. While overall membership has declined, affiliation levels have been held constant at the old figures. Some unions affiliate at low levels, as we suspect has the TWGU, so as to avoid the reproach of domination of the Party by over-heavy block votes. Others under-affiliate in order to register their disagreement with its policies, as seems to have been the case with the Electricians and Plumbers Union, which joins 420,000 people to the TUC, but only 180,000 to the Labour Party. Since these figures have remained constant over a number of years, it is clear that they reflect a substantial and presumably deliberate decision.

It is rather difficult to arrive at clear and strictly comparable data concerning the affiliation of trade unions to the Labour Party. True, the Certification Officer publishes the Annual Membership Returns of trade unions, and reports on the proportions of their members who contribute to the political levy. These reports appear up to two years after the year to which they relate. Meantime, trade unions have affiliated to the

Labour Party on the basis of the latest figures they have to hand, in accordance with the Labour Party's own timetables for the collections of monies and the registration of voting rights. The result is that there sometimes appear to be great discrepancies between the numbers of people affiliating to the Party and the numbers contributing to the political fund. However, quite a number of these discrepancies are the result of 'fiscal drag' resulting from the mismatching of different accounting years. Probably this problem had a smaller significance when trade union membership was steadily growing. Nowadays it is falling very sharply in some unions, and this provides part of the explanation for apparent over-affiliation, in which unions subscribe to the Labour Party on behalf of more members than pay into their political funds. Table 4.7 shows what proportion of the memberships of the larger unions pay the political levy, and what proportion are later affiliated to the Labour Party. A few unions affiliated on levels substantially below the numbers of members contributing; however, this appears to be a declining trend. The most conspicuous cases involved are the Metal Mechanics, the NGA, SOGAT, the Fire Brigades Union and the EETPU. As we have seen, the EETPU charges a very low rate of levy, and, allowing for its contributions to regional and local constituency parties, its political income will be rather restricted. Smaller unions like those of the firemen and metal mechanics, may well have other economic difficulties at a time of serious membership loss and economic decline.

At the beginning of the campaign for political fund ballots, *The Sunday Times* ran a front page story about trade unions which were systematically purchasing larger block votes than those to which they were entitled.[27] In fact 14 of the unions featured in this table had affiliated at more than 100 per cent of the number of people contributing to the political fund. However, a number of these contributions are easily accounted for by fiscal drag. The extent of this phenomenon, at a time of declining membership rolls, becomes clear if one calculates the proportion of Labour Party affiliations rostered against the previous years' numbers of contributors to the political levy. We cannot be sure that all unions affiliate to the Labour Party on the basis of the same year's membership statistics. This depends on their own internal recording and audit systems, and their relative efficiency. For this reason, the figure in brackets in table 4.7 may well be the 'corrected' figure for certain of the unions listed.

But, while marginal differences can be reasonably explained, there are some large differences which do amount to a consistent over-representation. The AUEW Engineering Section is the second largest trade union affiliated: 850,000 members is 157 per cent of the actual total of contributors. The 307,000 phantom engineers who do not contribute to the political fund, but who are represented in the AUEW's block vote,

Table 4.7 Percentage of members paying political levy and percentage affiliated to the Labour Party

Union	Total members	Contributing to General Fund	Paying political levy			Labour Party affiliations		
			No.	% of total	% of General Fund payers	No.	% paying levy	% 1982 levy payers
Bakers, Food & Allied	37,487	37,487	36,558	98	98	36,000	98	(98)
Ceramic & Allied Trades	28,873	28,873	28,496	99	99	28,000	98	(98)
NACODS	17,079	17,079	16,856	99	99	18,000	107	(102)
Communication Workers	196,426	196,426	183,325	93	93	187,000	102	(100)
UCATT	259,873	259,873	171,000	66	66	171,000	100	(100)
EETPU	405,041	383,829	295,254	73	77	180,000	61	(50)
AUEW (Constructional)	23,856	23,856	17,268	72	72	15,000	87	(82)
AUEW (Engineering)	943,538	735,960	542,584	58	74	850,000	157	(130)
(Foundry)	41,287	41,287	19,230	47	47	27,000	140	(100)
AUEW (TASS)	215,052	182,795	113,000	53	62	a143,000	127	(93)
Fire Brigades	43,405	43,405	26,999	62	62	16,000	59	(63)
Footwear, Leather & Allied Trades	41,897	38,115	36,879	88	97	39,000	106	(100)
FTAT	58,244	51,788	35,529	61	69	32,000	90	(86)
GMBATU	875,187	875,187	759,856	87	87	b725,000	95	(84)
SOGAT	216,639	193,710	121,176	56	63	76,000	63	(60)
NGA	133,949	113,619	59,457	44	52	31,000	52	(55)
COHSE	222,869	222,869	203,730	91	91	200,000	98	(94)
ISTC	93,175	44,296	40,165	43	91	70,000	174	(142)
ASLEF	23,589	23,589	21,954	93	93	24,000	109	(104)
Metal Mechanics	29,076	27,076	24,078	83	89	16,000	66	(73)
NUM	318,084	208,051	200,453	63	96	237,000	118	(107)
POEU	129,950	129,950	98,451	76	76	95,000	96	(94)

APEX	100,177	100,177	68,868	69	69	85,000	123	(111)
NUPE	689,046	689,046	670,736	97	97	600,000	89	(88)
NUR	143,404	143,404	138,529	97	97	151,000	109	(104)
NUS	28,511	28,511	22,523	79	79	23,000	102	(98)
USDAW	403,446	403,446	369,547	92	92	385,000	104	(100)
Tailors and Garment Workers	76,130	76,130	67,247	88	88	55,000	82	(81)
Textile Workers	15,273	15,273	14,540	95	95	17,000	117	(93)
TGWU	1,547,443	1,547,443	1,517,782	98	98	c1,361,000	90	(85)
TSSA	56,476	56,476	46,648	83	83	48,000	103	(96)
TOTALS	7,414,482	6,939,026	5,968,718	81	86	5,941,000	100	(94)

Table does not include unions with less than 10,000 affiliates to the Labour Party; ASTMS, whose membership shows a static 410,000 and who affiliate on 132,000 members (no political fund figures available from the Certification Officer since 1980).
Certain unions, recently amalgamated, do continue to affiliate separately to the Labour Party, but their membership is not shown separately by the Certification Officer.

[a] TASS includes 42,000 affiliates from Sheet Metal Workers.
[b] GMBATU includes 75,000 affiliates from Sheet Metal Workers.
[c] TGWU includes 75,000 affiliates from Agricultural Workers and 36,000 from Dyers and Bleachers.

Source: All figures are from *Report of the Certification Officer, 1984* except numbers of Labour Party affiliates, for which source is the Labour Party Annual Report, 1984.

do actually outnumber the total number of real members of the constituency section in the Labour Party. This means that individual members, contributing at the rate of £8 a year and carrying through all the Party's activities at the local level could have their influence largely cancelled by a fictional membership counted in the AUEW's block vote. In the iron and steel union (ISTC), over-affiliation reaches 174 per cent (falling to 142 per cent), while in the left-wing AUEW/TASS, and the right-wing APEX respectively, over-affiliation runs at 127 per cent (falling to 93 per cent) and 123 per cent (falling to 111 per cent). There was a lower level of over-affiliation by the NUM, the Textile Workers and the NUR. The smaller these unions are, the less this fictional representation actually matters. An augmentation of the Textile Workers 14,500 fund paying affiliates by 17 per cent is possibly capable of being understood as being a result of accounting disproportions: but even if it were to have been the result of an arbitrary decision, the shift of power towards the Textile Workers block vote would offer them minimal advantage. But

Table 4.8 Percentage of total membership contributing to political fund and affiliated to the Labour Party

	1976	1980	1981	1982	1983
No. of unions with political funds[a]	81	69	68	63	58
No. of unions affiliated to Labour Party[b]	59	54	54	50	47
No. of members	9.4m	9.5m	8.9m	8.0m	7.9m
No. of members contributing to political funds[c]	7.6m	7.7m	7.2m	6.5m	6.5m
No. of members affiliated to Labour Party[d]	5.8m	6.4m	6.3m	6.2m	6.1m
Members contributing to political funds (%)[e]	81	81	81	81	82
Members affiliated to Labour Party (%)	62	67	71	77	77
Fund contributors affiliated to Labour Party (%)	76	83	87	95	94

[a]Includes returns separately for four areas of NACODS and four areas of NUM as well as NACODS and NUM national returns.
[b]Some unions register political funds more than once, as local federated unions also file returns. (See [a].) The decline in numbers of unions affiliated otherwise reflects mergers between unions. *Source:* Labour Party Report 1984, p. 104.
[c]For 1982 and 1983 numbers do not include ASTMS, which made no returns.
[d]*Source:* Labour Party Report 1984.
[e]The 81–2 per cent figure is consistent and reaches back over the whole period of Certification Officer returns.
Source: Except where otherwise stated, the source of these figures is the *Report of the Certification Officer, 1984.*

the over-affiliation of a giant union poses radically different problems, and does represent a usurpation of power and authority.

These issues understood, it is possible to present global data on the proportion of all members of affiliated unions who contribute to the political funds, and the (different) proportion actually affiliated to the Labour Party. These figures are contrasted in table 4.8.

It need hardly be said that all these complexities have done nothing whatever to bring individual trade union members closer to the political Party to which they have been corporately affiliated. In fact, there has been a steady diminution of personal involvement by trade union members in the active work of the Labour Party over a rather long period of time. To trace this, we have to trace the evolution of the federal structure of the Labour Party, and the gradual dilution of federal principles.

The Labour Party as a Federation

In February 1900, at a meeting in the Memorial Hall in London, there was established a Labour Representation Committee. Today, we know that this was the organization which was to become the Labour Party. Millions of people have recognized this Party as their own, either by joining it, or by voting for it. Its power has grown to the point where on seven separate occasions it has gained the largest number of seats in Parliament and formed the government. But in 1900 no crystal gazer would have foreseen any of this. W. C. Steadman presided over a gathering of 129 people, drawn in the main from trade unions, but also representing a handful of socialist organizations. Ramsay MacDonald, a more famous participant in that first gathering, later recalled that 'Discretion moved the Conference . . . to adopt the title the "Labour Representation Committee" rather than one more definitely Party. Organized labour was by no means ready to plunge into the task of Party making. . . .'[28]

The 129 agreed that working class opinion should be represented in the House of Commons 'by men sympathetic with the aims and demands of the labour movements'.[29] They hoped that these movements would promote the candidatures of suitable people, and affiliate to their committee. They hoped that those elected would establish 'a distinct Labour Group in Parliament, who shall have their own Whips, and agree upon their policy'.

While maintaining their independence, members of such a group were expected to cooperate with any party which 'for the time being' sought to promote legislation which was helpful to the labour cause.

The founding conference established a committee of 12, composed of seven trade union representatives and five members of socialist societies. Of course, this gave the socialist societies a totally disproportionate influence. Something over half a million trade union members were represented in the conference, as against less than 23,000 socialists from three societies. But the socialists were keen to establish a political body unifying labour interests, while a goodly number of the trade unions were, to put it mildly, lukewarm. Some present in the Memorial Hall had been delegated to attend, but hoped that the organization might not succeed. Others were not totally unsympathetic, but none the less somewhat agnostic. A proposal for an executive of 18, twelve of whom would come from the unions, was amended in favour of the smaller committee, even though it was obvious that trade union numbers greatly exceeded the puny force of the socialists.

Something closer to the real relationship of forces emerged during the following months, when the membership of the committee was formalized. It was found to comprise 41 trade unions with a membership of 353,070, seven trades councils and three socialist societies with 22,861 members. One socialist society quickly defected. The Social Democratic Federation, claiming 9,000 members, had, right at the beginning in 1900, sought to commit the new organization to a specifically socialist programme. It failed, and left. Its departure meant that by 1902 the socialist influence came only from 861 Fabians and 13,000 members of the Independent Labour Party. But the trade union affiliation began a steady rise, first to 65 national organizations and 21 trades councils, then, by 1903 to 127 unions and 49 trades councils. Although trade union involvement was henceforth to fluctuate, by 1912 there were 130 national unions affiliated, representing well over 1.8 million members. There were also 146 trades councils or 'local Labour Parties'. A local Labour Party at this time was a kind of miniature Labour Representation Committee, strictly federal in composition. By 1916, there were over 100 trades councils associated with the new party, and there already existed 75 local federations. Common sense and practical considerations meant that the initial federation was simply structured, and hardly rule-bound. Changes were made ad hoc. After the departure of the Social Democrats, only three socialist society representatives remained on the executive, two from the ILP and one from the Fabians.

The first constitutional change came in 1905, after a trade union delegate tried to secure a reform which would provide for the election of the executive by a ballot of all the delegates to the conference. This proposal was rejected, but the societies agreed that henceforth they would be jointly represented so that the executive could earmark places for three representatives of the socialist societies, rather than designating spaces for the separate affiliates.

The 1906 General Election brought a major breakthrough. Twenty-nine Labour candidates were victorious, even though only 50 seats had been contested. In the seats where contests took place, Labour took 37 per cent of the total poll. The Labour Representation Committee resolved to call itself the Labour Party, but the Committee structure of the new organization remained the same, even if it was being formalized by precedent, as the federation developed. In 1914, at Glasgow, the constitution of the Party was revised, but it still began: 'The Labour Party is a federation consisting of trade unions, trades councils, socialist societies and local Labour Parties'. Both trade unions and socialist societies were expected to pay a penny per member per annum to sustain the Party, and each was entitled to be represented at the annual conference by one delegate for each 1,000 members. Although trade union representation was temporarily dislocated by the Osborne judgment, so that the Party reported that 'it was impracticable to compile membership statistics for 1913', none the less the interruption of trade union involvement proved only temporary. In 1912, as we have seen, 130 national trade unions with 1.8 million members had been affiliated. By 1914, after the Liberal Government's Trade Union Act had passed on to the Statute Book, 101 unions were still affiliated, with more than 1½ million members. The following year, the total affiliated membership passed the 2 million mark for the first time.

Following the war, the Party Conference of January 1918 agreed to seek a broader organizational basis and a sharper set of objectives. As Henderson reported, in spite of its successes in elections, the Party 'had never in the proper sense claimed to be a national political Party'. But the wartime mobilization had afforded the Movement great possibilities of expansion. Moreover extensions of the franchise would double the number of voters, and the Party needed to open itself to them. Could the federal structure cope with the organizational needs of a truly national Labour movement? Hitherto, the highest number of Labour candidates standing at any one time had been 78. Henceforth with the vast expansion of the working class electorate, Labour candidates would find a response everywhere they stood. Was it not necessary to create a new political organization, admitting individual membership? In the event, Henderson thought that it would be impolitic to abandon the federation, but that it was necessary 'to graft on to it' a form of membership organization which would enable individuals to join in each constituency. The new hybrid would consist of affiliated organizations 'together with those men and women who are individual members of a local Labour Party and who subscribe to the constitution and programme of the Party'. To govern this body it would be necessary to modify the executive. Now it would be enlarged to 23 persons, 13 of whom would represent affiliates (12 trade unionists and one socialist society), five of whom would speak for the new local Labour Parties and four of whom would represent women members. These, in addition to the treasurer, would all be elected by vote of the whole conference. Thus, the federal principle remained sovereign and the trade unions who comprised the main forces in the federation could determine who should occupy the seats on the executive, from among nominations offered by the other sections.

Yet, although the unions could decide between them who could gain access to the executive, they were deeply suspicious of the proposal to admit local Labour Parties, even to so dilute a form of 'representation'. Robert Smillie successfully moved the reference back of the proposed reforms, even though a general election was imminent. As a result, there was a hurried reconvention at a one day meeting a month later, when the new constitution was finally agreed.

The federation had survived. Now, the socialist societies were reduced to token membership of the new executive at the pleasure of their trade union colleagues. Although constituency Labour organizations would grow throughout the country, their access to the new executive was also at the pleasure of the trade unions. This situation was to continue through to 1937, although it became increasingly difficult to support, as the constituency parties gained in influence and solidity.

As local Parties developed within each constituency, the number of individual members grew. At the same time, the local government presence of the Party required cooperation between different constituency organizations. The Party had to lay down rules governing such cooperation, and these very sensibly established joint borough parties, which were themselves federal in character. On the borough organizations, ruling committees would be elected on the principle that the trade unions should have the sole right to elect their representatives from among the trade unions that were affiliated, and that the constituency parties should have similar rights. The London Labour Party, for instance, involved more than 60 separate constituencies as well as the widest range of trade unions. The London executive was comprised of trade unionists chosen from the trade union wing separately, and the constituency representatives appointed in the same way.

An even larger federation grew up in Scotland. Basing themselves on such precedents as these, representatives of constituency parties began to question why their members of the national executives of the Party should be elected on a trade union block vote. Successive Party Conferences were pressured: resolutions began to proliferate both at national and regional assemblies. A lobby was organized. In 1936, the National Executive Committee agreed to consult about proposals for reform and at the 1937 Conference it recommended that the constituency section of the NEC should be enlarged to seven members, who would be elected by the votes of the constituency members only. At the same time, it was agreed that the socialist society member would henceforth be elected by the votes only of affiliated societies in that division. Still federal, this modified franchise for the NEC formalized the idea of distinct constituencies within the movement taken as a whole. The agreement of 1937 persisted, and still determines the general framework of the present day Labour Party.[30]

It marks the third phase in the history of the federation. First, from 1900 until 1918 there was a federal alliance between unions and socialist societies. Secondly, from 1918 until 1937, the federation was under the ultimate control of the trade union block vote, while individual members began to be organized. Thirdly, the federation assumed its fundamental bi-polar characteristic of an alliance between trade unions and Constituency Labour Parties based on individual membership.

This situation continued in force for almost 30 years. The Labour Party did not enter the fourth stage of its constitutional development until 1965, and at the time the changeover was barely noticed.[31]

Prior to 1965, each CLP was itself a federation in which every national affiliated organization might participate as of right. The most simple organization in each Party was the ward committee. Constituencies were expected to establish one such committee in each ward within their territory. Enrolled at this level would be the individual members of the Party 'and such members of affiliated societies as enrolled themselves'. Both individual and affiliated members were required to live in (or be registered in) the local government ward in which they took out their membership. Starting at this basic level, members of affiliated trade unions and associations were entitled to participate at each higher level of the Party's organization. They could be directly represented on general management committees, or at borough party organizations or in the regional organizations; and they were, of course, entitled to representation at the annual national conference.

In 1965 all this was changed. Membership at the ward level, and at every higher level, was henceforth restricted to persons holding individual membership. In other words, an affiliated member could not exercise his rights within the Labour Party's structure unless he paid twice: once into a political levy as an affiliated member, and once in the form of a personal subscription to a CLP. The fact that the political levy amounted only to a derisory sum no doubt made this reform seem the more reasonable.

The opposition at the Blackpool Conference that year mustered only 44,000 votes altogether. The related reform which required participants in the annual conference to be individual members aroused stronger resistance: 295,000 votes were cast against it.[32] This seems to indicate that national trade union delegations were less concerned about the constitution of the Party at the grass roots than they were about their own potential access at the level of the annual conference.

The effect of the 1965 reform was to dilute the significance to individual contributors in the unions of affiliated membership. At the time, individual membership subscriptions were very low, but the gap between them and the level of political fund subscriptions in affiliated bodies was subsequently to widen dramatically. The clear intention of the reform was to encourage more affiliated members to take out individual subscriptions. However, it cannot be said to have been particularly successful in achieving this objective. It has until very recently been impossible to obtain reliable data about the real level of individual membership, because CLPs were required to affiliate on the fictitious expectation that their minimum membership would be 1,000. All informed commentators agree that in fact individual membership of the Labour Party declined after 1965, rather than expanding. But if the intentions of the reformers were not realized, none the less the reform had an effect which was no less serious for being unanticipated. This was to devalue the status of affiliated membership to a dangerously low point. What used to be an almost unrestricted right of personal access was now restricted to a right of collective representation, which might be extremely attenuated.[33] While some trade union organizations carried on a lively discussion about political matters, others, to put it gently, were rather torpid. The result of this process was to make it more and more difficult to maintain the value of the political levy as a proportion of trade union membership contributions. More and more the levy became a tax on trade union members, rather than an active contribution.

This is a damaging situation for the Labour Party trade union connection, even during times when it is relatively unquestioned; but it becomes perilous when that connection is under sustained and remorseless attack. To the extent that the trade unions are able to maintain their political funds in the ballots that will take place during 1985 and early 1986, the Labour Party would be well-advised to restore some of the personal rights that attached to trade union affiliates before 1965. Naturally, it is arguable that corporate affiliation at a very low level of subscription ought not to attract the same voting rights as individual membership at a relatively high cost. But this need not be an obstacle to the effective working of a federation, if a system of financial voting is introduced. This would make it quite easy to weigh corporate affiliates on one scale and individual members on another, in accordance with the actual payments made by each. This done, a few simple rules would greatly improve access and potential involvement.

First, at the collective level, affiliations to the Party should correspond as closely as possible to the true numbers of persons contributing to the political levy. Unions should not buy votes by over-affiliating but nor should they save or reallocate money by affiliating at lower levels of membership, leaving some persons effectively unrepresented. Secondly, all those who pay into the fund might reasonably be entitled to participate at some relevant level of the Party's organization whether or not they agree to make a further individual contribution. With a differential voting system, affiliated members could indeed once again resume an active presence at local, constituency, city or county, regional and national levels.

APPENDIX 4.1   SOME PROPOSALS ON THE LABOUR PARTY'S STRUCTURE

What follows is an excerpt from evidence offered to the Labour Party's inquiry into its organization and structure, established in 1981.

Supposing that the difference between individual and corporate membership fees represented a ratio of one to ten. Then corporate bodies would cast votes which weighed one-tenth as heavy as individual members, and the federation would become in fact an alliance of two roughly equal halves of corporate affiliates and individual members.

If we suppose that affiliated members should have their status clarified, it becomes possible to set a series of rights and duties which might apply to *all* members, whether affiliated or individual, although such rights may be exercised differently in the separate categories of membership. First, membership might entail the right to a share in the determination of policy, either through the criticism of existing policy of performance, or through the development of constructive alternative proposals. Policy could be influenced by simple resolutions, or by more elaborate submissions to relevant committees. The right to determine policy could normally apply at local, constituency, regional and national levels. Secondly, membership could entail the right to an appropriately weighted voice in the election of relevant spokesmen at all the above levels in the Party's structure, from management committee through to annual national conference. Thirdly, membership might involve the right to participate directly in the selection of appropriate candidates to represent the Party in electoral contests, from parish council through to Parliamentary elections. This particular right might be restricted to nomination or extended beyond this, if the constitution were changed. But no change in the constitution towards enabling greater participation in selection conferences is logically possible without prior reform in the field here discussed, unless affiliated members are to be effectively excluded. Fourthly, membership clearly entails the duty to support the Party financially, to work for it in relevant ways, to abide by its democratic rules and to support it against its opponents. The listing of rights and duties is probably uncontentious. Other rights and duties might well be added, but they would probably generate some controversy. For instance, members might well expect to have their democratic rights made enforceable by an appropriately autonomous disciplinary system. This is an issue which has been discussed at various levels in the Party, and remains unresolved. It is not important when the Party regulates its affairs with a tolerant disposition, but it would become important if policy were to be interpreted rigidly as has sometimes happened in the past.

In the light of a charter of membership rights, we may evaluate the teeming proposals for the reform of party structure rather differently than they have often been evaluated in the recent past. First of all, in relation to leadership, every proposal which complicates the direct accountability of leaders to members is an impediment to democracy. Leaders need to be directly elected by their relevant memberships, and the most obvious and sensible criteria for such elections turn around policy discussions. It may therefore seem quite inappropriate to have an over-sectionalized national leadership. Whether a person represents the Party as a Member of Parliament, a councillor, a school governor, or a member of a health authority is an accidental question within the Party itself compared to the fundamental question of his or her membership. If members are to exercise differential rights according to the public offices they hold, then the principle of the equality of membership disappears and the democracy of the Party is in jeopardy. MPs discharge their constitutional function inside Parliament, where they must have an appropriate status to do this effectively. Outside Parliament, they should have the general public status they have earned, whether in Party organizations or other voluntary bodies. The responsibility of serving in the legislature does not entitle one to legislate outside it. If it did, parliamentarians would become semi-feudal grandees.

The same argument applies within the affiliated section of membership. It is in fact the case that the majority of trade union representatives on the present Labour Party NEC are either Members of Parliament or full time employees of their unions' head offices. It would be possible to argue that there should be spaces reserved in this section for shop stewards, branch officials, dues collectors or various other categories of membership. Such arguments would be analogous to those seeking representation for, say, councillors, as a special category. They are not acceptable proposals. It is more important to ensure that the electoral processes which determine the membership of the executive do involve a real degree of membership influence within each affiliated organization, than it is to attempt to legislate for a precise mix of responsibilities and experiences.

The simplest structure for the national executive, if it is directly to reflect the membership of the Party, is one involving parity between individual members and affiliated members. It would seem to be invidious to seek to tell either category of membership whether it should choose activists working in national or local affairs, or having any other exceptional characteristics. Of course, there is no reason why this approach should not be combined with special rules to ensure adequate representation for women, by, for instance, stipulating that half the persons elected in each of these two sections must be women. It might also be possible to mark off proportional space for representation of ethnic minorities. But in these cases, special quotas would be open to all relevant members, and not earmarked for people who occupied particular roles in government or union administration: a person's function would not, in itself, win representation, because all contests would be equally open to all qualified electors within the constituency involved.

Notes

1 Lord MacNaghten, in the Osborne Case, *ASRS v. Osborne*, 1909, AC 87.
2 Sidney and Beatrice Webb, *Industrial Democracy*, Longmann Green & Co., 1920 edition (first published 1897).
3 Ibid., p. 247.
4 From *The Pioneer*, organ of the Owenite trade unionists, 1833.
5 V. L. Allen, *The Sociology of Industrial Relations*, Longman, 1971, part III, pp. 119 et seq.
6 House of Commons Official Report, Standing Committee F (Trade Union Bill), 21 February 1984.
7 TUC Congress Report, 1910, Chairman's opening speech.
8 Winston Churchill, House of Commons Debates, 30 May 1911.
9 TUC Report, 1911, p. 169.
10 TUC Report, 1912, p. 53.
11 Ibid., pp. 172–3.
12 Ibid., p. 173.
13 TUC Report, 1913, p. 88.
14 Ibid., p. 153.
15 Martin Harrison, *Trade Unions and the Labour Party since 1945*, Allen and Unwin, 1960, p. 23. See also Lewis Minkin, 'Polls apart', in *New Scientist*, December 1984, p. 8.
16 Harrison, *Trade Unions*, p. 26.
17 Cited in K. D. Ewing, *Trade Unions, The Labour Party and the Law*, Edinburgh University Press, 1982, pp. 50–51. See also Labour Research

Department, *Union Freedoms Under Threat*, LRD 1983, p. 23. (PRO., CAB 24/182).

18 House of Commons Debates, 5s col. 840, quoted in Martin Harrison, *Trade Unions and the Labour Party*, Allen & Unwin, 1960, p. 26.

19 Ewing, *Trade Unions, the Labour Party and the Law*, p. 61.

20 For an account of sponsorship, see William D. Muller: *The Kept Men?*, Harvester, 1977. For the functioning of the group of sponsored MPs, see Irving Richter, *Political Purpose in Trade Unions*, Allen & Unwin, 1973, chapter 8, pp. 146 et seq.

21 Ken Coates and Tony Topham, *Trade Unions in Britain*, Spokesman, 1980, p. 306.

22 *Labour Research*, May 1985, p. 136.

23 DATA, *Evidence to the Royal Commission on Trade Unions and Employers' Associations*, 1965, pp. 57–8.

24 ASTMS, 'The case for our political fund', Speakers' Notes, 1985, appendix II, p. 2.

25 Martin Linton writing in *Labour Weekly*, 8 June 1979.

26 Ibid. When Linton wrote his careful analysis of these complexities he then found only two unions who affiliated automatically on the exact number of members who paid, or who were eligible to pay, the political levy. These were UCATT and ASTMS. However, he also found that three unions were paying on more than 100 per cent. Top of the league was the NUR, affiliating on 110 per cent of levy contributors. 'We affiliate on a round number' a spokesman of the union told him. 'I don't suppose the Labour Party are ungrateful.'

27 Michael Jones, 'Labour's phantom union votes', *The Sunday Times*, 28 April 1985.

28 J. R. MacDonald, *A Policy for the Labour Party*, p. 24, cited in R. T. McKenzie, *British Political Parties*, Heinemann, 1964, p. 287.

29 Margaret Stewart, *Protest or Power?* Allen & Unwin, 1974, p. 54.

30 For more detailed accounts of the constitutional changes up to this time see McKenzie, *British Political Parties*, pp. 286 et seq. and 456 et seq.; and G. D. H. Cole, *A History of the Labour Party from 1914*, Routledge and Kegan Paul, 1948, pp. 71 et seq. and pp. 335 et seq.

31 A fifth stage was opened in 1981 with the establishment of an electoral college for the election of the Leader and Deputy Leader of the Party. This is considered in chapter 6.

32 Labour Party Conference Report 1965.

33 The restrictions which applied prohibited two categories of people from participating: members of parties opposed to the Labour Party, and members of organizations on a 'proscribed' list. Subsequent to the 1965 reform the list of proscribed bodies was abolished. It had consisted of bodies considered to be under Communist or Trotskyist influence.

5 The Campaign to Retain Political Funds

In the aftermath of Labour's general election defeat of 1983, the Movement's industrial wing had to face difficult choices about future strategy, including the nature of its response to the Bill which became the 1984 Trade Union Act. At the TUC Congress of 1983, a strong call was made by some leading spokesmen of 'non-political' and right-wing opinions for the TUC to distance itself from the Labour Party, the connection with which, it was thought, hampered the unions in their search for an accommodation with the government. The continued alliance with Labour, it was also argued, no longer reflected the actual politics of trade union members as revealed in the general election voting patterns.

This view was to be partly echoed by the TUC General Secretary, Len Murray, who affirmed in a TV interview that Labour's policy making was no affair of the TUC. This was an assertion which hardly squared with the experience of the TUC–Labour Party Liaison Committee, not to speak of the close ties sustained over a much longer history. This strand of thought soon acquired a status and a label – 'the new realism'. In tune with it, the TUC published a discussion document on 'strategy' which elaborated a distinctly cautious, corporatist approach to the future and hinted at a cooling-off in relations with the Labour Party.[1] However, a series of critical collisions, involving the use of the Employment Acts of 1980 and 1982, as well as the government more directly, soon put 'new realism' to the test.

In the dispute between the National Graphical Association and Mr Eddie Shah, proprietor of a chain of provincial newspapers, the TUC retreated at the last moment from supporting the print union's decision to resist the enforcement of the Employment Acts with a general strike of Fleet Street. In this case, the fundamental capacity of a trade union to defend its negotiated wage rages, and the level of its membership, through closed shop arrangements, was at risk. This is not to mention the jeopardy in which its financial assets were placed, subject as they were to large fines, damages, and sequestration. At the height of the crisis, the NGA stood on the verge of liquidation and closed shop

147

arrangements became demonstrably unenforceable against an intransigent employer. The TUC was forced to debate again its own Special Congress decision of 1982, to provide active support wherever a union, pursuing Congress policy of non-comformity with the new legislation, found itself under threat from court action, 'if necessary, calling for industrial action against the employer concerned, or more widely . . .'

During the Wembley conference which endorsed this commitment, some very strong words had been uttered from the rostrum. David Basnett, for instance, declared:

> This movement has always co-operated with the law but this Government is using the law to destroy consensus on which our society depends. To duck that challenge would be to betray our eleven million members – working people of this country. We shall not do so, and if we say that and we say it here today, for God's sake let us mean it.

Roy Grantham, of APEX, told the conference that: 'In 1971 opinion polls said there should be law, but when people saw the law, and when people saw what a mess the law was, people said "away with it and away with this Government".' Bill Sirs, of the ISTC, was also incensed: 'I do not think we are being strong enough . . . my union will support it 100 per cent on the basis that it does not go far enough.'[2]

These rhetorical declarations were nullified in the TUC General Council's decision to withhold support for the NGA. This was carried by a majority of 31 votes to 20. (The general council had recently acquired a number of new members, some from 'non-political' unions, under a novel 'automaticity' rule under which general council seats had been allocated according to a scale of categories based upon the numbers of members in each union, rather than through the long-established block voting system of election.) With the decision in the NGA case, industrial militancy and non-compliance with the new laws were rendered inoperable as a general strategy, long before the miners strike had broken out, and before its subsequent failure to evoke mass sympathetic support actions from other unions and the TUC itself.

The government's ban on trade union membership at the GCHQ intelligence centre at Cheltenham followed soon afterwards to expose still further the limits of a strategy of militant industrial resistance, whilst giving no comfort whatever to the 'new realists'. For while the government noted 'new realism' with satisfaction, it was not at all inclined to extend any kindnesses at all in encouragement of that tendency. Under the impact of these events, the general council was so far overcome as to decide upon a symbolic and temporary withdrawal of the TUC representatives from attendance at meetings of the National

Economic Development Council, the founding prototype of modern corporatist institutions. This withdrawal was strongly led by a leading spokesman of former consensus, David Basnett.

There remained on the TUC agenda the question of non-conformity with the 1984 Trade Union Act. But having, in the NGA case, bowed before the authority of the 1980/82 laws, what was left of non-conformism? Failure to hold strike ballots as required by the 1984 Act would be followed by employers' actions in court (as happened later in Austin–Rover in 1984, and then in the teachers strikes of 1985), which put at risk the very solvency of trade unions, and which led in the event to more cases of compliance as unions held their pre-strike ballots. For after the NGA, and later the miners cases, there was no real possibility of sympathetic action compelling judicial retreats, as had happened under the Heath laws of the early 1970s. Failure to ballot for union executive positions under the same 1984 law could in future produce a string of court actions by disaffected members. In stronger circumstances, there remained a case for sustaining non-compliance in the case of political fund ballots. This would have compelled the courts to intervene in the constitutional arrangements of the main opposition party in Parliament and caused a quickening of awareness on the constitutional implications of the Trade Union Act, in which wide pluralist sensitivities would have been touched. But the preceding retreat of the TUC and the unions before the combined weight of the law and their industrial weakness as a result of mass unemployment dictated a compliant response, and the Movement decided without very much discussion to hold the political fund ballots.

Moreover, the TUC's only initiative to head off the threat to political funds consisted of a negotiated agreement with Mr Tom King, the Employment Secretary, which tended to endorse the legislation. At an early stage in the Bill's preparation, the government had spoken of its disquiet at the alleged difficulties encountered by trade union members who wished to contract-out of paying the political levy, and hinted at a return to contracting-in as it had applied between 1927 and 1946. The TUC joined in talks with Mr King to reverse this apparent intention, and claimed to have won a vital concession from him when he agreed not to proceed with the change. But in return, the TUC agreed to circulate to all unions a 'Statement of Guidance' on the strict application of procedures to facilitate members' right to contract-out. Yet it was very clear before this stage had been reached that the government had its sights set not on contracting-in, (this could if necessary come later), but on the requirement for new ballots on the political fund itself, with a much more disruptive potential for the future of Labour Party finances, to say nothing of the Party's constitution. In fact, had it been known, complaints to the Certification Officer had reached an all-time low at the very time of the King negotiations, and certainly did not justify 'disquiet' of any kind.

During the negotiations, no counter-demands were made by the TUC in return for its 'Statement of Guidance' although a number of bargaining positions were possible. They might for instance have demanded that if a ballot went against the political fund, the minority remaining in favour should have the same rights now enjoyed by contractors-out, and be able legally to continue to collect and administer a fund, through contracting-in. They might have withheld circulation of the 'Statement of Guidance' unless the government agreed to modify the legislation, in this or other ways. They could have insisted that the government compelled the private company sector to declare their political contributions and to hold ballots of shareholders and employees on their continuation. None of these options found their way into serious public debate. By concentrating on the secondary question of contracting-in, the TUC allowed the government to obscure its own main intention, which was to put at risk the survival of any kind of political fund, whatever the mode of its collection. The last point of possible resistance to the new law had been passed, and the trade unions turned their attention to preparing a campaign for an affirmative vote in the ballots, to be held during 1985 and 1986.

There are 54 unions which currently have political funds, 47 of which are affiliated to the Labour Party. Most of them rallied to the support of a Trade Union Co-ordinating Committee Campaigning for Political Funds, set up under the chairmanship of Bill Keys (until that time general secretary of SOGAT), with an office in Transport House a full time coordinator, Graham Allen, and a modest budget of £150,000. The campaign had to function over a considerable period of time; all unions which had not balloted in the past ten years had to do so before April 1986, but each union chose its own preferred dates for voting; SOGAT itself successfully initiated the process in April 1985, and most unions were scheduled to have completed their ballots by the end of that year.

(At the time this book went to press, the ballotting process was well under way. Sixteen trade unions had completed their ballots and the results of these, which reflect the views taken by over 3 million union members, are given in chapter 9, 'Afterword'.)

In framing the tone and content of the campaign, the organizers weighed the Labour voting by trade unionists in recent general elections. The results were not initially encouraging for a 'yes' result in the ballots (see table 5.1 which gives the changes in the numbers of trade unionists respectively voting Labour and affiliated to the Labour Party in general elections held between 1964 and 1983).

The campaign took some encouragement however from polls taken early in 1985, which showed that a bare majority (54 per cent) had returned to the fold and would vote Labour had a general election been called at that time. But they also showed a less than perfect correlation between voting intentions and support for union political funds. At the end of February 1985 MORI conducted a poll for Channel 4 TV's *Union World* programme. The results for some of the largest unions are shown in table 5.2.

Table 5.1 Trends in Labour voting among trade unionists

Election year	Trade unionists voting Labour No.	(%)	Trade unionists affiliated to Labour No.
1964	6,077,980	73	5,502,001
1974	5,501,100	55	5,787,467
1979	6,185,280	51	6,511,179
1983	4,098,900	39	6,101,438

Table 5.2 Poll response to the question: Would you personally vote for your union to have a political fund?[a]

Union	Would (%)	Would not (%)	Difference (%)
NUM	52	37	+ 15
AUEW	48	41	+ 7
GMBATU	41	48	− 7
TGWU	38	50	− 12
EETPU	36	50	− 14
NUPE	32	53	− 21
ASTMS	32	56	− 24

[a]Poll conducted end of February 1985.

Among white-collar workers, 57 per cent opposed political funds; among blue-collar workers 59 per cent were opposed and only 40 per cent declared that they would vote for continuing their fund. Trade unionists who also voted Labour supported political funds by two to one. The 45 per cent who voted Conservative or Alliance in 1983 were overwhelmingly opposed to the levy. A substantial majority of 60 per cent however, supported the use of political funds for campaigns against government policy affecting their own pay and jobs, but only 28 per cent supported a campaigns on issues not linked to jobs and pay. A small minority of only 14 per cent supported their unions in assisting the Labour Party in national elections, with 36 per cent agreeing to such help for local elections. Only 39 per cent supported their union affiliating to the Labour Party, and 36 per cent supported the practice of sponsoring MPs.

With this evidence to guide them, the trade union campaigners decided that their theme should be: 'Yes to a Voice in Parliament'. They also determined: first, that it should be a *trade union* campaign; secondly, that it was about the right to have political funds; thirdly, that it would only be won in the workplace. That is, the Labour Party link was not to be stressed, and the Labour Party in fact agreed to refrain from major 'electioneering' during the campaign, and to play only a minor, supportive role.

The media's expected influence was to be countered by encouraging a steady, persuasive debate in the workplace, led by 'campaign contacts' recruited from lay trade union activists. These were supplied with a flow of posters, leaflets, cartoons and speakers' notes. Training courses and workshops were organized, and regular ammunition was also offered in the form of widespread coverage of the question in union newspapers and journals.

In their advice to the campaign contacts, the organizers stressed the need to canvass at work (model canvass cards were designed and supplied) and to identify and get out the 'yes' vote, while avoiding fruitless debates (which would heat the atmosphere) with 'the workplace bigot'. Members were also advised that the unions did not intend to become involved in a high-level national advertising campaign, nor even to use outlets in the local press, or to organize public rallies. Thus a very heavy weight of persuasion was to be thrown on the activists at workplace level.

A further critical decision was that the campaign should not offer 'promises'. That is, the future political goals and aspirations of trade unionists should not be raised. Instead, heavy emphasis was to be placed on past achievements of trade unions' political activities, and equally on the current defensive role of trade unions in resisting the job losses, closures, public sector cuts, threats to the welfare state, the health service and terms and conditions of work, initiated by the Thatcher Government and only to be withstood through trade union political action. Yet it was also stressed that this should not be a specifically anti-Tory campaign; nor should it set out to 'sell' the Labour Party.

A range of arguments was suggested to the campaign contacts. They were advised to point out to members that they could vote 'yes' and still contract-out of the levy, and that those who opposed the levy should do so, in order not to deprive their fellow-members of their right to have a fund. ('Don't vote away the rights of your colleagues'.) Some unions claimed to have evidence that Tory members and branches had indeed decided to adopt this recommendation. Complementing this approach, the campaign was anxious to point out that the ballot was not about affiliation to the Labour Party. This was a separate decision taken within the union's normal constitutional procedures.

Closely related to this point was the insistence on the need for unions to engage in lobbying and public campaigns on single issues, regardless of their Party affiliation. Such activity had been made more urgently necessary because of the far-reaching nature of the economic crisis, unemployment and government cuts. Equally strong was the campaign's emphasis on the positive role of union-sponsored MPs in Parliament; contacts were urged to deploy examples of their own union's MPs casework on matters directly relevant to the union's occupations and industries. A final theme, on which much data was supplied, was the extent of political finance, subject to no legal constraints or democratic controls, supplied by companies to the Conservative Party.

We assembled campaign material relating to the national campaigns of some 30 unions together with the unions' journals and newspapers at the start of the campaigns. Most of them follow closely the organizers' recommendations summarized above. There are variations to be found; unions such as the TGWU and NUPE did not mute their Labour Party affiliations to the same extent as some others, for example. The weight of the evidence from the literature suggests that there is support for a prediction made by Peter Hain, concerning one of the consequences of the 1984 Act.

> Ironically, the Tories may also have done the labour movement something of a backhanded long term favour. By instituting regular political fund ballots, they are effectively legitimising political activity and discussion within trade unions, and this could well prove the most lasting consequence of the legislation. By attacking political funds, they will force union leaders to give a priority to political education which, instead of being a luxury option, will become a necessity.[3]

Our own view, developed in chapter 8, is that while the current campaign has chosen to focus upon past and present political roles, a continued development of the political education of trade unionists must include the discussion and canvassing of future objectives, which may prove far less contentious than seems to have been assumed by some unions.

THE Political Fund ballot for the GMB will be held during the two weeks, June 14-28 — shortly after the Union's Congress in Blackpool, which is in the first week of June. The Central Executive Council has decided to adopt a workplace ballot procedure for the vast majority of membership. In the rare cases where this is not possible, postal votes will be allowed. The CEC has stressed the extreme importance of winning a 'YES' vote in this crucial ballot — not just to ensure that the Union's voice is heard in Parliament and in Local Council chambers, but to retain our right to campaign on issues affecting unemployment, low pay, pensioners, the National Health Service, ethnic minorities and a host of other subjects . . . MAKE SURE YOU VOTE 'YES' . . .

POL
WHY IT M

A DAY IN THE LIFE OF A SHOP STEWARD

MEMBERS who say unions should keep out of politics, should read the following — "A Day in the Life of Kay Drew", an imaginary shop steward at a fish processing plant.

Kay rushed her breakfast so that she could catch the seven o'clock bus. She used to be able to leave at 7.30 but the privatisation of her bus route meant services had been cut (1984 Transport White Paper). Her daughter and son had to be taken to the child-minder first. Kay was not happy about leaving the children with a minder, but the local school no longer had a nursery (Education cuts).

Being shop steward was very time consuming, but Kay felt it was a worthwhile job. As soon as she arrived at work, Jim Carter met her to say that the conditions in the gutting room were unsafe because the floor was too wet and slippery.

Kay had been aware of this problem for some time and had been trying to get in the factory inspector, but so far she had failed (Government cuts in the number of factory inspectors).

While she was trying, yet again, to get a visit from the inspector, she received a phone call from one of her members who was on maternity leave.

She had informed the employers of the date of her return to work and had been told her job was no longer open since she failed to reply within 14 days to their letter asking if she still intended to return to work.

This had surprised her since when she had had her previous baby, in 1979, she had not needed to do this, so she had not understood the importance of replying (change in procedures, 1980 Employment Act).

Kay promised to take her case up, but had to tell her that legally the Company was within their rights.

Just as Kay was settling down to her tea-break she remembered she had to see Tony Hayes, who had recently lost his job. Her full-time officer had told her that he had a good case on unfair dismissal,

but since the Government had extended the qualifying period from six months to a year for taking the case to a tribunal and Tony had only worked for the company for nine months, it would not be possible to take the case.

Kay was just beginning to think her day couldn't get any worse when her husband rang to say that their son had had an accident at the minder's and had been taken to casualty at Braining hospital. The hospital was ten miles away since the local hospital casualty department had been closed (NHS cuts).

After visiting the hospital, Kay returned home to find that the roof of her council house was leaking. She contacted the local council and was told that it could be a week before it was repaired since the work was contracted out rather than being done by a Direct Labour Organisation.

When Kay was finally able to sit down and have a cup of tea a thought crossed her mind: "Who says politics don't affect our everyday life?"

SET OUT, below, is an example of what it could be like, should we get a "NO" to the Political Fund in the forthcoming ballot . . .

■ It is a monthly Branch Meeting. In keeping with

What a "NO" vote could mean to you and your Union

the usual agenda, the Chairperson calls for reports.

A shop steward from the local hospital informs the Branch that he wishes to make an urgent report:

"Today the District Health Authority held a meeting, where it was decided to seek private tenders for our cleaning, catering and laundry services.

"Should this happen, we stand to lose 182 jobs.

Implications

"Along with other shop stewards, I have attended a meeting earlier this evening to discuss the implications for our members.

"We all feel that the present Hospital Administrator was put there by friends of the Government because it is his recommendation the Health Authority have acted on.

"As a steward, I represent 59 workers in the Laundry Department and we demand that this Union mount a campaign in de-

"Brothers and Sisters. I need to bring to the attention of the Branch, the situation currently prevailing at our General Hospital.

fence of our jobs."

Under a law that had removed our political fund; the legal response would be as follows. The Branch Chairperson would have to say:

"What you've told us, Brother, is in strict legal terms, out of order. Although we have great sympathy for your cause, what you are asking us to do is 'political'.

"If we campaign on your members' behalf to stop their jobs being privatised, we are deemed to be in direct conflict with their laws, because what you are asking us to do is campaign against their laid down policies.

"If, however, we still had a Political Fund, there would be no problem. The Tory Government knows exactly who still has Political Funds and who does not.

"If we act in a political manner — i.e. attempting to stop your job losses to privatisation by mounting a campaign of leaflets,

petitions and public meetings — we will most certainly end up in the dock, resulting in severe financial penalties being placed on this Union."

The steward replies:

"Are you telling me that because we don't have a

Political Fund any longer, we are virtually powerless on campaigning to save members' jobs threatened with privatisation?

"If I'd have known that, I would have voted "YES" in the ballot. Almost everyone at my hospital voted "NO", because we were under the impression that all the Political Fund was donated to the Labour Party."

(From an original idea by ROY BEAKE, LONDON REGION.)

"Don't let unions join the silenced majority".

"No free speech for Trade Unions! Thank goodness it couldn't happen here".

Figure 5.1 The centre spread from the GMBATU's newspaper for March/

T SURVIVE . . .

TU campaign ambulance on tour of Lancashire

A LOBBY of the Burnley, Pendle and Rossendale Area Health Authority against privatisation saw the unveiling of a campaign ambulance, recently purchased by the Lancashire Health Service Trade Union Co-ordinating Committee.

The vehicle has been decorated with the Red Rose of Lancashire by volunteers, is fitted with a public address system and was used to great effect touring Burnley Town Centre publicising the lobby of the District Health Authority meeting held at Burnley General Hospital.

It is hoped to tour the whole of the seven Lancashire Districts.

■ Pictured with the ambulance are John Hursthouse and Paul Hoggarth, District Officers, Burnley and Pendle Branches.

Without a political fund this lobby could become illegal

TORIES – Keeping their cake intact and eating ours as well

THERE is no proposal to introduce democracy into the activities of Employers in the Trade Union Act, which requires unions to ballot on whether or not to contract to have a Political Fund.

SHAREHOLDERS are not given extra rights in the Act to have any say in the political donations made by their company.

COMPANIES give far more money to the Conservative Party than trade unions donate to the Labour Party.

CONSUMERS: Every time you go shopping in the local high street, and spend money on goods or services, you are contributing to the funds of the Conservative Party. Consumers have no control over this . . .

The story below helps to show the extent to which we are all forced to contribute to Conservative Party funds. The companies in brackets donated the sums indicated to the Conservative Party in 1983.

They are only a small representative number of the total number of companies who made such political donations. The Conservative Central Office does not give full details.

★ ★ ★

■ Susan and Steven Smith came back yesterday from their honeymoon in Majorca (HORIZON TRAVEL, £10,000). They need supplies and drive to the shopping centre in their recently acquired car (BRITISH CAR AUCTION GROUP, £10,000; ROYAL INSURANCE, £35,000) passing the jewellers where they bought their wedding rings (H. SAMUEL, £2,000; CON-SOLIDATED GOLD-FIELDS, £50,000).

They buy food at MARKS AND SPENCER (£50,000) and other goods at DE-BENHAMS (£25,000). Feeling tired they go to a cafe for tea (BROOKE BOND, £42,630) with sugar (TATE AND LYLE, £18,250) and biscuits (UNITED BIS-CUITS, £43,000).

On the way back to the car park they buy a loaf from the bakery (RANK-HOVIS-McDOUGALL, £30,000) and call in at the bank where they have secured a mortgage for their new flat (NATIONAL WESTMINS-TER BANK, £9,235).

They deposit their shopping at home (GEORGE WIMPEY, £34,000), where they find a letter from the insurance company referring to their contents policy (GUARDIAN ROYAL EX-CHANGE, £79,234).

They leave again to visit Susan's mother in the newly-built general hospital (TAYLOR WOODROW, £79,035), where Susan also works as a catering assistant (PRITCHARD SERVICES, £10,000).

After visiting time is over, they cannot decide whether to go to the cinema (RANK £45,000) or have a meal at the local steak house (TRUSTHOUSE FORTE, £41,000).

To make up their minds they call in at the pub for a drink (SCOTTISH AND NEWCASTLE BREWERIES, £5,000).

★ ★ ★

They agree on the cinema and on the way home later they buy fish and chips (ASSOCIATED FISHER-IES, £2,000).

The day has been hectic and Steven has developed a headache. He takes a couple of painkillers (BEECHAM, £20,000), while Susan has a quick look at the evening newspaper (UNITED NEWSPAPERS, £10,000).

Steven has to be up early the next day for work at the factory (RACAL, £75,000) so they retire to bed at 11 p.m. (STAG FURNITURE, £6,000) with a cup of cocoa each (ENGLISH CHINA CLAYS, £10,000; CAD-BURY SCHWEPPES, £15,000).

**"So we're agreed these unions shouldn't be involved in politics".
". . . now about our company's next £100,000 donation to the conservatives".**

"Unions don't need MPs and campaigns to fight their battles . . . We have a free press".

April 1985, campaigning for a 'Yes' vote in the political fund ballot.

WHERE'S HER CHOICE?

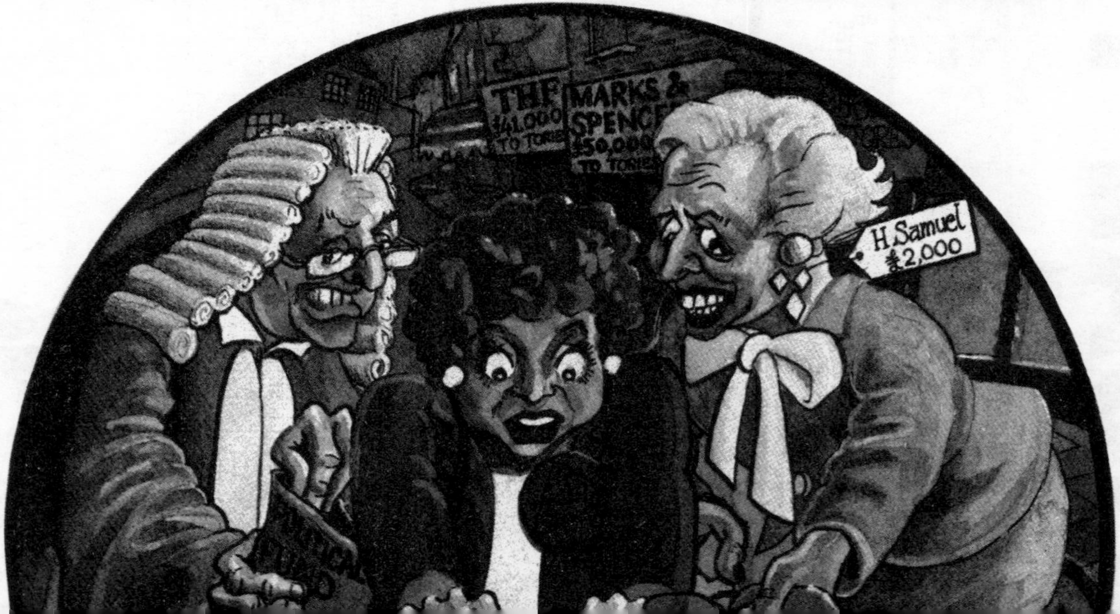

SAY YES TO A POLITICAL FUND

Even before the political fund ballots, every trade union member has a clear choice whether or not to pay into the Political Fund because of the statutory right to contract out.

But almost everyone in Britain is helping to fund the Tory Party whether or not they are aware of it and regardless of their wishes because of the cash given by big companies to the Tory Party and its close allies.

Every purchase from Debenhams or Woolworths, British Home Stores or Marks & Spencer, B&Q Do it Yourself or H. Samuel Jewellers, leaves something in the till for the Tories.

If the weekly shopping list contains PG Tips or Tetley Teabags, Bisto or Oxo, Colmans Mustard or McDougalls Flour, Mother's Pride or Hovis Bread, Mr Kipling Cakes or McVities Jaffa Cakes – there's a slice for the Tories.

Chocolates for Mothers Day – Milk Tray or Terry's All Gold, Lyons Maid Ice Cream or KP Nuts for the children – it's the Tories who are licking their lips.

Take a drink – a pint of Ansell's or Tartan Bitter, a Skol Lager or a Teacher's Whisky; a glass of Harvey's Bristol Cream or a Babycham – the Tory Party is saying "Cheers".

Eat out at a Trust House Forte Restaurant with wine from Grant's of St James', or in a Wimpy Bar with a One-Cal fizzy drink, and you leave a tip for the Tories.

Go teetotal with Britvic fruit juice, and some of your cash ends up "Sssh – you know where" (Yes they're on the list too.)

Company donations to the Tory Party come from the pocket of every shopper in Britain.

Companies are under no duty to ballot on political donations, and there is no right to opt out for their shareholders or customers.

The total extent of Company political donations is not known. Gifts of less than £200 do not have to be published.

But it is known that in the most recent available Annual Reports some 384 Companies have admitted giving over £3½ million to the Tory Party or to bodies closely allied to it. Even the SDP/Liberal Alliance is getting in on the act, with over £30,000 from 9 companies in 1983-84.

It is hardly democratic for a Tory Government to attempt to restrict the political funds of the Trade Union and Labour Movement when they gain so heavily from Big Business at the expense of all shoppers and consumers.

How your weekly shopping funds the Tory Party

Latest available figures for Political Donations linked with Brand Names quoted above are as follows:

Debenhams, £25,000
Woolworth (B&Q), £5,000
British Home Stores, £1,000
Marks & Spencer, £50,000
H Samuel, £2,000
Rank Hovis McDougall (Bisto, One-Cal Drinks, McDougalls Flour, Mother's Pride, Hovis, Mr Kipling Cakes), £30,000
Allied Lyons (Ansells, Skol Lager, Harvey's, Babycham, Britvic, Tetley's Tea, Lyons Maid, Grant's of St James, Teacher's Whisky), £82,000
United Biscuits (McVities, Crawford's, Terry's, Wimpy, KP Nuts) £43,000
Brooke Bond (PG Tips, Oxo), £39,000
Reckitt & Colman, £26,000
Cadbury Schweppes, £15,000
Trust House Forte, £41,000
Scottish & Newcastle Breweries (Younger's Tartan Bitter), £5,000

Figure 5.2 Say 'Yes' to a political fund says the NUPE *Journal* of May 1985.

The bulk of the campaign literature confirms its defensive nature, even when, as in several cases, all the skills and experience of trade union journalists, and their education and training departments, have been brought to bear in what are obviously intensive educational drives. NUPE, for example, produced a lengthy training pack designed after the model of its advanced shop steward training methods. The POEU's campaign kit was professional and glossy. The NUR put out a string of campaign newsletters; the GMBATU held regional training courses; USDAW established a 'network' of campaigning contacts from headquarters to the shop floor; APEX promised to arrange branch visits by their sponsored MPs, although there were only three of these. All the unions selected examples of their MPs at work, or detailed their own relevant political campaigns of recent years. The NUR wrote up its campaign on pension rights for British Rail staff, on job cuts on the railways, and on the privatization of bus transport. The ACTT spoke of legislation on cable TV and the Video Recordings Bill. USDAW drew attention to the Sunday Trading law and the threat to the future of Wages Councils.

The style and content of the GMBATU's literature is illustrated in figure 5.1. An example of NUPE's literature is shown in figure 5.2.

In assessing the merits of the campaign literature it has to be borne in mind that there is strong evidence of widespread ignorance among trade unionists about the political work of the unions. Polls have suggested that less than half the members know of the existence of a political levy or that they pay it. Our own discussions with union activists suggest that even shop stewards are frequently unaware of the forms of the relationship between their union and the Labour Party. Of course, a reading of the campaign literature tells us nothing about its impact on the shopfloor and no one knew in advance what effect it would have on the results of the ballots. Equally, it was not easy to assess the weight and effect of the counter-campaign in the anti-Labour press, which predictably signalled its intention to ignore constitutional niceties about the distinction between the vote for the political fund, and affiliation to the Labour Party. Thus the *Daily Express*, 8 January 1985, declared: 'The union rank and file get their chance to cut off Labour's lifeline: Vote with your pockets! The day of reckoning is at hand for the Labour Party. It could be about to lose its union paymasters . . .'

To contradict this malign forecast, two small unions gave encouragement to the 'yes' campaign by winning political fund ballots in 1983 and 1984. They were the Society of Telecom Executives, whose 28,000 managers and professional workers in British Telecom recorded a 55 per cent vote for a fund in an 83 per cent turnout, and the Amalgamated Society of Textile Workers and Kindred Trades, which voted by 1,011 against 673 to re-instate the political fund which had earlier been abolished.

A significant additional factor could be the attitude of trade unions which up to now have not had political funds, but which want to avoid legal restraints on their right to lobby and campaign on single issues without necessarily becoming involved in Party affiliations. The largest such unions are the NUT and NALGO. Both have considered the redefinition of 'political objects' in the 1984 Act, and have taken legal opinion about the continued legality of lobbies and campaigns. They believe that they will probably continue to be able to spend general fund money on such campaigning, provided that they do not imply in its course that particular parties or candidates should be favoured by an electorate. They do not therefore propose to hold a ballot on the establishment of a political fund at present. But they will keep the question under review, particularly if case law undermines the interpretation of the Act upon which they are basing their reliance. (NALGO ballotted its members in 1983 on the question of affiliation to the Labour Party; there was a nine to one result against.) A third, small, union, the Northern Carpet Trades' Union, also without a political fund, has adopted a similar 'wait and see' position, and will continue with its normal practice of lobbying MPs.

Of the political party responses to the ballot campaign, the Labour Party, as we have seen, adopted, at the request of the unions, a modest role, leaving the campaigning to the unions themselves. It therefore mounted no campaign of its own, but encouraged its members in the constituencies to offer advice and evidence for the local union campaigns. In particular they were to help to demonstrate the practical value of political work in Parliament and in local affairs. The general secretary, Jim Mortimer, wrote to constituencies to stress the autonomous union lead in the campaigns, and to encourage his members in a restrained, supportive role. Regional Labour Parties also mobilized support activities and the new Labour Party workplace branches in particular obviously were more closely involved.

The Conservative Party and Government declared they would remain neutral in the campaign, since they wished merely to provide a new opportunity for union members to express their own choice on whether political funds should continue. They did not, however, adhere consistently to that declaration. On the one hand, Mr Tom King told *The Sunday Times* that 'it was now for union members to decide whether or not to have a political fund under his 1984 Trade Union Act and it was not for him to tell them how to use their right.'[4] Yet he had himself issued a press release a month earlier (30 March) which weighed in very heavily in favour of a 'no' vote.

With the political fund provisions of the 1984 Trade Union Act coming into force this weekend, Employment Secretary Tom King today urged trade union members to consider the implications carefully.

He said: 'My advice to trade union members is: "Vote whichever way you wish but make sure you know what you are voting for". And that quite clearly is the question: "Do you want your trade union to engage in party politics?" '

The political fund provisions of the Trade Union Act come into force on Sunday 31 March, 1985 . . .

These provisions would enable union members themselves to decide whether their unions should actively engage in party politics, Mr King said. He continued:

This was a right given to their grandparents in the Trade Union Act 1913. But under that Act it was sufficient for unions to ballot their members just once – on setting up their political funds. This means that most present day union members have never been able to exercise this important choice.

And the importance of that choice must not be obscured. It is not simply a matter of union leaders acting as power brokers in the affairs of a political party, armed with massive block votes bought with millions of pounds from their unions' political funds. A union's involvement in party politics profoundly influences the whole way in which it behaves. The opportunity is now there, for the first time in many generations, for union members to decide just what sort of organisation they want to belong to.

But the basic question clearly is this: Do union members want their leaders not only to spend money, but also to dissipate time and energy, in playing party politics; or do they want them to get on with the important job which trade unions were set up to do – representing their members' interests?

I am aware that there have been suggestions that unions can only properly represent their members' interests if they have a political fund. Misleading claims of this sort were to be expected. But these claims are no more true now than they were in 1913.

In particular, it is quite untrue to suggest that the 1984 Act has prevented unions financing campaigns on Government policies from their general funds. The only circumstances in which expenditure on campaigns must come from a union's political fund are when the main purpose is to persuade people to vote for or against a particular political party or candidate. Campaigns on matters like jobs, health and safety and other issues affecting the members' interests may certainly be financed from unions' general funds provided that their main purpose is not to persuade people to vote in a particular way.

There is nothing whatever in the 1984 Act to stop trade unions lobbying their members of Parliament if they do not have a political fund. Several trade unions with no political funds currently retain Parliamentary advisers, paid for from their general funds, and there is nothing in the 1984 Act to change this. As before, only payments to MPs which amount to 'maintenance' – for example, for MPs 'sponsored' by a trade union – need come from political funds.[5]

There are three points to be made about this. First, we must ask why, if no change or new restriction was intended other than those in the 1913 Act, the government found it necessary to amend the definition of political activity? Secondly, we can point to the already existing interpretations on the limits of legitimate political activity as decided regularly in cases of complaint reaching the Certification Officer. We summarize these cases in an appendix 5.1 and draw attention to the 1981 case involving Mr Richards and the NUM, and the POEU's case of the same year, wherein the Certification Officer's comments have serious implications for the future legitimacy of supporting or donating to single-issue campaigning bodies which may take issue with government policies on, say, spending cuts. Finally, it is right to maintain a cautious scepticism about Mr King's assurances. Not only do these come from a partial source, but they can in no degree guarantee the direction of future judicial interpretation of the 'political objects' clauses of his Act. Indeed, a Junior Minister admitted, during the committee stage of the 1984 Act in the Commons, that actions such as NALGO's 1983 campaign against public spending cuts, which included national newspaper advertizing, could be illegal under the Act because NALGO has no political fund.

The NALGO campaign was subjected to much attention in the Commons debates, and the exchanges are instructive. Alan Clark, MP, the Minister in question, subjected the union's campaign literature to detailed scrutiny.

Mr Clark   The text says: 'The latest cuts mean only one child in three will be lucky enough to get a nursery place. The Government grant' – everybody reading this advertisement would have known which party was in Government at that time – 'for new buses will be cut for £71 million.' It goes on to list a series of other cuts and then say: 'The Government says that we can't afford to spend more money on the Welfare State. Then how come they've constantly increased spending on defence since they came to power?' In other words, since *they* won the last election. The clear inference from that is that it is at elections that one's fate in these four respects is decided. Then, just to confirm that impression, there is a sort of mock-up ballot paper with an X on it and a slogan saying 'Put people first' and then 'If this gets your vote make sure you use it'. There can hardly be a clearer example of a tendentious political advertisement . . .

Mr John Smith   We shall deal with the merits of NALGO's campaign later, but this is probably the most important single question we shall ask the Minister and I should like him to think carefully about it and to give us a definitive reply. In his opinion, will the changes proposed in this Bill mean that the NALGO anti-cuts campaign would have to come out of a political fund?

Mr Clark ... there is a definition in subsection 3(f): 'seeks to persuade any person to vote for or, as the case may be, not to vote for a political party or candidate'. The whole Committee will see that this NALGO literature is as good an example as one is likely to get of something which comes into that definition.

With their apprehensions thus confirmed, Opposition speakers continued to press the case of the NALGO campaign, and the Minister began to hedge his bets.

Mr Clark There is an undertow of people saying 'Like NALGO'. It is incredible that Opposition Members will not admit that NALGO's advertisement was overtly political and tendentious. The right hon. and learned Gentleman has talked about anti-privatisation campaigns. Unless couched very carelessly, such campaigns could be funded from the general fund. The right hon. and learned Gentleman is irresponsible to go on the rampage and portray any normally legitimate expenditure on a campaign as something that will no longer be allowed if the political fund resolution is not renewed.

Mr Smith I am surprised at the Under-Secretary. I thought that he had boldly steamed into the harbour, smoke stacks a-blazing and that there he was, confidently tied up. But as soon as he gets a little rattled he tries to ease out again and says that the NALGO campaign is different from other campaigns. It does not matter tuppence whether, as a Conservative and a Minister, he likes NALGO campaigns or thinks that they are tendentious. These are highly subjective matters which form the heart and core of political debate. If in one breath a Minister tells me that he does not like something and in the next he tells me that it is to be made subject to political and legal restriction, I begin to wonder whether it is Britain that I am living in.

Mr Alan Clark The test is clearly set out in paragraph (f). Does the material set out to 'persuade any person to vote, or as the case may be, not to vote for a political party or candidate'? Campaigns against privatisation and so on are not in that category, as the right hon. and learned Gentleman knows.

Mr Smith The Minister is saying that one can campaign against privatisation and the revolutionary effect that it may have on one's wages and conditions, provided that one does not criticise the Government while one is at it.

Mr Alan Clark Provided that one does not seek to persuade people to vote for or against a party.

Mr Smith I see. One can campaign against these dreadful proposals, but one is not allowed to take that final step of saying, 'This Government caused the change in your conditions'. One cannot even invite people to protest by criticising the Government. I am not sure just what it is that one is allowed to do, but there is a little bit about not encouraging people to vote against the Government. The Government seek to protect

themselves in the legislation, and seek to do so in the most unsavoury
way. That is why this is a matter of great importance.[6]

But Dr David Owen and his Liberal allies were also very concerned
to put over an interpretation of the Act which reassured non-political
unions of the invulnerability of their campaigning roles. He also initiated
a debate on trade union ballots in the Commons on 23 April 1985, at
the height of the publicity surrounding the ballot rigging allegations in
the elections for the TGWU general secretary, first conducted in 1984.
He sought to use this case to support the argument for an exclusive
compulsion to conduct all ballots under the 1984 Act by post, since,
he claimed, the TGWU experience had discredited workplace ballots.
This seems an unwarranted conclusion; the opportunities for ballot-
rigging exist also in postal balloting, as do the much more serious,
because more likely, problems of administrative efficiency. We have
discussed this in chapter 3. David Owen was in pursuit of a simple party
advantage: to identify left-leaning trade union leaders with electoral
malpractice, and to force on the unions the most privatized, least
participating form of election method, the postal vote, from which he
anticipates that the Left will suffer disproportionately.

We have to assert, against these positions, two simple propositions:
(a) that whatever the purpose, state intervention in trade union rule
making is extremely dangerous; and (b) that ballot-rigging, whatever
the purpose, is wrong. Defective union rules, and ballot-rigging alike,
are only to be legitimately corrected by a thorough-going development
of democratic, participative involvement of the membership in trade
union decision-making; postal ballots tend, if anything, to diminish the
collective, participative elements in this process. But clearly, in the
wake of the TGWU case, trade unions and their leaders and
administrators will feel the need to enforce their balloting rules, if they
are not to see further incursions by the state into their independence.

Shirley Williams, the president of the SDP, joined in the campaign
with a letter to trade union general secretaries, some of whom published
it together with their replies in union journals. She repeated the claim
that lobbying and campaigning will not be disqualified from finance out
of general funds under the Act, 'so that there is no need for unions to
have political funds to carry out . . . these activities'. She also affirmed
a preference for contracting-in, where there is a political fund, and a
demand for a separate union ballot on the issue of affiliation to the
Labour Party. Failing this, she promised a 'no' campaign by the SDP.

At the time of writing, we are not certain about the outcome of all
the union ballots, which are taking place as this book goes to press. In
a temporary sense, it may seem a disadvantage to be unable to deal with
the outcome of the campaigns. But it can be foreseen that, should the

ballots be won, the unions will have entered a more political future, in which policy questions will be more widely debated than before. On the other hand, were any union to lose a ballot, the issue would by no means end with an adverse result. The Act does not prevent a repetition of the ballot at any time of the union's choosing, and a failure to win the ballot by the methods and strategy summarized above will compel unions in that position to address again the need to campaign positively and to demonstrate the urgency of political action for future policy choices.

A programme which stands in its own right, but which could also help in such campaigns, concerns us in chapter 8. Included therein should be a renewed debate about the 1913 Trade Union Act and its incorporation in the 1984 Act. We showed earlier that the imposition of special restrictions (balloting, a separate political fund, and contracting-out/in) on the trade union role in politics was widely regarded as unjust and discriminatory by the generation which accepted it as a temporary compromise. The 1984 Act has compelled a reopening of this question, as Jim Mortimer, Labour's General Secretary at the time, recognized in a paper for the Party on the eve of the ballot campaign:

> It is not sufficient to ask for the repeal of the Employment Act 1980, 1982 and the Trade Union Act 1984. Something new has to be put in their place. . . .
>
> Some Labour strategists argue that new statutory rights might be more politically appealing than simple repeal of widely popular legislation.
>
> Such a move might be seen to usher in a new era of industrial relations rather than a simple restoration of the 'bad old days of the 1960s and 70s.' Any new rights could be balanced by giving unions new responsibilities, it is argued.
>
> Mr John Prescott, Labour's employment spokesman, said yesterday: 'I approach the issue with an open mind. People should not assume that it will be a simple return to the legislative position of ten years ago.
>
> 'It's time to look afresh at the issue of industrial citizenship and the rights of trade unions in our society.'
>
> Mr Mortimer, a highly respected former chairman of the Advisory, Coniliation and Arbitration Service points out in his paper: 'The assertion of statutory rights has the apparent attraction of providing a framework of readily understood rules.
>
> 'Thus, such a framework of rights might include the right to organise a trade union, to bargain collectively, to strike, to seek to provide solidarity action, peacefully to demonstrate and to seek to persuade others in the course of a dispute and to conduct the affairs of a trade union without state interference.'
>
> But in a strong argument against such a course, Mr Mortimer says: 'It is not possible simultaneously to provide positive legal rights, but yet to

keep the courts out of industrial relations . . . the interpretation of these rights falls to the courts.

'The almost universal experience of other countries is that the courts come to see it as their duty to lay down the limits of these rights. Judicial interpretation may be very different from that intended by the legislature.'

Mr Mortimer also points out that the provision of positive rights would go against the grain of previous industrial relations legislation, which had been intended to exclude trade disputes from judicial review by the courts. Substantial parts of this legislation are still on the statute book.

Although attempting to present a balanced review of the choice facing the Labour movement, Mr Mortimer apears to prefer restoration and extension of immunities while finding a means of introducing supporting legislation 'which without inviting the frequent intervention of the courts, would nevertheless encourage trade union organisation, trade union recognition and collective bargaining.'

Mr Mortimer suggests repealing the Tory Government's employment legislation, reintroducing the immunities which those statutes abolished and introducing 'state sponsored props' to collective bargaining, such as the right of representation already enshrined in the Health and Safety at Work Act.

The paper also suggests a radical overhaul of trade unions rights to spend money on politics, by calling for an end to the distinction between a union's political and general funds under the Trade Union Act, 1913.

Mr Mortimer comments: 'The trade union movement lived with the 1913 act not because it was acceptable in principle, but because in practice it did not seriously impede most unions from pursuing political objectives.

'Now that the Conservative Party has deliberately upset this arrangement without any corresponding limitation on companies, there is no reason why the Labour Party should feel inhibited in changing the law to restore to unions their full right to determine how to spend their money.[7]

APPENDIX 5.1 COMPLAINTS ABOUT THE ADMINISTRATION OF POLITICAL FUNDS

The interpretation of political fund rules under the complaints procedure operated by the Certification Officer shows that, even before the government's 1984 Bill became law, unions were already closely supervised and restricted in their decisions on how their funds should be spent. The Trade Union Act extends this control to the surveillance of 'the production, publication or distribution of any literature, document, film, sound recording or advertisement which taken as a whole' seeks to influence voting for a political party or candidate. Scrutiny of the Certification Officer's Reports of recent years shows that this kind of control has already been foreshadowed in some significant cases.

Under the 1913 Act any trade union member who alleges that he is aggrieved by a breach of a political fund rule may complain to the Certification Officer, who may order a formal hearing, and if he considers a breach to have occurred, may make an order for remedying it. Unions may appeal against such orders to the Employment Appeal Tribunal, and subsequently to the Court of Appeal.

The number of complaints made in the most modern period, covered by the existence of the Certification Office, have been as follows:

1976	3	
1977	18	
1978	12	
1979	105	(76 of which were from one branch of the TGWU)
1980	20	
1981	12	
1982	24	
1983	21	

Thus, the general level of complaints has been very low. In 1984, while all the advocates of legislative intervention in trade union political affairs were making their most strident speeches, it hit rock bottom. Most complaints concern grievances by individual trade union members, usually that their right to contract-out of the political fund has been transgressed in some way. The great majority are resolved by correspondence, without the need for formal hearings. The appearance of regular reports of formal hearings dates from 1979.

From the point of view of the freedom of trade unions to make decisions on their own expenditures, the most significant complaints are those which allege that unions have spent money on 'political objects' from the general fund, and not from the political fund. Several important cases have been brought, and in some unions have been ordered by the Certification Officer to refund certain monies from their political to their general fund.

In the first such case, heard in 1980, Mr B. P. McCarthy complained on four grounds that his union, APEX, had spent money from its general fund on political objects as set out in its rules. The first complaint concerned money spent on a Special General Election Issue of the union's journal. The relevant union rule does refer to '. . . the distribution of political literature or political documents of any kind . . .' and consequently the Certification Officer found:

1 That there *was* a 'distribution' of the election issue.
2 That this issue *was* 'literature or a document'.

3 That this literature or document *was* 'in support of any such candidate or prospective candidate' *because the issue supported Labour candidates who were members of the union.*
4 That the issue *was* 'political' literature or a 'political' document because it supported candidates of a particular political party.
5 The election issue was not a normal issue of the journal and that its main purpose was not to further the 'statutory objects' of the union.

The Certification Officer therefore found the complaint 'well-founded'. In the same case, he also found justified a complaint that a special election issue of the union's area and branch circular should not have been financed from the general fund. APEX was ordered to transfer £1,022.10 from its political to its general fund, and the union complied.

In 1981 an important case concerned Mr W. Richards and the NUM. Mr Richards made four complaints, one of which was directed specifically against the Nottinghamshire Area of the NUM. The first complaint was that the union had spent money from its general fund on sending union official and members to take part in a march and lobby of Parliament organized by the Labour Party as part of a campaign against government public spending cuts: £11,501.63 was spent on the hire of a special train, on payments to those attending, and on consequential payments to cover contributions to the pension schemes of those attending. The Certification Officer upheld the complaint on the grounds that the meetings were 'political' and their purpose could not be 'statutory' since they had been organized by the Labour Party 'and not by the Trades Union Congress'. So he ordered the refund of the sum involved from the political to the general fund of the union. The second complaint was that the union had spent £550 from its general fund to send a colliery band to attend the same march and lobby. The Certification Officer duly ordered a refund in this case also.

A further complaint was that the union had paid £73,924 from its general fund to a trade union consortium for the development of premises at Walworth Road for use as a Labour Party head office. Although the union argued that this was not expenditure but an investment, and moreover an investment not in politics but in property, the Officer found the complaint justified, and again ordered repayment.

In another case of the same year Mr R. N. Coleman argued that his union, the POEU, was in breach of the rules by paying an affiliation fee of £8 from the general fund to the Canterbury and District Trades Council for a campaign against the cuts in public expenditure. Here the decision was apparently more favourable. The Certification Officer cited a 1925 case in which the Chief Registrar of Friendly Societies had said that 'political' means the adjectival form of 'party politics' and not of 'polity'. Hence, activities on matters of public concern were not always 'political' in the terms of the 1913 Act, and he rejected the complaint.

However, he went on the reflect less liberally on the case. He referred to the 'statutory objects' provision which appears in the union's political rules and which derives from the 1913 Act. (All unions with political funds have a similar rule.) The rule states that furtherance of the political objects of the union shall include:

> the holding of political meetings of any kind, or . . . the distribution of political literature or political documents of any kind, unless the main purpose of the meetings or of the distribution of the literature or documents is the furtherance of statutory objects within the meaning of the Act, that is to say, the regulation of the relations between workmen and masters, or between workmen and workmen . . .

The Certification Officer's Report on the case summarizes his comments on this as follows:

> He said that (the 'statutory object') proviso relates to the purpose of the body distributing literature or holding meetings, and not to the purpose of the union in making a payment to the body in the first place. By their nature bodies which are not trade unions are less likely to distribute literature or hold meetings for a purpose within the statutory objects. He warned that unions need to be careful about paying money to other bodies likely to spend it on political objects; the 'statutory objects' escape route was unlikely to be open to unions in those circumstances.[8]

In 1983, the Certification Officer received four complaints about general fund contributions to the purchase of a block of properties in Walworth Road to provide the Labour Party with headquarters, on its move from offices rented from the TGWU in Transport House. All of these related to the Officer's decision in an ASTMS case on this question, which took the same form as that in the NUM case already cited. When ordered to repay the sum involved, ASTMS appealed to the Employment Appeal Tribunal. This appeal was rejected in July 1983, following which ASTMS announced that it would take the case to the Court of Appeal. The Certification Officer's ruling has very wide implications, since more than £700,000 worth of investment by trade unions in the Walworth Road headquarters has to be paid out of political funds acros to general funds as a result. The case against ASTMS was originally brought by a Conservative member of the union, Mr Loudon Parkin, who received assistance from the right-wing lobby, the Freedom Association. In the course of the case, ASTMS affirmed that the trade union consortium which raised the money had received legal advice that it was permissible to employ general funds in an investment in the office building as long as the loan was made at a commercial rate of return. The Certification Officer ruled that the investment had indeed been commercial, but since it had been for a political objective it should therefore have come from the political fund. In spite of litigation, up to the time of writing the Certification Officer's ruling remains in force.

Now, these cases reflect the state of law and its interpretation as things stand under the 1913 Act. They reveal an extraordinary, even humiliating, state of affairs. This is the status of trade union political activity which has prevailed for 70 years. Such intervention has come to be regarded as 'normal', although company subventions for political purposes are quite free of any such regulations. Surely it is hardly reasonable that a union should be subject to the kind of imposition revealed in these cases, where even the hiring of a band may be subject to legal dispute, and where the financing of a campaign on public spending cuts is seen as contentious, since its precise legal implication may be doubtful. But as pointers to the situation that would prevail if any unions were to lose their future ballots on political funds they are quite sinister. For at the moment, the worst that can happen when cases of this kind go against the union, is that it is required to make a payment into its general fund from its political fund. That is restrictive enough. But if a union has no political fund because it has lost the ballot, the same kind of case would immediately call in question a huge, complex and entirely integral part of a union's normal functions. In the case of the union band, and the union's special train to the march and Parliamentary lobby, they would quite simply be illegal; there would be no way in which the union could finance such activities at all. A similar fate would befall union journals which carried any direct political message, while the flow of donations and subscriptions which unions make to a vast range of causes would be in jeopardy. The grossly illiberal nature of the pre-1984 legislation raises very serious fears about the intentions of the 1984 Trade Union Act.

Notes

1 See chapter 2.
2 TUC Report, 'Special Wembley Conference' (5 April 1982), pp. 388, 398, 404–5.
3 Peter Hain, in *Marxism Today*, November 1984.
4 *The Sunday Times*, 28 April 1985.
5 Department of Employment, Press Release, 30 March 1985.
6 House of Commons Official Report, Standing Committee F (Trade Union Bill), 28 February 1984.
7 *Guardian*, 30 April 1985.
8 Report of the Certification Officer, 1981.

6 The Block Vote and TULV

The Block Vote and the Concentration of Power

In 1900 there were 373,000 trade unionists affiliated to the Labour Representation Committee. They represented 41 unions. By the middle 1950s the number of trade unionists in the Labour Party exceeded 5 million: the number of unions involved, however, had only doubled. During the 1980s, while the proportion of actual trade unionists voting for the Labour Party was declining seriously, the statistics of trade union affiliation remained high, over the 6 million mark. But the number of organizations providing these ghostly corporate members had once again diminished, near to the original levy of 1900.

During more than 80 years, important changes had come about, no less in trade union organization than in the structure of industry and political institutions. We have commented elsewhere on the notable concentration of scale which became necessary in trade unions from the 1960s onwards. Unions were getting bigger, or going to the wall. Mergers and takeovers flourished, and, among trade unionists adhering to the Trades Union Congress, fusions and combinations actually halved the number of organizations between the 1960s and the 1980s. This, then, has been the age of the great block votes.

The creation of large trade unions certainly improved the level of specialized services available to many workers, although such improvements were not always unambiguous. Many people think that the growth of giant trade unions involved some loss of individual expression and local control over events. It is unwise to dogmatize about this problem: the internal democracy of different trade unions has varied significantly, and some were far more successful than others in the business of involving active membership participation. However, what is quite undeniable is that the leaders of larger trade unions were able to exercise greater and greater powers within the councils of the Labour Movement. At the end of the Second World War six trade unions had already built for themselves a mass membership which afforded their block votes an unchallenged hegemony over all the rest. When the

170

Transport and General Workers Union, the National Union of Mine-workers, the Amalgamated Engineering Union, the National Union of General and Municipal Workers, the Shop Workers and the National Union of Railwaymen all acted in unison, their combined vote was unbeatable at the Labour Party Conference. Even when the leaders of these unions entertained disagreements one with another, their separate influence remained formidable.[1]

Each great union was like a comet, with a tail of followers from among the lesser fry, joining (and sometimes trading) their support for whatever political advantage it was worth. Thus throughout the lifetime of the immediate post-war Attlee Labour Governments, and indeed until the middle 1950s, the biggest unions were able to act with almost monolithic solidarity. Their power having been centralized during the pre-war years of unemployment, they were able to ride the influx of new members because there were tangible advances to be had for the asking, in the new age of full employment. Dominated by a triumvirate consisting of Messrs Deakin, Williamson and Lawther of the TGWU, NUGMW and NUM respectively, this trade union block policed Labour Conferences, monopolized Conference Arrangements Committees,[2] determined what should be discussed and what not, and provided unfailing support for the Party leadership whatever it did.

In the late 1940s and early 1950s, as the cold war division of Europe was registered and reinforced, the Labour government was committed to the Marshall Plan, the North Atlantic Treaty, the presence of American troops in Britain, German rearmament and political control of trade between Eastern and Western blocs. At home this brought first the restriction of wage-bargaining and then expensive arms programmes. Almost all opposition was steam-rollered absolutely flat. The only defeat registered by the Party leadership at Conference concerned the need to abolish tied cottages for farmworkers. True, when Aneurin Bevan broke ranks with his Cabinet colleagues, a political argument rent successive Party conferences, and began to divide the unions themselves.[3] Ultimately Bevan was to seek to consolidate this division by contesting the Party treasurership, for which union votes were the decisive influence. But the pretorian guard remained firm.

These were the years during which Sir William Lawther became immortal for his contribution to the art of chairmanship: 'Shut your gob' he said. After Arthur Deakin left the TGWU his successor (in 1955) died almost immediately upon assuming office. In 1956, Frank Cousins became General Secretary of the TGWU and a process of renewal began to democratize the structure of the union and then, by example, slowly to influence the procedures of other trade unions as well.[4]

The collapse of the hard core of the pretorian guard took time. It was an uneven process. For a long time its traditions were continued by Lord Carron, the president of the engineers' union, whose creative abuse of his delegation's votes was a marvel of ingenuity.[5] On one occasion he frustrated his opponents on the Left by actually voting both ways on one particularly contentious motion, and thus cancelling the union's commitment to it. As a result, the unwanted motion was defeated. But the advance of plant bargaining and the development of a resourceful and independent-minded shop stewards' movement received strong official support from the TGWU, and began to open up attitudes in other unions as well. As a result of a strenuous campaign for union democracy, centring on the more obvious abuses of votes at Labour Party and TUC gatherings, Hugh Scanlon emerged as a 'new broom' president of the engineers, and for several years he and Jack Jones ('the terrible twins') were seen as a combined radical influence on Labour policies, replacing the steady conservative hand of Deakin on the tiller.[6]

All of this has reinforced the view that the predominant trade union block votes have carried prodigious political influence. Of course, there have been shifts within the ruling cabal. After the war, the NUM mustered 687,000 votes, and was a force to be heard. Raging pit closures in the 1960s and subsequent steady contraction of the workforce had reduced these numbers to 180,000 by the middle 1980s, so that there was no longer any automatic expectation that a mineworker would figure among the leaders of Labour's national executive. Indeed, manoeuvres among the oligarchs actually displaced the NUM altogether for a time, after Mr Sid Weighell of the railwaymen miscast his vote and brought about the defeat of the miners' candidate. However, the NUR itself was a victim of prolonged decline, and its own block vote a wasting asset.

On the other hand, the growth of local authority trade unionism brought NUPE and NALGO to the front rank, both numbering more than 700,000 members. NUPE, which unlike NALGO was affiliated to the Labour Party throughout, did not easily inherit the right to representation on the Party's national executive committee, and had to struggle hard to overcome the inertia which had dominated the negotiations about voting for the trade union seats. The results of horse trading among trade unions about the composition of the 12-strong trade union section of Labour's NEC have never directly reflected the precise political affiliations of the different unions. But it is quite clear that, over the years, there has been a succession of different schools of thought among the grandees of the major unions which have, in turn, exercised an overwhelming influence, not to say power. The modes of this operation were informed, apparently relaxed, and rather private.[7]

The Background to Trade Unions for a Labour Victory (TULV)

The latest of these schools emerged in the late 1970s, and was led by David Basnett of the general and municipal workers. In the initial phases this current of thought resembled its predecessors in exercising its dominion mainly by informal agreements. But by the end of the decade, the polarization of the Labour Party became such that it was felt necessary to depart from precedent by creating a visible and structured movement. This emerged under the name of Trade Unions for a Labour Victory (TULV), a conscious rupture with a tradition in which union leaders preferred blunt but private deals in smoke-filled rooms to semi-public factionalism.

Critics found a careful ambiguity in this formula. The centre right faction in the Labour Party had already, under the impetus of growing divisions between the Parliamentary leadership and the members in the constituencies, organized itself into a pressure group under the title Campaign for Labour Victory (CLV). The right and centre of the Party were deeply fragmented. Not only were they at odds about Britain's membership of the EEC, but they were also unable to agree about the nature of the crisis in the Party. Some of the most vociferous leaders of CLV were subsequently to defect in order to form the Social Democratic Party. Two contemporary historians (who are anything but sympathetic to the Left) cite an anonymous prominent front bencher on the 'Campaign' in the following distinctly uncomplimentary terms:

> The Campaign for Labour Victory was disastrous and an awfully elitist organization . . . it sent out messages to its few contacts saying what its policy was. [Its] failure was threefold . . . it was London based, a leadership organization . . . had the Common Market obsession which to a degree I share but is not the basis of the socialist programme and . . . also had a lot of personality problems.[8]

The idea of Trade Unions for a Labour Victory clearly evoked a sense of connection with the Parliamentary faction of a similar title. But at no time would it have been easy for trade unions to take up an open commitment to this kind of factional alignment. Unions always contained their own internal divisions, and were now more prone than ever before to contest too-blatant abuse of the block vote. Even the giant hierarchs of the fifties and sixties had got into trouble for making free with the powers vested in them by their vast corporate affiliations. In the late 1970s it was even more hazardous to seek to lock whole organizations to one side or another in an inner-Party struggle.

After the intervention of the International Monetary Fund in the affairs of the Labour Government, the initial hopeful phases of the Wilson Government's social contract were checked and reversed.[9] Tight control of incomes, coupled with rising unemployment, brought about the 'Winter of Discontent' in which many trade unionists were radically disillusioned with government policy. For different reasons, even the modest successes of governmental policies of income redistribution alienated many skilled workers, and revived bitter disputes about differentials.[10] On the other hand, low paid workers suffered worst from high inflation, and had every cause to rebel. For one reason or another, trade union members were no less disenchanted than constituency Labour Parties, and no more prone to be conscripted as lobby fodder.

It was entirely within their traditions that prominent general secretaries should take the initiative when the Labour Party found itself in crisis, but their control of their respective machines was very much less complete than had been the case in the earlier decades of the post-war period. Moreover, all the time the political commitment of their members to the Labour Party was being dangerously eroded.

In the engineers' union, as Hugh Scanlon came to the end of his term of office, there was a celebrated rumpus about his mistaken miscasting of the union's vote at the 1978 Party Conference, which prevented the adoption of a motion calling for regular selection conferences even in the constituencies of sitting MPs, which would have ensured that a choice of candidates were interviewed by a selection conference once in the lifetime of every Parliament. This proposal would have ended the situation in which, once chosen, a Parliamentarian has had every expectation of survival right up to the moment of electoral defeat, or retirement, whichever has been the earlier. As it happened, as a result of a contentious vote, a compromise proposal was accepted, requiring sitting members to win a formal vote of confidence if they were to avoid appearing before a selection meeting. The argument about this issue was obviously not finally settled, and it was further developed during the next months in a variety of publications and meetings, after which the interim decision was changed.

However, an even more crucial issue was raised in the course of the 1978 ballot on this question. The reselection vote *would* have been won, had 877,000 votes of the engineers' union been cast in accordance with the repeated decision of the union's Conference delegation. As things went, the mandatory reselection motion received 2,672,000 votes, and was opposed by 3,066,000. But the AUEW abstained. As *Tribune* reported:

> As soon as the vote had been taken, the AUEW president, Hugh Scanlon, came to the rostrum to say that his delegation had abstained by mistake.

They had intended, he said, to vote in favour of mandatory reselection and had they done so the outcome would have been reversed.[11]

Hugh Scanlon's version is, however, disputed by some AUEW delegates. They say that the delegation leader deliberately abstained, in defiance of the clearly expressed will of the delegation, at a meeting held only hours before. One AUEW delegate, Jock MacPherson Quinn, was also a conference teller. He says that when he offered the ballot box to Scanlon, Gavin Laird and John Boyd – who were sitting together – they replied that they weren't voting. When Quinn reminded them that they were mandated he was told to get on with his job as teller. By way of confirmation, a similar story had been featured in the *Guardian*:

> One Union that might be angrily considering making its leader stand for re-election with the same regularity as some trade unions want Labour MPs to do, is the Amalgamated Union of Engineering Workers. When the votes were cast yesterday after the debate on reselection, there were some angry allegations that the outgoing president, Mr Hugh Scanlon, had not carried out the mandated wishes of his members, coupled with some claims of high-handed and peremptory behaviour by the president-elect, Mr Terry Duffy.
>
> Last Sunday all four sections of the AUEW met and voted to support an amendment concerning MPs reselection. But yesterday afternoon, just before the debate began, the union delegation was summoned to talk things over with its executive who had opposed the decision, and it was asked to reconsider. The delegates reconsidered – and decided by an even more decisive vote to stick to their original decision.
>
> At this, Mr Duffy is reported to have got very angry, and a slanging match followed.
>
> When it came to the actual vote after the debate a teller, who happened to be from the AUEW, approached Mr Scanlon so that he could cast the engineering section's vote. Mr Scanlon said he was abstaining on this amendment and waiting for another which had not yet been debated. The teller protested that this was not what the delegation wanted, and said he was told by Mr Scanlon to 'go and do his job'.
>
> It is being claimed that if the crucial 870,000 votes that Mr Scanlon had in his hand had gone the way the union had decided it would have made all the difference to the final result.[12]

After inquiry, it is difficult to be certain about the reason for Hugh Scanlon's abstention, which some put down to confusion, while others still believe it to have been deliberate. Although, whatever might have been the cause, this was a sad event, there is no point in pursuing its motivation here. What is more important is the fact that the union executive was so concerned about this motion that it tried to secure a constitutional reversal of the delegation's decision to support it, and that a recalled delegation meeting was set up entirely for this purpose. This second meeting confirmed its original decision by 26 votes to 19, and when this happened,

> Duffy in the words of one observer 'went bananas'. He told them that they were overturning a unanimous decision of the union's executive (which is not true) and that nothing like this will happen in the future after he takes over.[13]

Of course, the engineers' union has a history of controversy upon this matter, and indeed, before the election of Hugh Scanlon to the presidency, there was a long-running dog-fight on the matter of 'Carron's Law'.

This story was summed up by David Edelstein and Malcolm Warner in their authoritative study, *Comparative Union Democracy*:

> It is one thing to make policy, but another to see that it is carried out.... A... serious and more pervasive loss of the national committee's policy-making powers to the president took place under Lord Carron's right-wing rule, and ended only with Scanlon's election in 1967. It was made conspicuously evident by Carron casting the Engineers' massive block vote at conferences of the Trades Union Congress and the Labour Party in defiance of decisions of the national committee, under what became known as Carron's Law. However, a similar conflict between the national committee and executive council began in 1955, the year before that of Carron's election as president, over the question of support for the left-Labour Aneurin Bevan's bid for office in the Labour Party. The decision of the primarily rank-and-file delegation which was involved to the Labour Party conference was over-ruled by the executive council, which was represented in the conference delegation and claimed the power of decision in such matters. The Engineers' rules permit the executive council to appoint representatives from among its members and, together with the president and general secretary, to call a meeting of the delegation prior to the conference (Rule 44:1,2) but we see no grounds for the council claiming decision-making powers.
>   On the contrary, the rules state: 'All decisions of the National Committee shall be final and binding on the Executive Council' (Rule 14:8). Later in 1955, a decision of the rank-and-file appeals court supported the majority of the conference delegation, but the entire sequence was repeated in 1956 when a new national committee decision to support Bevan was again defied by the executive council at the Labour Party conference ... Such defiance of the national committee, the Labour Party, TUC delegations and the appeals court was repeated under Carron's reign as president with differences only in detail: 'In 1965 the . . . National Committee carried a fervid motion pledging 100 per cent support for the Labour Government. What exactly constituted 100 per cent was not defined, but this difficulty did not embarrass Sir William. From now on,

the AEU vote was forever to be stacked behind he Government . . . In the 1966 Labour Party Conference . . . 100 per cent was still no less. Sir William put aside all plaints from the delegates that the union had, in fact, gone on record against the American intervention in Vietnam, and in favour of cuts in military expenditure. From the moment that the Conference opened, he kept firm control of the pad upon which the votes of the delegation are recorded, and remorselessly plonked the AEU's 768,000 votes . . . straight down the line for the platform.' (*Crisis of British Socialism*, Spokesman 1972, pp. 169–171)

The ridiculously mechanical nature of Carron's control at the conference is illustrated by what happened when he was called away on personal business; the pad for recording the delegation's black vote was passed to the most senior member, the left-Labour executive councillor Scanlon, who then proceeded to poll the delegation. The result was that the Labour Party conference did indeed pass resolutions for reducing military expenditure and against American intervention in Vietnam, with the support of the Engineers, a support which would have failed had Carron been present.[14]

These abuses of the union's votes at TUC as well as Labour Party Conferences resulted in a series of appeals to the Final Appeal Court of the union.

In a series of judgements in relation to Resolution 16 of the 1966 National Committee, it ruled against the Executive Committee's decision not to recall, and the failure to allow the TUC delegation its voting rights. In practice this was of as little immediate help to Carron's political opponents as had been the previous court decisions against him. As far as Carron was concerned the Final Appeal Court was stacked with his political opponents who were misusing the Constitution of the Union: if they were in his position they would be as against the Government as he was for it, and would use the union vote to disregard National Committee policy entirely. At this stage anyway, with only a year to retirement, he could afford to ignore the Court.[15]

Carron was twice censured by the Appeal Court, which was vested, constitutionally, with ultimate authority on the matters which came before it. As Minkin reports, this made no difference:

At the Party Conference of 1967 Carron made his last stand with an effrontery which had one AEU delegate waving his crutch in rage. At the Saturday morning delegation meeting, he refused a discussion on the economic and incomes policies and then when delegates demanded a second meeting closed the meeting with a 'We'll see'. There was no second delegation meeting, and, on the floor of Conference, no pad was passed round the delegation despite yet another rowdy demonstration by members of the delegation.[16]

Norman Dinning has repudiated the suggestion that he 'waved his crutch' but otherwise, this is a fair description of what happened. All the protests of AEU delegates achieved little indeed, until the Carron regime came to an end. Also in 1967, Sir William withheld the vote of the engineers from A. J. Forrester, who had been nominated for the National Executive Committee of the Party by DATA, the draughtsmen's organization. The engineers' delegation had not only voted to give support to Forrester, but confirmed this decision when Hugh Scanlon queried the result at the delegation meeting. A recount took place, which underlined the delegation's support for Mr Forrester. The vote, at that time numbering 768,000, was none the less withheld and Sir William never made any explanation as to why.

Was Carron's Law to be restored, under a new name? If this were what Terry Duffy was threatening in 1978, the matter clearly concerned not only members of his own organization: 877,000 votes was more than the number in the hands of the whole constituency section of the Labour Party, taken together. If all the individual members of the Party were to have their wishes cancelled by one functionary, riding arbitrarily over the desires of his members, then there would obviously be a real political crisis.

After the mix-up in the 1978 voting, the Labour Party's NEC decided, the following July, that the three issues of reselection of MPs, election of the Party leader by a wider franchise than that of the Parliamentary Party alone, and the determination of the election manifesto would be placed before the 1979 Party Conference.

The AUEW's National Conference met in Eastbourne, in mid-September, after this NEC decision but before the annual Party conference. Because it would have been impossible to have foreseen these developments at the previous AUEW gathering, in January 1979, the Eastbourne Conference wished to arrive at a collective view in time to influence the decision about how to vote in the Party Conference at the end of that September. Since the union would have no clear policy unless the issue was discussed on the spot,

> . . . in response to representations within the sections, delegates to the Conference drew up an emergency resolution, which was accepted by the Conference Standing Orders Committee. This said: 'That this National Conference supports the principles of mandatory re-selection of M.P.'s by their Constituency Labour Party, the determination of the contents of the Manifesto by the N.E.C. of the Labour Party as the representatives of the Labour Party Conference decisions, and the election of the Leader of the Party by the whole of the Party. National Executive Council are therefore instructed to ensure that this Union votes accordingly at the 1979 Labour Party Conference in light of the Labour Party N.E.C. recent decisions to place this matter on the agenda of this Conference.'

This resolution was reported to the Conference in the Standing Orders' Committee report.

No one doubts that this resolution would have been carried and become the policy of our amalgamated union, binding on all delegations and the national leadership.

In the face of an obvious majority of delegates being in favour of the demands for more democracy in the Labour Party, the Chairman refused to allow the Standing Orders Committee report on this issue to be put to Conference. When the Conference voted against this dictatorial approach, the Chairman ended the proceedings, thus denying Conference its right to decide policy on a whole range of other issues as well.[17]

It was in this fraught climate that Labour's constitutional reforms were considered, and many unions were sharply divided about what to do. Dissatisfaction with the policies of the Labour government had risen, as we have already pointed out, since the International Monetary Fund had imposed an abrupt change of course. Unemployment was rising, there was open mutiny about the issue of wages in many sectors of the public service and further afield, and the overall condition of social and welfare policies was causing some concern. These were the years of proto-monetarism, a happier time in retrospect than they seemed to contemporaries, for whom they were acutely uncomfortable and disconcerting. Indeed, they were in fact the thin end of a wedge which was soon to drive home to dreadful effect under a restored Conservative administration.

Already many unions had become involved in the lobby to make the Party leadership more accountable, and more responsive to the wishes of its supporters.

NUPE, for instance, had in 1975 affiliated to the Campaign for Labour Party Democracy (CPLD), a pressure group which had been formed to advance the cause of reselection of MPs, first broached in the so-called Rushcliffe amendment moved at the London Conference of the Party in 1974. Somewhat reluctantly at first, this group widened its scope to include support for the demand for a wider franchise in leadership elections. The NUPE executive decided to affiliate to CPLD because they felt that the Party leaders were insufficiently responsive to the campaign their union was waging against public expenditure cuts. This decision was reported to the union's biennial conference in 1977.[18] It was not contested. The following year the union went over to a new procedure of annual conferences, so in 1978 the executive was able to report again, on its failure to secure progress on the issue of reselection through a Labour Party NEC subcommittee which had been established to report on the subject.[19] In 1979 the issue rose again, when the conference of the union was faced with several motions calling for disaffiliation from the Party, in reaction to the events of the 'Winter of Discontent'.[20]

Early during the debate on leadership elections, during the winter of 1977–8, the NUPE executive committed itself to the solution of an electoral college.

If we take the debates of the general and municipal workers' union (NUGMW), we find that in 1977 there was an attempt to oppose the reselection of Labour MPs. Motion 407 at the union's conference sought to condemn moves 'to displace sitting Labour MPs on purely ideological grounds, and in spite of years of devoted service to the Labour Party which such members have given'. The motion proposed that it should be impossible to displace a sitting Labour MP without first giving him the

> opportunity to appeal to an impartial Committee appointed by the Party Leader which shall not include any MP nor any member in any way connected with the constituency affected. If the decision of the Appeal Committee is not accepted by the General Management Committee of the Constituency Party or by the MP concerned, the issue should then be submitted to a secret ballot of all individual and affiliated members of the Labour Party who are registered electors in that constituency, the result of which would be binding on all concerned.[21]

Mr J. S. Cook, moving this motion, made the point that general management committees which selected Parliamentary candidates might prove to have had fewer than a hundred people, while successful candidates would subsequently win 'from 15,000 to 20,000 votes upwards'. He went on to express concern that the National Executive of the Labour Party, which was constitutionally charged to inquire into the results of selection conferences in which Members of Parliament were displaced, 'simply concern themselves with whether the rules have been carried out'. Their preoccupation with whether the decision had been taken according to due protocol seemed to Mr Cook to be erroneous. He thought that the political reasons for the displacement needed also to be examined, as he put it 'impartially'.

David Gladwin, the vice chairman of the union's conference, and himself the longstanding chairman of the Labour Party's Conference Arrangements Committee, intervened in the debate to thank the movers of this motion for agreeing to remit it for consideration by the executive. In accepting the remittance, he said 'We recognize the concern . . . but we are not sure about the solution'.[22]

Perhaps the National Executive Committee of the Labour Party should be reorganized, he mused. For example, should the constituency section consist only of members of the Parliamentary Labour Party? Should not the Parliamentary Party be represented in its own right? Could regional councils and local councillors be represented? Should the trade union members be in a minority on the NEC 'when we contribute the lion's share of their expenditure?' It was with this platform enrichment of Mr Cook's motion that the issue went back to the NUGMW's executive.

In 1978 the union's general secretary's report included a paragraph on his executive's treatment of motion 407.[23] This neatly trimmed about the adoption and reselection of Parliamentary candidates. While not considering that an MP 'should be allowed to assume that he had a seat for life', neither should he be 'arbitrarily removed by unrepresentative bodies'. Since they believed that Constituency Labour Parties may have been taken over by unrepresentative groups, the executive had tabled a motion at the Labour Party Conference itself. 'That motion was not in fact considered at Conference, but was referred to the Labour Party NEC. Subsequently, following representations by the General Secretary, the NEC decided to take up the idea proposed in the motion of a review of the structure, finances, organization and democracy within the Labour Party'.[24] None of these motions validated the move to establish a new formal alliance of trade unions. In fact, as Larry Whitty explained:

> With the collapse of finances for the Walworth Road, virtually all major unions became anxious at the financial and managerial state of the Party. It was a GMWU suggestion that eventually led to it being put on a viable union-based footing. That experience is a major factor behind the unions' demands for an Inquiry – at least as important as any political motivation.
>
> The Committee, established to oversee the finances on Walworth Road, inevitably became drawn into wider matters of finance and organisation, and in anticipation of an Autumn 1978 Election, re-established itself as Trade Unionists for a Labour Victory (with the addition of Bill Keys of SOGAT). In that form they organised the TULV Campaign in the May Election. Whilst David Basnett, as Chairman, was a major initiator, all unions on the Committee were involved, both in the election campaign – which again revealed serious weaknesses in Party organisation (and trade union political organisation) and all members of the Committee were equally well convinced of the need for a wide-ranging Inquiry. It is not primarily a GMWU initiative.[25]

TULV is Formed: Subsequent Controversies

It is not contested that the Labour Party's permanent financial crisis had reached a particularly severe point when it had to find new offices after the TGWU was compelled to reclaim the space it had for so long allocated to the Party in its headquarters at Transport House. Suitable premises were quickly found in Walworth Road, but the cost of conversion was prohibitive. In order to raise the necessary funds, a consortium of trade unions was brought together to buy the building and finance its development, as Larry Whitty explained. It was in this consortium that the formal organization of Trade Unions for a Labour Victory took root. Thirteen general secretaries, including most notably Moss Evans, David Basnett and Clive Jenkins, began regular meetings in order to concert their reactions to a succession of events: the prospect of the 1979 Election; the proposal for an inquiry into Labour Party organization; the presentation of evidence to that inquiry when it was eventually agreed. Throughout these deliberations the argument about the reform of the Labour Party's structure was reaching fever pitch. Soon, as we have seen, it was to culminate in the decision that Members of Parliament would not escape the process of reselection, and in new procedures for the election of the Party leader and deputy leader.

While not restricting itself to these matters, the inquiry sought by TULV unions was certainly related to them. By 1980, 'TULV was taking so much of general secretaries' time that they elected heads of union research departments to staff three working parties'.[26] It was in these that the constructive work of liaison for practical campaigning originated.

At this point, the general and municipal workers' union took the initiative to suggest a permanent committee with a formal constitution. Trade unions with more than 100,000 members would each be entitled to a seat on the governing committee, and smaller unions would share a total of five seats between them, the occupancy of which would be determined by an election. Certain unions were reluctant to commit themselves, and the right-wing leaders of the EETPU, APEX and the AUEW were notably cautious. Later there was to be an abrasive confrontation with the NUM, for very different reasons.

In its earliest years, the TULV organized a loan of £¼ million to the Labour Party, and established a special fund, as it said, 'to provide further finance to the Party'. However, since such funds as would be made available through this mechanism could already have been transmitted direct to the Party, there were suspicions about this initiative. On the one side it was reported that David Owen and other Party leaders who were contemplating the creation of a new Party were deeply distressed about the power being exercised by a group of 'conservative' trade union leaders, while on the other side, constituency activists who had been faced with a series of manoeuvres (not all of which originated in the unions) to prevent the constitutional reform of the Party, suspected a right-wing plot to orchestrate the block vote.

The levy fund was established in the summer of 1981. Twenty-three unions representing 83 per cent of the Labour Party's affiliated membership contributed £234,859. By the end of a financial year which had been determined to coincide with the 'annual' meeting of TULV as an organization, 35 unions had associated themselves. Eleven of these, however, found great difficulty in making financial contributions, because the terms of their political funds made it impossible for them to participate.

The target of the first circular appeal was an annual contribution of 10 pence per affiliated member. Some unions paid in full, while others paid at half or a quarter of this rate. Some made a fixed donation, simply in order to set the fund off. There was a problem about how to handle all this money: this was resolved by the establishment of a limited company which was known as the 'Trade Union Management Company Limited'.

The first such money was spent on a major publicity campaign called 'Plan for Jobs', to which TULV paid £95,000 out of a total cost of £122,000 incurred by the Party. There were also payments to three by-election campaigns, and additionally the organization met the cost of the first TULV/Labour Party NEC Conference in January. Having successfully operated for a year, a second appeal was undertaken. This raised £306,000. By 1983–4, income for a period of six months had gone up to £450,000.

At the end of 1983, there was a strong complaint from the NUM that the 'growing influence of the TULV' was to the 'detriment of the constitution of the Labour Party and of the democratic principles of accountability within the Party'.

The NUM argued that trade unions already had very adequate means of participation in the work of the Labour Party. They furnished 12 out of 24 of the ordinary members of the National Executive Committee of the Party,[27] and in addition were able to participate in the TUC Labour Party Liaison Committee, which brings together leaders of both organizations, and the spokespeople of the Parliamentary Labour Party.

The NUM was understating the influence of trade unions on the Party machinery, since five members representing women on the NEC, and the Party Treasurer, are all chosen by a vote of the entire Party Conference, and trade union votes determine who these representatives shall be. This means that the effective representation of the trade union block on the NEC is 17, or even 18, not 12.

The NUM was particularly concerned that TULV might not be 'neutral' in respect of policy. The union brought the following charges:

1 In December 1983 at a meeting of TULV in the House of Commons, TULV met and discussed the forthcoming Special Assembly Conference on the Electoral College, for the election of a Leader/Deputy Leader of the Labour Party. The method of voting was fully discussed and 'the paramount need to avoid a contested election this year'.

2 Prior to the 1983 Annual Conference of the Labour Party the views of TULV were expressed to [the General Secretary of the Party], Mr Mortimer, that no increase should be sought for the Trade Union

contribution to the Party. As a result no motion was discussed on Trade Union contribution, however, it will be recalled that CLPs were asked to raise their level of contributions. It was for this reason that the National Officials recommended to the delegation that the NUM should abstain on this motion at the 1983 Conference.

3 TULV is an alternative service of funding for the Labour Party, and as such can determine how to grant money to the Party, and on what terms. This power over the purse strings has frequently led to discussions between TULV and Mr Mortimer on matters of policy.

4 There have been established a number of regional TULV Committees who are responsible to the main Committee. There is strong evidence to suggest that some Regional TULVs actively campaigned against the selection of certain candidates, and elsewhere have used their financial clout to influence regional parties.

5 The TULV has encouraged Political Education at a regional level, and on finding it out of line with its political aims, there is strong evidence to suggest it has withdrawn its support.

6 Parliamentary Elections: There is evidence to suggest that TULV has chosen to support certain candidates against others by providing physical and financial assistance when considered useful. For instance in the by-election in Bermondsey no help was given, whilst in Darlington there was a massive TULV input.

In reply to the NUM's charges, TULV circulated two responses. The first draft characterized all these points as 'dubious, if not utter nonsense'. A later reply gave more considered answers. The date given in the NUM's first point was 'presumably an error', but the substantive charge made in point 1 presumably, it said, concerned a meeting

> between TULV and the Shadow Cabinet. It is the only occasion on which TULV met the Shadow Cabinet on its own and it was at the then Leader and Shadow Cabinet's request. The issue of the electoral college was raised by Shadow Cabinet members, but TULV members made it clear that they could not commit their unions and that there would be no collective TULV view. That has remained the position of TULV on Leadership and Deputy Leadership elections and on any other elections both before and since that meeting. There has been no co-ordination of votes or attitudes on the form of the electoral college or on subsequent leadership or deputy leadership elections, or NEC elections. A cursory examination of the now recorded voting patterns would make that clear.

The TULV draftsmen who formulated this reply were probably mistaken. The erroneous reference in the NUM's letter almost certainly concerned not any joint TULV–Shadow Cabinet conference, but a committee meeting of TULV itself, which had been held in December 1980 (on 17 December at 4.00 pm). Present at this meeting had been the general secretaries of the NUGMW, the AUEW, the TGWU, NUPE,

ASTMS, SOGAT, COHSE, USDAW and the NUR. Substituting for the general secretary of the POEU was John Golding, MP, who was the only person from the Parliamentary leadership to be present.

The minutes of this meeting report 'There was a lengthy discussion of the position of various unions, the NEC and the PLP, on the leadership issue.' The same minutes continue with a report on an exchange concerning the composition of the proposed electoral college, which was to be established in order to conduct leadership elections within the Party. Union votes appeared to be gravitating in favour of two distinct proposals, either to give equal representation to the Parliamentary Labour Party, the trade unions and the Constituency Labour Parties, or to confer half the votes on Parliamentarians and divide the remainder equally between unions and constituencies.

The TULV committee apparently discussed the mechanics of leadership elections, and the desirability of compelling constituencies to vote on a 'one member, one vote basis'. Had Constituency Party representatives been present, they would have observed rather wryly that there appears to have been no discussion about how to enfranchise trade union affiliates in this same way. TULV agreed to inform the Parliamentary committee

1 That there was no agreement amongst the unions on the *proportions* for the Electoral System but attempts would continue to be made prior to Conference to seek a consensus.

2 That the majority of the unions felt it was not right to lay down how CLPs took their vote, whilst it should be made clear that each CLP had the option of going for individual ballot.

3 That there should be no election or Special Conference before October, and that on balance, the view was that this time round voting should take place at this year's Annual Conference – preferably on the Monday morning – *unless* there was a decision otherwise by Special Conference, the position on future elections could then be resolved.

4 That the strong view was that the Party should avoid a contested election this time round and that the current leadership should be maintained in office.

Judging by these minutes, TULVs reply to the NUM is conscripting necessity in order to declare its virtue. It is true that, at the later joint meeting with the Shadow Cabinet, they insisted that there could not be a collective view on the constitution of the proposed electoral college. In other words, the members of TULV disagreed with one another. But certainly they tried to reach agreement, so that even if they 'could not commit their unions', this was not to mean that they believed, as they implied in their reply to the NUM, that they should not seek to do any such thing.

Concerning the argument about the level of trade union affiliation fees to the Labour Party TULV replied that

> the General Secretary [Mr Mortimer] did indeed meet TULV – at the request of the Finance Committee of the Party – to sound out union views on the possibility of an increase in affiliation fees. TULV was a useful vehicle for this discussion. The General Secretary would otherwise have had to go and ask individual unions on a separate basis. But he would have received the same answer, and the results as far as proposals to conference are concerned would have been the same.

It was strongly denied that any attempt was ever made to put pressure on the Party by controlling the purse strings.

> The allegation that the power over the purse-strings has led to discussions between TULV and the General Secretary and writers of policy is totally false. There has never been such a discussion on any policy issue. The projects on which TULV have been asked and given assistance are agreed with the NEC and the Party Leader. They are clearly recorded in the accounts of TULV and are available to all TULV unions, the NEC and the NUM.

The argument about regional TULV committees provoked a request for evidence.

> The reference to the 'strong evidence' that Regional TULVs favour particular candidates in selection processes is unsubstantiated. No such allegation has ever been brought to the attention of the National TULV Committee. The only occasion reported (in *Tribune*) concerned a meeting in Bristol which was completely disavowed by the National Leadership of the TULV, and should not have used the TULV name. On no other occasion has there been any allegation of TULV interference in selection processes. As to using 'financial clout' to influence regional parties, this is absurd since in most cases regional TULV have not had any significant funds whatsoever to use in this way, even if they had wished to. Again, no evidence has been produced.

This complaint of the mineworkers had concerned a regional initiative in Bristol. Redistribution of boundaries had changed the city's political geography. In the most winnable Bristol constituency, trade union support was mobilized for the Chief Whip, Michael Cox, in preference to Tony Benn. *Tribune* published a front page reproduction of an advertisement from the *Bristol Evening Post* inviting votes for two candidates in the name of 'Bristol TULV'.[28] The claim that trade union involvement in this argument was really the work of an informal caucus rather than an initiative 'by the national leadership of the TULV' may well be strictly true. But TULV had itself emerged as an informal caucus at a higher level, and was not brought into being by any collective decision of the Labour Party Conference, or even through debate in the constituent trade unions themselves.

Those on the left of the Labour Party regarded it as hardly fortuitous that a group of regional officers wishing to concert their political efforts should do so under the auspices of TULV. The address given in the *Bristol Evening Post* advertisement was that of the Bristol office of the NUGMW. All the ambiguity of the relationship between the faction originally called Campaign for Labour Victory, and the trade union alliance of so similar a name, reinforced their suspicions. When the national body said that these people 'should not have used the TULV name', such critics remained unsatisfied, because *de facto* an initiative had been taken by subordinate officials of TULV unions, and there was no way in which this could be rectified after the event.

There were also rather more convincing replies to the other two points made by the mineworkers.

On political education, the NUM charge was mistaken, said TULV. There had never been courses for a political indoctrination, but there had been training courses for agents and trade unionists, which had proved both expensive and difficult to organize. It was these technical courses which might be abandoned, but for technical reasons, not as a means of political suppression.

Finally, concerning Parliamentary elections, the reply was:

> It is not true that TULV has 'chosen to support certain candidates against others'. As the Party can confirm, TULV help was available to all candidates in 'Key Seats' irrespective of their political position within the Party. It also provided help to all by-elections including Bermondsey. This is quite clear from the minutes and circulars from TULV which have of course also been received by the NUM.

The NUM had asked the question 'What is the constitutional position of TULV?' As a limited company it was not accountable either to the Labour Party or to the TUC, but 'to the unions who comprise its membership'. Since they felt it was 'bringing financial and political pressure to bear on the Labour Party to amend policy', the miners decided upon a course of 'principled opposition' to TULV. The response of TULV was, if not to cry 'witch-hunt', at any rate to imply mis-representation.

> TULV is not a pressure group, does not have individual members, but is a device to act as liaison between all unions to try and ensure (i) that the practical side of organisation can be carried through effectively (setting up efficient non-duplicate circulation networks amongst the unions;

encouraging union officials and lay members to give practical support to constituency work; recruiting new members for the party; etc) and (ii) that every possible source of finance is made available to the Party, whether that be through the Levy Fund or by other means.

The NEC and the TUC/Labour Party Liaison Committee cannot do the work done by TULV. No-one but an ostrich would deny that TULV has filled gaps that had remained unfilled for decades – the unions were just not pulling their weight in many aspects of Labour Party organisation, particularly at election time. There is a great deal that could be said about the type of jobs done by TULV to assist the party which would not have been done if TULV had not existed.

Critics, however, remained unmollified by this protest.

For all that, we may say that in general there was little evidence of effective policy or constitutional coordination by the unions constituting TULV. As the organization insisted in its reply to the NUM, it had not arrived at common policies concerning the constitutional reforms which passed through the Labour Party Conference (much though it tried, as it did not insist in its reply to the NUM). It was not even particularly successful in concerting policies for the inquiry into Labour Party structure, although it surely made the effort. Whether the convergence of general secretaries which it represented might have brought financial pressure on the institutions of the movement is a more open question. Certainly they bypassed, and thereby undermined, the Party's duly elected treasurer, for whom many of them had cast their own unions' votes.

But in materially affecting the reform of the Party, TULV was less than a major influence.

Trade Unions and the Labour Leadership Controversies

Precisely how fragmented and discordant the different union policies were is now a matter of record. There were three issues at stake in the debate on Labour's constitution: first, how should te leader be elected? Then, how far must MPs be exposed to repeated reselection? And lastly, who should draft election manifestos? During the 1980 Blackpool Labour Conference the majority of union leaders agreed on one thing, which was the need to block the last of these proposed reforms, concerning the future drafting of election manifestos.[29] This they did. But a procedural move by APEX to reverse the previous year's decision on the reselection of MPs did not succeed. There were elaborate manoeuvres and countermanoeuvres about the composition of the proposed electoral college, which, it had been agreed, would be set up to elect the Party leader and deputy leader. Various formulaes were advanced, contested and modified. At the end of the bargaining and canvassing, the change of rule was deferred for three months in order to allow adequate time to allow unions to consult their members.[30] This postponement also allowed adequate time for Mr Callaghan to resign, and for a new PLP election to be held under the old rules, thus bringing Michael Foot to office.[31]

In the run-up to the recalled (Wembley) Conference in February 1981, the right-wing organizations and MPs sought an electoral college with a majority of votes going to the Parliamentary Labour Party. This was the policy of the AUEW. The centre right, and David Basnett, proposed that 50 per cent of the votes should go to the PLP, the rest being split equally between unions and constituencies. The Party executive favoured the largest proportion (40 per cent) going to the unions, and the remainder being divided equally between the PLP and the constituencies. ASTMS favoured parity between the three sections. Some unions favoured a 50 per cent share going to the unions. The Campaign for Labour Victory canvassed the idea of an individual members' postal ballot, confined to members of one year's standing. In its proposal, nominations would require the endorsement of 10 per cent of the PLP.

Within the months after October 1980, various groupings changed their views: the NEC moved over to parity; debate was keen.

At Wembley, the proposal of CLV received only 400,000 votes against 6 million plus. Then Eric Heffer, speaking for the NEC, proposed parity between the three wings, with a 1 per cent allocation to socialist societies. The TGWU supported this solution. COHSE proposed 40 per cent to the PLP, with the remainder equally divided between unions and constituencies. USDAW countered with the move for 40 per cent to the unions. The NUGMW and UPW proposed 50 per cent to the PLP and 25 per cent each to the other constituents. At this point, Terry Duffy moved that the PLP should have 75 per cent, the unions and the constituencies 10 per cent apiece and the socialist societies 5 per cent. The AUEW, he announced, would support no other proposal, since all others gave the PLP less than 51 per cent, which was contrary to their policy. Thus immolated by their own decision, the AUEW watched the decision shift inexorably towards the USDAW formula. After a succession of ballots, this carried.

The next problem for the unions was what to do when the new procedures were put into operation. The test came quickly with the nomination of Tony Benn as a candidate for deputy leader. Michael Foot made it abundantly plain that he disapproved of this contest, but in the event there were three candidates: Denis Healey, the incumbent, Tony Benn and John Silkin. Now the unions had to devise ways of fixing upon their votes. All the previous discussion about enfranchisement of individual members had turned upon the behaviour of constituencies (and indeed, it continued to do so, even though many of them in fact took elaborate pains to discover members' opinions). But the unions themselves had to represent six million alleged voters, and their mechanics of consultation were, to say the least, often ill defined.

Two trade unions attracted most of the adverse commentary on this matter. As might have been anticipated, both were unions which sought to consult their members, and became locked in controversy as a result. Unions which were content to take a decision in caucus, either in their executives, or in their conference delegations, were not so vulnerable to criticism. However, there is no doubt that some union leaders acted independently to secure the result they personally wanted. There was a strong complaint from *Tribune*[32] that Bill Sirs of the ISTC 'had apparently nominated Denis Healey, without consulting either his conference or his executive committee'.

At the opposite extreme the POEU conducted a ballot of all members, even including those who contracted-out of the political fund. The union had received legal advice which persuaded it to follow this rather strange procedure. The result was a very strong decision for Denis Healey. More commonly, decisions were taken at union annual conferences. This was the procedure adopted by APEX. The NUM conducted a pithead ballot, which came out strongly for Benn.

NUPE conducted a ballot of their 1,600 branches, and voted by a margin of 55 per cent to 39 per cent to support Denis Healey. Undoubtedly the NUPE leadership contained a majority of people who had wished to vote otherwise, and the result of the ballot was not announced until the last possible moment, so that it did not influence decisions that were being taken elsewhere. Reg Race, a NUPE-sponsored MP, thought that the members would have voted differently had the NUPE executive made a positive recommendation. Interviewed on television, he said: 'The only friends that Denis Healey had were the press. Many members of trade unions have been influenced by newspapers. The press have no inhibition in saying who they want members to vote for. The leadership of trade unions ought to make it clear which of the candidates really supports the policy that the union fights for'.[33] In fact, on one of the policy questions closest to the interests of NUPE members it was not absolutely clear where any of the three deputy leadership candidates stood.

NUPE has been at odds with other trade unions, even similarly left-wing ones, because it has consistently campaigned for a national minimum wage. For some unions this smacks of an incomes policy, which they are determined not to support. Tony Benn had reached an agreement with the left-wing trade union leaders, in which he affirmed his opposition to incomes policy, without it being plain that he supported action on behalf of low paid workers. Thus, while no one should doubt the intentions of newspaper proprietors in this particular election, there is a deeper explanation for the result than that put forward by Reg Race. Had Tony Benn been campaigning for a national minimum wage, media attacks upon him would perhaps have reinforced NUPE members in their resolve to support him. Against this, it could be argued that Michael Meacher, who has always been a staunch campaigner for the low paid, also failed to win the public employees' vote when he stood for the deputy leadership in 1983.

The TGWU decided to take 'soundings' of branch opinion before determining how to vote in the 1981 election. Other unions followed a similar policy, notably the seamen. The TGWU's consultations were accident-prone. The issue was not put to the biennial conference, but was referred to branches through their regional offices. Seven of the ten regions supported Denis Healey. There followed an intense argument about the weight of support within each region, and the balance between regions. The left wing argued that the larger regions had voted for Benn; the right wing contested this, pointing to differences in the turnout in the different regions, showing that Denis Healey tended to poll very heavily in the areas that supported him, while Tony Benn polled less well in his regions. The argument about the interpretation of this consultation gave the impression that it had been a less than adequate exercise.

Matters were not improved by the struggles at the conference itself. The union's general executive committee had made an unambiguous recommendation that the union's votes should go for Benn. The delegation, after a cliff-hanging argument, plumped for Silkin, a TGWU-sponsored member. When Silkin was defeated, in the first ballot, the delegation then voted to support Benn.[34]

All these difficulties arose because no preliminary decision was taken about how members of the union were to be involved in the choice of their Party's leaders. The union's procedures had to be pressed into service to cover contingencies which had never been foreseen. At the same time, of course, there was a bitter struggle to win supporters of the left and right at every level. The result satisfied no one. In March 1982 the union executive decided to settle the issue once and for all, by decreeing that henceforward the delegation to the conference would decide how to vote having heard the executive's recommendations.

In the engineers' union there has been a consistent centralization of decision-making power, and from 1981 onwards delegations to the Labour Party Conference were elected by divisional committees rather than union branches. Undoubtedly this change was calculated to increase the influence of the leadership on the behaviour of the conference delegation.

The lessons of the 1981 deputy leadership contest did produce some improvements in the conduct of the ballot for leader and deputy leader, after Michael Foot's resignation in 1983. During that contest branch ballots were held in NUPE, COHSE, the POEU (which thus cancelled out the incongruities of its earlier response), APEX, USDAW and the NUM. Even the ISTC progressed to the point where it decided to invite all candidates to address its executive before the decision was reached. 'Consultations' of branches took place in GMBATU and some other unions. Conference delegations were left to decide in UCATT and the AUEW/TASS, together with the TGWU. What is quite clear is that no standard modes of procedure have been agreed, so that contributors to the different political funds have markedly different roles to play in determining Labour's leadership, depending on which union they belong to.

In the constituency section of the Labour Party constitutional change which widened the franchise for the leadership elections was warmly welcomed, and accepted as a serious advance. For the unions it has been no such unambiguous progress. If the reform enfranchises only union leaderships or executives, it will not succeed in increasing the feeling of participation which has developed within constituencies. At the very least, it might be thought that this problem is a worthwhile topic for discussion at union annual conferences.

An Evaluation

If TULV was not a conspicuous success in co-ordinating either the unions' response to the Labour Party's constitutional reforms, or the mode of implementing those reforms once they had been put into effect, none the less, it claimed to have discharged other functions than these. How did it fare in these chosen fields?

There is, of course, great scope for coordination in improving the performance of trade unions in Labour Party activities. However, scrutiny of the result of the TULV's work is not all that encouraging. In its review of the 1983 General Election campaign, the organization claimed 'a substantial improvement' on the campaign of 1979. In particular, the efforts made by regional TULVs in certain key seats were singled out for praise.

In 1983, it will be remembered, the proportion of trade unionists voting for the Labour Party hit an all-time low, at something between 38 per cent and 39 per cent. This overall result clearly overshadowed the different regional reports. In London, despite 'a good campaign' in which more literature and meetings put out the Party's message 'the result was desperately disappointing'. In the North West, many full time officers had helped in the marginals but 'involvement of lay members . . . had not been good'. From the Eastern region, the report was dismal: 'many organizational failures', 'many unions did not cooperate', internally 'there was still a fear of TULV in the constituencies' and even inside TULV itself few unions 'were positively active. Slightly less negative lessons were drawn from the experience in the East Midlands, where the campaign had 'clearly shown a lack of political organization within trade unions and a lack of professional organization within the Party'. In the North things were better, mainly because full time officers worked well in most cases; however, 'the main drawback . . . had been the lack of lay activists'. In Yorkshire, too, officials had been deployed effectively but 'much of the propaganda material went over the heads of ordinary trade unionists'.

If the electoral results of this coordination were not encouraging, neither were the results in recruitment of Labour Party membership and improvement of Party organization an unmitigated success.

On 24 November 1983 the AUEW decided to withdraw from TULV on the grounds that it could 'better plough [its] money direct into the Labour Party'. As if he were exercising his usual capacity to let cats out of bags, Mr Duffy said in his letter of resignation to David Basnett:

> As you are aware, we eventually persuaded a reluctant Executive Council of the need to affiliate to TULV because we were concerned that the NEC of the Labour Party at that time were acting in a manner which, to say the least, did not enhance our financial stability.
>
> Our Executive Council now feel that with the new NEC and Leadership, our cause would be better served by giving whatever political money we have to the Labour Party direct, because they are convinced that the present NEC and the Leadership are acting in a far more responsible manner.
>
> Let me assure you that if subsequent events indicate that we should change our mind, I give the guarantee that I will immediately resurrect the cause of affiliation to the TULV.

Supporting his president, Mr Gavin Laird, the AUEW's general secretary, told the *Guardian* that the union had withdrawn from the TULV because 'it was no longer a successful organization'. Mr Laird added that 'the AUEW was very happy with the composition of the Labour Party's National Executive and that the job of TULV had become irrelevant'. Some people thought that Mr Laird's statement reflected a considered move to damage TULV, and to undermine the influence of the general municipal workers, so that they were less than certain that Mr Duffy's remarks were as careless as they seemed.

Shortly after the engineers' decision to leave the committee, at least two other unions (the tobacco workers and the bakers) wrote to the NUM accepting the need for a consultation about what to do about TULV.

The tobacco workers' general secretary, Douglas Grieve, said that 'the TULV seems to be assuming rules which are the prerogative of the Labour Party'. Joe Marino of the Bakers' Union, while accepting the value of 'discussions on this matter' sternly insisted that 'our short association with TULV is over'.

In spite of these arguments, TULV survives, and continues to associate most of the main trade union forces affiliated to the Party. The various disputes which continued up to 1985 ensured that the organization was not sufficiently comprehensive to take on the duty of coordinating the union campaigns to win their political fund ballots, and yet another new ad hoc liaison network had to be established for this purpose.

There have been two themes throughout this short history. First, union leaders clearly wished to regulate and restrict the changes in relationships between Labour Parliamentarians and the Party at large.[35] But they could not coordinate effective counteraction to the reforms proposed (mainly by Constituency Labour Parties) for two reasons. They disagreed about the extent to which reform was needed, or should be tolerated, and they exercised differing degrees of influence over their own organizations. Secondly, as a result of the drift away from active rank-and-file participation by union members in the CLPs, unions could indeed improve their political liaison and preparedness for elections. The technical functions of training and education were, no doubt, better discharged for having been discussed within the regional TULV framework, even if this came into being under a certain cloud.

However, old quarrels are unlikely to continue unchanged. Early in 1985 David Basnett announced his early retirement from the general secretaryship of the NUGMW-Boilermakers amalgamation (GMBATU), shortly after the announcement that Larry Whitty, one of his most capable adjutants, had been chosen as incoming secretary of the Labour Party. Union elections were replacing Moss Evans by his successor, and were about to determine a new president of the AUEW. A new cast of actors was assembled to contend with the burnt-out landscape of industrial relations following the defeat of the miners strike and the inauguration of the latest and most swingeing trade union laws.

Notes

Throughout this chapter quotations without annotation are from minutes circulated by TULV.

1 For a balanced discussion of this, see Martin Harrison, *Trade Unions and the Labour Party since 1945*, Macmillan, 1960, ch. 5, pp. 195 et seq.

2 The authoritative study of the role of trade unions in the Labour Party Conference is that by Lewis Minkin, *The Labour Party Conference*, Allen Lane, 1978.

3 Cf. Mark Jenkins, *Bevanism: Labour's High Tide*, Spokesman, 1979, particularly p. 113 et seq. Also Leslie Hunter, *The Road to Brighton Pier*, Arthur Barker, 1959.

4 Cf. Geoffrey Goodman, *The Awkward Warrior: Frank Cousins, His Life and Times*, Spokesman, 1984.

5 J. David Edelstein and Malcolm Warner, *Comparative Union Democracy*, Allen & Unwin, 1979, pp. 263 et seq.

6 Hugh Scanlon's commitment to workers' control is summed up in the very first pamphlet to be published by the Institute for Workers' Control, immediately after it was founded in 1968. 'The Way Forward for Workers' Control' is a resolute and clear-headed statement of the policy of trade union encroachment on what had previously been seen as managerial prerogatives. Jack Jones was to become a consummate master of the politics of the TUC. Cf. John Elliott, *Conflict or Co-operation*, Kogan Page, 1978.

7 Harrison is at pains to deny the notion that Labour Party policy could be controlled by a handful of people 'in a smoke-filled room' (*Trade Unions and the Labour Party*, p. 209 et seq.) However, R. T. McKenzie's more sceptical view in *British Political Parties* (Heinemann, 1955, p. 502) certainly appears to fit the early post-war years. After all, the unions were uniting to defend what they saw as the achievements of a Labour government.

8 Kogan and Kogan, *The Battle for the Labour Party*, Kogan Page, 1982, p. 68–9.

9 Cf. Michael Barratt Brown, 'The record of the 1974–9 Labour Government – the growth and distribution of income and wealth', in Ken Coates (ed.), *What Went Wrong*, Spokesman, 1979, pp. 34–73.

10 One of these is reflected in the correspondence between Jeff Rooker, the MP for Birmingham, Perry Barr, and Sir John Boyd, the former General Secretary of the AUEW. Mr Rooker had agreed to speak at an unofficial committee organized by Roy Fraser, the spokesman of the rebellious skilled men whose differentials had been eroded during the period of the Social Contract. Cf. Jack Eaton and Colin Gill, *The Trade Union Directory*, Pluto Press, 1983, p. 96.

11 *Tribune*, 6 October 1978, p. 7.

12 *Guardian*, Blackpool Diary, 4 October 1978.

13 *Tribune*, 6 October 1978, p. 7.

14 Edelstein and Warner, *Comparative Union Democracy*, p. 289.

15 Lewis Minkin, *The Labour Party Conference*, p. 197.

16 Ibid., p. 198.

17 AUEW Oppositional Broadsheet, distributed at the 1979 Labour Party Conference.

18 NUPE, Biennial Conference Report, 1977, p. 22.

19 NUPE, first Annual Conference Report, 1978, p. 20.

20 NUPE, Annual Conference Report, 1979, p. 142 et seq.

21 NUGMW, Annual Conference Report, 1977, pp. 496 et seq.

22 Ibid., p. 498.

23 NUGMW, General Secretary's Report, in Annual Conference Report, 1978, p. 53.

24 Ibid.

25 Letter to Ken Coates, 3 January 1980.

26 *New Statesman*, 23 January 1981.

27 In addition there are five other members. One of these is elected by a handful of socialist societies, one from the Young Socialists' organization and a treasurer is elected by the votes of the whole Conference. The Party Leader and Deputy Leader, after the reform of the Party rules, have been chosen by an electoral college consisting of trade union and constituency representatives, and the members of the Parliamentary Labour Party.

28 *Tribune*, 25 June 1982; *Bristol Evening Post*, 4 June 1982. The two candidates were contesting the chairmanship and secretaryship of the Bristol District Labour Party: they were Bob Hewlett of the TGWU and Maurice Rea of NATSOPA.

29 This proposal was defeated by only 117,000 votes. See Labour Party Annual Conference Report, 1980.

30 For an account of the movements behind stage, see Chris Mullin, 'Two days that shook the Labour Party', *Tribune*, 10 October 1980.

31 In spite of a public warning from David Basnett that the PLP should not make any permanent change in the leadership during the interim period.

32 Chris Mullin, *Tribune*, 25 September 1981.

33 Kogan and Kogan, *The Battle for the Labour Party*, p. 116.

34 Chris Mullin, 'Labour's longest day', *Tribune*, 2 October 1981, p. 3.

35 See the interview between David Basnett and Chris Mullin, in *Tribune*, 23 January 1981. 'Q The inquiry had political purposes, didn't it? A Did it? What was the political part? Q The argument over democracy in the Party, for example. A Yes, that's right. I can see what you mean by political . . . as being political.'

7 Class Politics and the General Strike that Did Not Come

The Movement Between Individual and Political Forms of Action

From time to time we have referred to the 'pendulum' theory of trade union history, once very popular in the Workers' Educational Association. The late G. D. H. Cole suggested that it was possible to identify a series of distinct periods during which the British labour movement was predominantly committed to industrial action. These periods, thought Cole, were interspersed by others, during which all priorities were explicitly political. Often this theory carries the implication that pendulum swings from industrial to political forms of action may be the result of disillusion with one or the other commitment. If so, we must always remember that some people are able to maintain their strong aversions even during times when these have become distinctly unfashionable. So, old Marxian socialists like Fred Knee, or the Socialist Party of Great Britain, were speaking contemptuously about collective bargaining throughout the years in which it was achieving its most evident early successes, while many a resolute syndicalist has held strongly to his view throughout all the political upheavals and mass popular movements we have witnessed in the last century. If pendulums carry many with them as they swing, they always leave some behind. Some of those who stay behind may well become influential in their turn, if they survive for long enough until the pendulum comes back.

None the less, it would, before 1984, have been difficult to resist the view that British workers were turning away from strikes as their chosen mode of self-defence. Having fallen from their 1979 peak, in which workers spent 29.5 million days in strikes, 1981, 1982 and 1983 saw a very low level of strike activity, with only 3.8 million days of strike involvement during the last of these years. As we have already seen, the actual number of strikes diminished considerably (see table 7.1).

Then came the big bang in the shape of the miners strike. For a whole year this extraordinary battle raged throughout the English coalfields. Even at the end, after many people had returned to work, the majority

Table 7.1 Number of strikes, workers involved and striker-days in the UK

Year	No. of strikes	No. of workers involved (thousands)	Striker-days (millions)
1966	1937	530	2.4
1967	2116	731	2.8
1968	2378	2255	4.7
1969	3116	1654	6.8
1970	3906	1793	11.0
1971	2228	1171	13.6
1972	2497	1722	24.0
1973	2873	1513	7.2
1974	2922	1622	14.8
1975	2282	789	6.0
1976	2016	666	3.3
1977	2703	1155	10.1
1978	2471	1001	9.4
1979	2080	4583	29.5
1980	1330	830	12.0
1981	1338	1499	4.3
1982	1528	2101	5.3
1983	1352	571	3.8
1984	1154	1375	26.6

Source: Department of Employment Gazette.

of those who began the strike were still resisting in spite of hunger, cold and large scale intimidation. Was this strike the beginning of a new phase of 'class politics'? Did it rehabilitate the commitment to industrial action as the main form of resistance? Or was it rather the last moment in a dying industrial wave following which the labour movement might once again swing over to political forms of action?

To some extent these questions remain open. Their answers will be determined by the extent to which constitutional remedies are seen to remain open. In the meantime, however, we do need to address the belief, widely canvassed by influential spokesmen of the Left in Britain, that the miners' strike required mass extension through solidarity strike waves, reaching up to and including a general strike. Such calls were heard in some major unions, but they were most coherently articulated by Tony Benn during December 1984, and supported by other Parliamentarians such as Dennis Skinner. The miners' leaders were in general more restrained in their appeals for support, although Arthur Scargill quite understandably called for action in sectors which handled fuel, and not only urged the TUC to fulfil its 1984 Congress promises, but appealed to union members to make the running in this process.

There is no doubt that, while some of these calls were intended simply to reinforce the industrial leverage of the miners – by interrupting coal movements to the main consumers in the steel and power supply industries – the general tendency implicit, and sometimes explicit, was to associate widening sympathy strikes with political goals, the rededication of the labour movement to its class alignments and the direct defeat or restraint of the Conservative government by industrial action. Given the strong evidence of managerial authoritarianism which marked the government's offensive, the call for sympathetic trade union action was entirely to be expected: but the response was very limited. For this reason, we need a serious discussion of the history and theory of the general strike, conceived as a method of turning out a government or of achieving a radical social transformation or revolution.[1] Since we wish to advance the case for a strong turn of the trade unions towards politics (whatever the position which the hypothetical pendulum has reached), we think it reasonable to look briefly at the experience and the theory of industrial politics, particularly the general strike.

Secondary and Solidarity Action and the Pluralist Tradition

The government's assumption that 'sympathetic', 'secondary' or solidarity action by trade unionists is unjustifiable in any circumstances has already brought about legislative action to remove immunity from civil proceedings for all such categories of action. This amounts to a general prohibition, in all circumstances in which the social temperature is cool enough to permit the courts to follow their wonted bent. But the fact that the law proscribes sympathy strikes does not mean that they should be so proscribed. Indeed, it is a measure of growing authoritarianism that even liberal opinion has been so slow, indeed so reluctant, to respond to laws having such far-reaching implications.

In an earlier age things were not so. We can enter the attitudes of a previous generation by following the argument of Harold Laski, who firmly defended the idea of political freedom as inhering in the single individual 'over and against the state'. But in his once best-seller *Liberty and The Modern State*,[2] he then extends the question to include associations of citizens, for the individual does not stand alone in society. 'The essence of liberty' lies in the freedom to combine. But what degree of control is the state justified in exercising over voluntary associations? Laski sets up the case for prohibition of general strikes as an unwarrantable extension of the rights of collective associations. Such arguments are pressed, he tells us, 'on the ground that this is an attempt to coerce the government either directly, by making it introduce legislation which it would not otherwise do, or indirectly, by inflicting such hardship on the community that public opinion forces the government to act'. So the critics insist

> If men want to obtain from government a solution other than the government is willing to attempt, the way to that end is not by the use of industrial power, but through the ballot-box at a general election. . . . The General strike, even a large sympathetic strike, is in fact a revolutionary weapon. As such, it is a threat to the Constitution and illegal as well as unjustifiable.

But Laski painstakingly rejects the 'illusive simplicity' of these arguments, and carefully distinguishes different grounds on which such action may be undertaken. 'That it cannot in any circumstances be justified I am not prepared to say until I know the circumstances of some given case.' In 1926, the government had abandoned 'even the fragment of a genuine search for justice', and was acting 'as the mouthpiece of the coalowners'.

He continues:

> There is no danger that the general strike will ever be other than a weapon of last resort; the occasions when it can be successfully used will be of the utmost rarity. But they may occur. I cannot accept the position that Government is always entitled to count on industrial peace, whatever its policy. Nor do I see why it is unconstitutional, as in 1926, to withdraw from work in an orderly and coherent way.

Of course, a general strike is an occasion of injury and hardship for the community. But in pursuit of their case, trade unions must perforce arouse a 'slow and inert public' to a knowledge of their position; the public 'has no sense of its obligations until it is made uncomfortable'. To win public attention and debate for the kind of issue that would provoke a general strike, requires an action of such a dimension.

Nor, says Laski, can there be some artificial distinction drawn between general strikes for industrial purposes (justified), and for political purposes (unjustified), for there is no formula available which could draw such a hard and fast line between the two.

> I should not agree that a general strike is unjustified to secure the eight-hour day, or to protect the payment of unemployment relief, or to continue the Trade Board system in sweated industries . . . Quite frankly, I should have liked to see a general strike proclaimed against the outbreak of war in 1914; and I conceive the power to act in that way as a necessary and wise protection of a people against a Government which proposes such adventures . . . I do not forget that the German Republic was saved from the Kapp Putsch by a general strike.

Moreover:

> A Government which meets the threat of a general strike is not entitled
> to public support merely because it meets the threat. It is no more possible
> to take that view than to say that all governments deserve support when
> they confront a rebellion of their subjects . . . everything depends on the
> purpose.

And finally:

> I do not of course deny that freedom of action in this field is capable of
> being abused. That is the nature of liberty. Any body of persons who
> exercise power may abuse it

including of course, governments. The omnicompetence of Parliament
itself would, if gravely abused, cease to be omnicompetence. 'The same
truth holds . . . of the liberty to proclaim a general strike'.

Laski's pluralism is out of fashion. Not only trade unions, but also
local authorities, find their powers melting away in the blaze of
governmental authority. But it is worth remembering the arguments
which used to carry conviction in this area:

> Freedom of thought, then, the modern state must regard as absolute; and
> that means freedom of thought whether on the part of the individual or
> of a social group. Nothing is more stupid than for the state to regard the
> individual and itself as the only entities of which account must be taken,
> or to suggest that other groups live by its good pleasure. That is to make
> the easy mistake of thinking that the activities of man in his relation to
> government exhaust his nature. It is a fatal error. The societies of men
> are spontaneous. They may well conflict with the state; but they will only
> ultimately suffer suppression if the need they supply is, in some equally
> adequate form, answered by the state itself. And it is tolerably clear that
> there are many such interests the state cannot serve . . .
>
> The state, as we have seen, is in reality the reflexion of what a dominant
> group or class in a community believe to be political good. And, in the
> main, it is reasonably clear that political good is today, for the most part
> defined in economic terms. It mirrors within itself, that is to say, the
> economic structure of society. It is relatively unimportant in what fashion
> we organise the institutions of the state. Practically they will reflect the
> economic system; practically, also, they will protect it. The opinion of
> the state, at least in its legislative expression, will largely reproduce the
> opinion of those who hold the keys of economic power. There is, indeed,
> no part of the community of which economic power is unable to influence
> the opinions. Not that it will be an absolute control that is exerted by
> it. The English statute-book bears striking testimony to the results of the
> conflict between the holders of economic power and those who desire its

possession; and, often enough, there has been generous co-operation behind the effected change. But the fundamental truth remains that the simple weapons of politics are alone powerless to effect any basic redistribution of economic strength. . . .[3]

If general strikes may indeed be justified, however, we are left with a number of questions. In what circumstances are such strikes possible and effective? How do they materialize? What do the general strikers and their leaders do, when the strike is established? What goals can be set, beforehand, for achievement through general strike action? And, for what purposes have general strikes actually been called in history, and what has been their outcome?

General Strikes and 'Mass Strikes'

Strictly speaking a general strike can take place at the national level, or may be confined to a particular locality. In common parlance, the term 'general strike' has come more and more to be understood as a national stoppage. But some of the most effective 'general' strikes have been localized in their scope, if not in their implications. One of the key examples was the strike in September 1913 in Dublin. This has been the subject of a major novel, and an extensive television serial.[4] James Larkin, the leader of the Irish Transport and General Workers' Union, was a powerful advocate of the doctrine of 'one big union', and exponent of sympathetic trade union action. The September strike erupted into dramatic confrontations. Lord Askwith cites contemporary newspaper headlines (more long-winded in those days): 'Dublin is now dramatically in a state of civil war between Labour and capital'.[5] There was no doubt where contemporary British labour leaders stood in this, for them, disconcerting battle. Philip Snowden pointed up a sad contrast:

> The old policy of the trade unions was to build up strong reserves: to refrain from exacerbating the public and the employers by never ceasing threats of strike: to exhaust every possible means of conciliation before calling out the men . . . the new policy is to enter upon a strike without any effort to obtain a settlement of the grievances by negotiation; to exacerbate the employers by every possible means; to indulge in wild and sanguinary language, which makes it impossible for a self-respecting employer to meet such leaders of the men . . . and to endeavour to cause as much public inconvenience as possible . . .[6]

But if the Labour Party was reluctant to offer sympathy, an important part of the trade union movement was at first in a different frame of mind. Seven thousand railway workers struck at Crewe, Sheffield,

Derby, Liverpool and Birmingham, because they did not want to handle goods that were blacked. The railway leaders ultimately persuaded their members to lift this action, on the grounds that 'many of the "tainted goods" had not come from Ireland'. The Trade Union Congress organized a ship full of food to support the Dublin strikers.

The Court of Inquiry which was established to examine the dispute was chaired by Askwith, joined by J. R. Clynes (of the unions) and H. F. Wilson (for the employers). Askwith found the employers intransigent and Larkin recriminatory. Worse, he reported, 'even during the sittings of the court, sympathetic strikes continued to occur'. Unsurprisingly, the court ruled,

> The sympathetic strike may be described as a refusal on the part of men who may have no complaint against their own conditions of employment to continue work, because in the ordinary course of their work they come in contact with goods in some way connected with firms whose employees have been locked out or are on strike . . . No community could exist if resort to the 'sympathetic' strike became the general policy of trade unionism, as, owing to the interdependence of different branches of industry, disputes affecting even a single individual would spread indefinitely.[7]

However, the union was not persuaded by this reasoning, and the strike continued. Further food supplies poured in from England, and Askwith was able subsequently to report, wryly, that Mr Larkin went to England in order to describe the leaders of the Labour Party as being 'useful as mummies in a museum'.

As the strike raged, this kind of radicalism intensified, and intransigence stiffened on both sides. In October, Larkin was sentenced to seven months' imprisonment for 'seditious speaking', although he had to be acquitted of incitement to revolt and larceny, and was subsequently released in November. In appealing for further sympathy action, Larkin brought down strong criticism on his head, from British union leaders, of whom he said: 'I never trust leaders, and I don't want you to trust leaders. Trust yourselves.'

The secretary of the Miners' Federation of Great Britain issued a public reproof, and both the miners and the railwaymen then declined to bring out their members in a general sympathetic action in support of the Dublin struggle. In the absence of such action, by February 1914 the dispute had 'melted away'. Askwith's judgement is interesting. 'The fervour of his [Larkin's] nature, probably led to some results though at very heavy cost of suffering, but his scheme of organization was not perfected, and connoted not only the organization of his own men, but counter-organization of employers.'[8]

The principles of one big union were not defeated with the end of the Dublin strike, however. The same reasoning was to echo and re-echo for many years to come.

A few years earlier, Rosa Luxemburg had published her classic study *The Mass Strike*.[9] For sure, she used the term 'general strike' widely throughout her text to characterize large strikes even though these may have been confined to single regions, towns or industries, but her own title was deliberately chosen. She described in graphic and kalaedoscopic detail a whole series of strike *waves* in Russia between 1896 and 1906, not a single, final and decisive event. She nevertheless saw in these actions an immense political significance and a single underlying theme of revolution. This, she thought, linked together separate strike actions spread across the length and breadth of the Russian Czarist empire over a period of ten years. Within this kind of view, Larkin's voice would have a different meaning from that understood by Askwith.

The General Council of the British TUC in 1926 was always careful to avoid the use of the term 'general strike', preferring the less apocalyptic-sounding 'national strike'. William Benbow, the English shoemaker, printer and radical friend of William Cobbett, who was the acknowledged father of the idea of the general strike, announced his ideas in a pamphlet entitled *Grand National Holiday and Congress of the Productive Classes* in 1832. The Chartists, who took up the concept, (and tried to implement it) spoke always of 'the Sacred Week' or 'the Sacred Month', those being the periods alternatively judged necessary to bring about the government's concession of the Six Points of the People's Charter. It was the English trade unions of the same period who transmuted this for the first time into 'the general strike'.

Of course, following them, the Bakuninist wing of the First International, and later the Syndicalists, chose the same term, which is why it thereafter always carried with it the overtone of insurrection, and the sense of a consciously chosen alternative to political and party roads to social revolution. Despite the TUC's terminology, this is also the unavoidable connotation whenever the British movement reflects upon the experience of nine days in 1926.

Yet, if we follow Rosa Luxemburg in examining whole periods of mass industrial militancy (which almost inevitably carry with them political implications) within the field to be considered, we must include, for example, the Polish events of 1980–81, the French mass actions of 1968, the Belgian strikes for the franchise between 1886 and 1913, the Italian factory occupations of 1921, to say nothing, in Britain, of the 'syndicalist' phase of 1911–14, and the strike wave which peaked to massive proportions in the 1970s (*see* table 7.1). It is evident that we are confronted with a class of social phenomena, not a unique type. Each occasion has its own character, and each has its own, specific outcome.

To begin at the beginning. William Benbow made high claims for the general strike; it was variously 'a plan of freedom' and 'a plan of happiness'. It would 'rid the world of inequality, misery, and crime'. In his pamphlet, he called on all workers to prepare for the 'national holiday' by laying in stocks of food for one week; he believed that success would follow such a long work stoppage. Each locality should appoint a committee to direct the agitation; a national congress should assemble for a month. It would undertake a kind of social audit, and 'put tyranny to flight'. If, after a century and a half, this programme should seem eccentric and more than a bit Utopian, no one can doubt that it carried great weight and influence amongst the Chartists between 1838 and 1842.

There were probably few Chartists who had not read it; its phrases were on every lip; Chartist speakers made use of it; and all the debates on a general strike and all attempts at its realisation in that decade are to be traced to Benbow's pamphlet.[10]

Moreover, the police and judiciary certainly took Benbow very seriously; he was gaoled for his part in the organization of the Blanketeers' march in 1817, again during 1819–20, once more in 1839, and was arraigned in 1840 for making seditious Chartist speeches.

His plan came nearest to realization in the so-called 'Plug Plot' of 1842, which, with 500,000 strikers involved at its height, properly deserves the name of general strike.[11] A series of strikes (immediately sparked off by wage cuts), spread from their originating centre in Lancashire, right across the North, through the Midlands and into South Wales and Scotland. 'Moral force' Chartists had just been rebuffed by Parliament's rejection of their mass National Petition, but Chartist agitation was still very active. At the same time, the Anti-Corn Law League was not averse to the spread of disaffection against a protectionist government. Economic discontent was readily able to grow over to advance wider political goals. Physically, the strikes were spread by a 'rolling' tactic, with strikers moving like flying pickets from mill to mill, striking out the boiler plugs to render production impossible, and raking out the fires beneath the boilers too. In a few days a mass meeting on Mottram Moor in Lancashire resolved that 'all labour should cease until the People's Charter became the law of the land'. Similar resolutions were passed at strike meetings throughout Lancashire, in Manchester and in The Potteries. The Chartists' national secretary, entering Manchester by train, observed the smokeless chimneys. 'Not a single mill at work! Something must come out of this and something serious too!' he wrote.[12] The Chartists in conference called on the strikers to remain out until the Charter became law. The Chartist executive declared for a general strike – the best weapon for achieving the Charter.

The social peace in the North broke down. There were attacks on industrial plant and gas works, houses were burned and trains were stopped. The Army responded with mass repression and shootings and the Chartist leaders were gaoled. Thus intimidated, and shorn of political achievement, the economic situation of the strikers asserted itself. The economy was in slump; markets for the mills' products were in collapse. In a few weeks the strike was over, without even achieving effective resistance to wage cuts. The Chartists returned to conference methods, and the drafting of a new Bill of Rights, amidst much recrimination.

The connection between general strikes in Europe and the struggle for political democracy is significant.

> Britain's very early general strike was not the only one to be linked with demands for the vote. At the end of the century one can find a whole series of intriguingly close parallels: in Belgium in 1886, 1887, 1892, 1902, and 1913, in Sweden in 1902, in Finland and Russia in 1905. Apart from the October strikes in Russia, none ever came near 1842 in its length, or in the absolute number of workers involved. Only a third of Belgium's industrial labour force, 350,000 workers, took part in the biggest of that country's strikes in 1913. In Sweden no more than 120,000 struck work in the four-day general strike of 1902. Yet all these strikes won at least a measure of fairly immediate change in representation.
>
> The reason for this contrast in achievement is certainly not that 1842 was somehow isolated and unprepared. In terms of scale and organization it was rather the culmination of a long period of struggle in which trade union activity and the movement for democratic rights had become closely interdependent. If we are looking for parallels to the initial patchy and part insurrectionary Belgian strikes of the 1880s, the best comparison is probably not 1842 but the Jacobin-inspired strikes of 1818 and 1820 or the two-day holiday of 1839. Nonetheless 1842 not only failed to secure any visible legislative response but, temporarily at least, marked the end of this form of action in Britain. Whereas in most other European countries the general strike was officially accepted in the later nineteenth century as labour's basic and final weapon in the battle of democracy, in Britain such use of strike action remained effectively outlawed in the trade union movement until after the First World War.[13]

Normally the national general strike has been seen as a direct political act, and it has most often been invoked in order to secure an extension of voting rights, or a General Election. But exceptionally the general strike has been put forward as a model for the replacement of existing society in one great anarchist upheaval. Between 1864 and 1872 this issue was debated constantly inside the First International by the two schools which ranged themselves behind Bakunin and Marx respectively. Echoes of their argument re-emerged during the great epoch of syndicalism, and are best summed up in the different views of Georges Sorel and Rosa Luxemburg.

Luxemburg greeted the massive Belgian strikes in favour of universal suffrage with the aphorism 'the working class must learn to speak Belgian'. Sorel, by contrast, was scathing about the Belgian experience, which, he maintained, did not constitute a proper general strike at all.[14] The Belgian workers were being manipulated by political puppet masters. The parties were harnessing proletarians to advance their interests and no beneficial change would come from this. The true general strike would reconstitute the entire society.

From roots like these, buried though they may be, the modern argument still draws inspiration. Sorel, and his forgotten mentors such as Tortelier and Pouget, were successful in generating what Sorel himself described as a 'myth' which re-emerged in 1968 in a new French uprising under the banner 'Imagination au Pouvoir'.

For all this, for the present authors at any rate, Marx and Luxemburg had the edge of the argument over Bakunin and Sorel. Today, the majority of young activists who drew their inspiration from the 1968 events in Paris are no longer to be heard arguing for the rule of imagination, although life would be better and more interesting if they were. Alas the rank and file of the barricades now treads in the mills of domesticity and mortgages, while many of the more colourful advocates of the late revolution are struggling with the minor burdens of office.

Rosa Luxemburg discovered the same dialectical relationship between mass strikes and revolutionary politics in Russia, as is evident in the 1842 strike. She reviewed, (for the benefit of dogmatic and schematic controversialists in the German Social Democratic movement) the experience of the mass strike in Russia leading up to the revolution of 1905. But she began her famous pamphlet with a general discussion of the concept, starting with Engels' criticisms of the Anarchist position (which the modern reader may more readily associate with syndicalism, which derives from the same political root). It is worth re-citing Luxemburg's extract from Engels:

The General strike, in the Bakuninists' programme, is the lever which will be used for introducing the social revolution. One fine morning all the workers in every industry in a country, or perhaps in every country will cease work, and thereby compel the ruling classes either to submit in about four weeks, or to launch an attack on the workers so that the latter have the right to defend themselves and may use the opportunity to overthrow the old society . . . at the Congress of the Alliancists at Geneva on September 1st 1873, the general strike played a great part, but it was admitted on all sides that to carry it out it was necessary to have a perfect organisation of the working class and a full war chest. And that is the crux of the question. On the one hand, the governments, especially if they are encouraged by the workers' abstention from political action, will never allow the funds of the workers to become large enough, and on the other hand, political events and the encroachments of the ruling classes will bring about the liberation of the workers long before the proletariat get the length of forming this ideal organisation and this colossal reserve fund. But if they had these, they would not need to make use of the roundabout way of the general strike in order to obtain their object.[15]

Luxemburg does not use this demolition of the Bakuninist vision to take sides in the German debate for and against the general strike; she regards both positions as being conditioned by the same assumption as was made by the Anarchists, which is that the general strike can be planned for, and ordered, from above, from a political or trade union hierarchy deliberating on and prescribing the great event. She distances herself equally from those who believe that the general strike will inaugurate the revolution, and those who would suppress and contain the instinct to mass strikes, if and when they occur, as being contrary to the supremacy of politics.

Her text reviews the historical experience of 1896–1905, in a vivid piece of original reconstruction of the confused, apparently chaotic chronology of the strike wave which swept Russia in that period. The strikes were nowhere called by the revolutionary political parties that were hard at their clandestine work, deep amidst the very communities which produced the strikes. The motivation of the strikers, often clearly economic initially, spilled over to embrace radical political goals, usually outdistancing and leaving standing those same professional revolutionaries. At key moments the strikes link up with the revolution, and directly express it. Incredibly, she finds that they also outlast the ebbing of the revolutionary movement, and turn in their final phases back to the economic. She concludes the factual account with this passage:

> The mass strike, as the Russian revolution shows it to us, is such a changeable phenomenon that it reflects all phases of the political action and economic struggle, all stages and factors of the revolution. Its adaptability, its efficiency, the factors of its origin are constantly changing. It suddenly opens new and wide perspectives of the revolution . . . it flows now like a broad billow over the whole kingdom, and now divides into a gigantic network of narrow streams; now it bubbles forth from under the ground like a fresh spring and now is completely lost under the earth . . . it is ceaselessly moving, a changing sea of phenomenon.[16]

She contrasts this historical picture with 'the rigid and hollow scheme of an arid political action carried out by the decision of the highest committees and furnished with a plan and panorama'. In real life Russia, in 1905, 'we see . . . a pulsating life of flesh and blood'. She concluded: '. . . in reality the mass strike does not produce the revolution, but the revolution produces the mass strike'. And, 'if the mass strike is not an isolated act but a whole period of the class struggle, and if this period is identical with a period of revolution, it is clear that the mass strike cannot be called at will. . . .' And she advises the political leadership: 'instead of puzzling their heads with the technical side, with the mechanism of the mass strike, the Social Democrats are called upon to assume *political* leadership in the midst of the revolutionary period.'[17]

Of course, a further and even more substantial Russian experience in mass strikes, that of 1916–17, should be added if we were to complete the story. It is noteworthy that in his *History of the Russian Revolution*, Trotsky largely followed the method of Luxemburg; he uses the chronology, statistics and nature of the strikes of those years to indicate the political temperature of the working class, not to demonstrate the powers of leadership or the influence of exhortation. What other analysis could explain how the political strikers of 1905 became the loyal chauvinists of 1914 ('In the factories in those days nobody dared to call himself "Bolshevik" for fear not only of arrest, but of a beating from the backward workers'[18]) and finally reverted to audacious mass militancy for ultimate revolutionary purposes in 1917, at a time when the Bolsheviks, with the exception of a handful of their leaders, had grave reservations about the revolutionary timetable?

A specific explanation is also required for the strike wave which swept British industry between 1911 and 1914. Several versions of syndicalist or revolutionary trade unionism inspired some of the best minds amongst trade unionists in those years. Tom Mann, James Connolly, Daniel de Leon, E. J. B. Allen and a host of other propagandists flooded the British trade unions with their literature, in which the general strike, and the 'training' role of lesser strikes, were advanced as the main method of working class emancipation. Here for example, is E. J. B. Allen, with an anarcho-syndicalist version of the role of the general strike:

> The industrial union is destined to become the most powerful instrument in the class struggle by showing the working class how to hold in check the rapacity of their masters and the tyrannies of the State by direct pressure of their collective economic strength; which power reaches its highest expression in the complete paralysis of the whole of the normal functions of capitalist society by means of the general strike. The use of the general strike must be amplified and extended, embracing a larger and larger number of workers in the actual combat; evolving that unity of action and sameness of inspiration which will make them *think and act as a class*, for the direct and forcible expropriation of the capitalists.[19]

James Connolly adopted the version of industrial unionism originating with Daniel de Leon in the USA. Here, he expresses the common view of a range of different tendencies within the movement for revolutionary unionism, about the negative role of politics:

> The political institutions of today are simply the coercive forces of capitalist society; they have grown up out of, and are based upon, territorial divisions of power in the hands of the ruling class in past ages, and were carried over into capitalist society to suit the needs of the capitalist class when that class overthrew the dominion of its predecessors.[20]

The syndicalists and industrial unionists were alike, too, in their will to transform the structure of trade unionism, in the direction of the principle 'one industry, one union'. They advanced this goal both as a means to unify workers for more effective industrial class warfare, and as a model for the self-managed socialist industrial constitution which they envisaged as their alternative to both capitalist and state-managed societies. It was in promoting such purposes as these, rather than in promoting the general strike, that they left an indelible mark on British trade unionism and socialist politics. It should be said too, however, that although the majority of trade union members of the period did not embrace syndicalist expectations of the general strike, large numbers were imbued with the syndicalist spirit of intransigent and militant disrespect for managerial and state authority.

In the period leading up to the First World War, there was a disillusion with the 'decorous' socialism of the infant Labour Party in Parliament, after its initial electoral gains and the success it registered in obtaining, through its Liberal allies, the Trades Disputes Act of 1906, which overturned the House of Lords' devastating ruling in the Taff Vale case. Equally, the working people's appetite for trade union organization and militancy was fed directly by their experience of inflation and lagging wage rates. As they moved to establish new trade union structures, such as the National Union of Railwaymen, or breathed new, more democratic life into old ones (such as the Miners' Federation, and the Engineers), they were impatient to apply those instruments to good effect, to win recognition from employers and to push up wages to match the rise in living costs. The legacy of that generation is an important element, holding back the encroachments of corporatism into trade union life, down to the present day.

The 1926 British General Strike

Moreover, although the general strike never acquired a mass appeal in Britain,[21] the syndicalist spirit survived and indeed matured during the war years, to hold out continued hopes of socialism by trade union insurrection among the activists of the post-war years, up to and including the 1926 General Strike. This episode has, of course, generated more debate and more heat than any other in modern labour history. Historians down to the most recent continue to confirm the main findings of successive generations.[22] These boil down to seven propositions. First, the strike was seen by its TUC leaders as a defensive, purely industrial struggle designed to promote solidarity in the unions around the resistance of the miners – and thence the whole working class – to wage cuts and longer hours. Second, the goals of the miners and their unions were also confined to economic defence. (The miners dropped their demand for a restructured or nationalized industry at an early stage.) Third, the strike was impressively solid and the strikers were almost totally loyal to their official leaderships. Fourth, the government was determined to resist the strikers and their demands. Fifth, the government was extremely well prepared for the strike, while the TUC had done little or no forward planning. Sixth, the strike was called off unconditionally and the strikers had no independent will or organization to sustain the strike after its official abandonment by the TUC.[23] Last, the effect of the strike was seriously to weaken the trade union movement, but not to destroy it, or to cause fundamental divisions within it, even though the miners' union was seriously damaged for over a decade by the Nottinghamshire splinter union which emerged.

Some of the myths of the strike have indeed been questioned in recent years, notably that which ascribes total intransigence (and 'impossibilism') to the miners' leaders A. J. Cook and Herbert Smith.[24] No one doubts that the strike was a failure, although its value as a symbol of heroic resistance and trade union solidarity remains. We do not have space – nor is it to our purpose – to attempt any original insights in this context. However, it should go without saying that the strike was not modelled on a revolutionary unionism, nor did any substantial body of trade union opinion hold that it should be directed towards a radical political purpose. The left wing, and rank-and-file bodies like the Minority Movement did, of course, advocate the general strike, but their influence was always limited, and it greatly diminished during the years after the defeat. Despite the solidarity of the strikers, it was a 'top-down' strike, initiated and called off to order of the TUC. There is a vast divide between the sociology of the British experience in 1926, and the kind of mass strike wave described by Luxemburg, or experienced at other periods even in Britain. It remains important to examine the relationship of the Labour Party to the strike, since this question was again raised in the context of the 1984–5 miners dispute.

At the superficial level, this examination is frequently confined to a study of the statements (or more latterly, the lack of statements) by Labour leaders. Such analyses would be more interesting if Labour leaders stood in any direct relationship to the trade unionists involved; of course, they do not. Political leaders within a democratic framework are bound to preoccupy themselves with political questions, first among which will usually be direct electoral matters. If the 1926 General Strike was about defending miners' wages and resisting the imposition of longer working hours on them, the voice of Mr Ramsay McDonald made little difference either way. If, on the other hand, it was about the revolutionary overthrow of bourgeois democracy, then there was no way in which Mr McDonald could be expected to support it. Parliamentary spokesmen cannot permit themselves the luxury of flitting in and out of their commitment to representative institutions. Indeed, their working class supporters would be among the first to criticize any such pusillanimity.

If a given constitutional framework becomes unworkable and unbearable, then this will be apparent whatever leaders might say. But in 1926 and after it workers were very anxious to elect Labour Members of Parliament in order to achieve quite specific and tangible reforms. The overwhelming majority of those who went on strike did not for one moment believe that in so doing they were abolishing future general elections. It is certainly true that in 1984 almost none of the miners, and hardly anybody outside the NUM, believed that the strike was an alternative to the electoral process. Thus, whatever the opinions of the leader of the Labour Party may have been, these were in no way a crucial datum: electoral processes were seen by most strikers as quite distinct from the industrial struggle.

The most serious casualty of the 1926 strike was the spirit and policies of the radical trade union generation which matured before it; Beatrice Webb actually rejoiced in this outcome in a famous entry in her diary:

> For the British trade union movement I see a day of terrible disillusionment. The failure of the General Strike of 1926 will be one of the most significant landmarks in the history of the British working class. Future historians will, I think, regard it as the death gasp of that pernicious doctrine of 'workers control' of public affairs through the trade unions, and by the method of direct action. This absurd doctrine was introduced into British working-class life by Tom Mann and the guild Socialists and preached insistently, before the war, by the *Daily Herald* under George Lansbury. In Russia it was quickly repudiated by Lenin and the Soviets, and the trade unions were reduced to complete subordination to the creed-autocracy of the Communist Party. In Italy the attempt to put this doctrine into practice by seizing the factories led to the Fascist revolution. In Great Britain this belated and emasculated edition of the doctrine of workers'

control will probably lead to a mild attempt to hammer trade union activities. Popular disgust with the loss and inconvenience of the General Strike will considerably check the growth of the Labour Party in this country, but will lead to a rehabilitation of political methods and strengthen J. R. M.'s leadership within the Party itself.[25]

Comparisons are odious and it should not be expected that history will precisely repeat itself after 1985. MacDonald, like the British Empire, is no longer with us. But the advocates of general strike responses in 1984–5 must of necessity consider 1926 again, and discuss their analysis of it. Among other matters, we would do well to reflect on the transparent contrast between the state's will to resist, including its technical, permanent readiness to do so,[26] and the trade unions' total failure to match that will or preparedness. That failure was, of course, made good partially and spontaneously in the hundreds of local 'Councils of Action' and strike committees which emerged during the nine days to assume considerable functions, with embryonic implications of 'dual power'. But how did these activities melt away within a few days of the official surrender by the TUC, despite all those years of syndicalist, and later, communist, teaching?

The strike never reached that duration and social gravity in which the ultimate questions about general strikes could have been asked and answered, namely: 'What do you do with a successful general strike and how can it make the transition from industrial to effective political action? What do you do if the government concedes your case? What do you do if the government continues to resist and to deploy its resources in expression of that resistance? To ask these questions is to demonstrate that history gives us no example, no model, from which to derive answers. Certainly we get no guidance from the one British excursion into this territory. This is not to argue, of course, that the strike should not have been called, or to deny its powerful place in trade union and labour history and lore. Its moral values are vibrant and profound, and their assertion wholly to be welcomed. This is quite another question from that of whether it is wise, or possible, to project such actions as a key element of socialist advance; this would be to substitute voluntarism to the point of fantasy for realistic and realizable strategic thought.

'General Strikes' after the General Strike

The TUC was vaccinated with powerful antibodies during those days: it successfully resisted all subsequent attempts to involve it in general strikes, or movements tending to that conclusion, after 1926, until very recently. In 1958, for example, the crisis surrounding an ineffective and stalemated strike of London busmen saw the General Council at its most timid and 'constitutional', when it advised Frank Cousins that no widespread sympathy action could be expected, however widely he pushed the strike into technically adjacent industrial sectors in which the TGWU had strong membership, such as the petrol tanker drivers and the workforce in electricity generator stations supplying power to the London underground. On that occasion the air in the General Council meetings was thick with references to the General Strike of 1926 and to the wholly negative lessons which the TUC derived from it.

Significantly, the post-war occasion when the TUC did contemplate a general strike call, in 1972, in protest at the gaoling (under the Heath Government's Industrial Relations Act) of the five 'Pentonville' dockers, was when a rolling strike embracing many industries and hundreds of thousands of workers was already spontaneously in progress. Before its official call could come, trade union members were voting with their feet. The government retreated, the dockers were released and the 'general strike' threat had achieved its limited and class-defined purpose.

In 1984–5 constant exhortations were made in a setting where hundreds of miners had been gaoled, fined, beaten up and generally intimidated by the law. This was by any assessment a much worse situation than that of 1972, but no spontaneous strike wave arose in the miners' defence, and in its absence all the exhortations were without effect. Moreover, where some conscientious and sympathetic trade union leaders did back sympathy action (albeit sometimes veiled in internal causes and grievances), as on the docks, the strikes petered out from lack of will or conviction among the 'secondary' strikers. It was devastating and demoralizing evidence of the toll taken of elementary militancy and solidarity by the dole queue. In that context, neither bottom-up or top-down strikes were of any avail. If we may learn from Rosa Luxemburg and from the England of 1842 that mass strikes are not engineered from above, we may derive another fundamental lesson from our more recent history; that sympathy action in an epoch of mass unemployment does not normally emerge spontaneously, and that its promotion from official sources is likely to be difficult, not to say eventually ineffective.

More recent supporters of what they call 'class politics' have implied that trade union political action might still topple governments, even if it fell far short of the degree of commitment involved in a general strike. To be sure, the interrelation between different industrial processes is so close that it is quite conceivable that certain groups of key workers could bring about devastating disruption if they so chose. But the example of such action which is most commonly given concerns the miners strike of 1974. In our opinion, arguments resting on this case have tended to produce a mythological version of these events. The truth seems to us to point a completely different moral.

The Myth and Reality of 1974

Michael Crick, the biographer of Arthur Scargill, rightly points up a paradox when he says 'the 1974 strike is the miners' dispute which people remember, simply because it led to a General Election and the downfall of a Government, but within the history of the Miners' Union it is less important than 1972'.[27]

The conflict with the Heath administration arose because the government was seeking to enforce phase 3 of a pay policy which did not give the National Coal Board scope to meet a union wage claim. War in the Middle East, and radical new policies of the Organization of Petroleum Exporting Countries (OPEC) increased oil prices by 70 per cent in mid-October 1973. The miners were feeling the pinch of inflation, in spite of their victorious settlement of 1972, because they had settled their pay deal within the government's incomes policy during the intervening year. Their demand was for a surface minimum wage of £35, an underground minimum of £40, and a coal face minimum of £45. This involved increases of between £8 and £13 a week. Evidently, this would not be easy to fit within the framework of the incomes policy, and the government would find itself caught between an oil crisis with considerable inflationary effects on the one side, and discontented miners on the other. The miners suspected that the incomes policy would seek to hobble them at a time when their market advantage was otherwise irresistible: speaking at the union's Annual Conference in the summer of 1973, Mick McGahey said:

> We reject any basis of negotiations with this Government and its so called anti-inflationary policy. It is not negotiations in Downing Street, but it is agitation in the streets of this country to remove the Government that is required. Ted Heath has laid down the guidelines. He has organized the football match, he has picked the teams, appointed a referee, made sure of the linesmen and has even decided the result, and that is why we say there should be no negotiations with this Government, but the need is to defeat it.

As Tony Hall, the popular historian of the coal industry has insisted, 'McGahey later went to great lengths' to qualify these remarks, in order to establish beyond doubt that his proposal to topple the government exclusively involved constitutional mechanisms. However, the press reported McGahey's remarks very widely, and this has given a certain degree of credibility to the myth that the 1974 strike 'overthrew the Government'.[28]

In fact, the president of the NUM went to some considerable lengths to try to avoid a strike altogether, while the union was beginning its preparations with an overtime ban. Mr Gormley even went so far as to offer some conciliatory advice to the Prime Minister. This was apparently misunderstood, and the misunderstanding prevented the conclusion of an agreement during the preliminary negotiations. It seems that Joe Gormley thought that a strike would quite possibly provoke a general election, which, in the midst of an energy crisis, might quite possibly be won by the government. But the miners were less and less prone to heed such warnings, as the news came in from the Middle East. Tony Hall cites one Chesterfield miner as saying to Eric Varley, then Opposition spokesman for Energy: 'I wish my pit was in the Persian Gulf – then we would get whatever we asked for and even have a say in the government's foreign policy as well.'

After negotiations with the Coal Board broke down, they were resumed at 10 Downing Street. Joe Gormley's secret weapon for the avoidance of the strike involved circumventing the pay policy by agreeing the concession of extra pay for the time spent changing, preparing to descend and leave the pit, and bathing after work. However, to his great annoyance, Harold Wilson publicly ventilated this proposal in the middle of negotiations, so that the government could not easily embrace it without conceding defeat. Accordingly a settlement was not achieved.

As the strike became more probable, the government took defensive measures. These were prepared in a very visible manner which itself constituted part of the official campaign. At the climax of these efforts, on 13 December, the Prime Minister announced the institution of a compulsory three-day week in industry. He argued that the miners' overtime ban was curtailing deliveries of coal to power stations by as much as 40 per cent. Oil markets were tight, and even increased oil supplies were inadequate to breach the resultant gap. Trouble in the power stations meant engineers there were restricting their own working hours, so that as a result of these combined problems the government needed to reduce power consumption by 20 per cent.

It was around the question of the three-day week that the major political battle took place. If it were possible to place the blame for the three day week on the miners, then Mr Heath could expect a substantial increment of votes. If, however, the three-day week could be seen as an instance of government incompetence and overreaction, then the electorate might choose differently. It was the outcome of a political argument on this issue, not the triumph of insurrectionary force, which toppled the Heath administration, and brought the Labour Party back into office. But perhaps because the idea of an insurrection is more exciting than that of a debate, the reality of the 1973–4 events is to a degree obscured by legend. Hence the notion that 'Mr Heath was defeated by the miners', which was to recur after a decade in the allegation that Mrs Thatcher sought to revenge that defeat. The real terms of the political argument which Mr Heath lost are more significant.

Immediately before the 13 December announcement, the Institute for Workers' Control had begun to receive information that the government was greatly exaggerating the disruption of coal supplies to power stations. Mr Heath was to report that 'so long as the industrial action of the coal miners and the train drivers continues . . . large scale interruption and disruption of electricity supply' would be unavoidable. But train drivers, workers in power stations and miners themselves were convinced that the actual rate of delivery to power stations was holding up much more than the government claimed. The Institute began to provide a constant flow of direct testimony on these matters to Tony Benn, who was the Shadow spokesman for Industry in the House of Commons. On 18 December he intervened in a debate to seek answers to these charges, which were not forthcoming.

Michael Barratt Brown, working on the official statistics, and collating the evidence from trade unionists in the energy sector, showed that there were in fact coal stocks which could last for 40 weeks of normal weather, which led him to the conclusion that the three-day week was not administratively necessary, and should be seen as 'a general lock out'.

On 12 December 1973, the day before the promulgation of the three day week, the IWC denounced 'the Government's entirely suspect claim about the state of power station supplies'.[30] It pointed out that the transport workers' leader, Jack Jones, had been complaining about an 'appalling shortage of diesel fuel for lorry transport, which has been making a nightmare of the long distance driver's life', but, 'ASLEF drivers report that two 1000-ton trains have gone from Saltend and two from Teeside respectively every day during the fortnight ending 11th December, carrying light oil to the Eggborough power station in the West Riding. That is 50,000 tons of inappropriate oil sent up the power station chimneys, directed to the purpose of putting the coal miners in their place, and in the process contributing to chaos in the transport system'.

The Institute called for a trade union inspection of supplies of fuel. It sought for 'an office . . . to collect and collate' all relevant information 'and to make the resultant picture available to politicans and public opinion'. Such an office it saw as

a powerful deterrent to anti-social behaviour whether by oil companies or by the Government itself. The men and women who man the computers which redirect oil tankers in mid-Atlantic may well prove more patriotic than the combines they work for, and may willingly inform their Unions of the manoeuvres which are being undertaken to profit their employers in spite of any adverse effects on the British economy.

In response to this call, the Labour Party established a special monitoring and information service, which requested Labour groups on local authorities, Constituency Parties, affiliated unions, Labour MPs and candidates to provide information about coal or oil production, imports, exports, movements and stocks. The head office of the Party circulated a ten-point questionnaire which also requested briefing on the effects of the three-day week in terms of short time, unemployment, loss of earnings, reductions of exports and changes in prices.

Train drivers, power station workers, dockers and others involved in the transportation of oil and coal made regular reports both to the Institute and to the Labour Party monitoring service. These reports offered accurate information about the state of coal stocks and the rate of deliveries.

On its side, the government maintained a flow of disinformation. Mr James Prior warned of the danger that power cuts might cause floods of sewage in the London streets. The IWC was able to report

> that all the sewers and ancillary pumps in Great Britain, running continuously, burn less than three watts a day per head of the population. Of course, an unknown but very high proportion of this miniscule amount of electricity is generated in the sewage works themselves from home produced methane. The very modest deficit in supplies which remains could easily be made up by . . . field generators of the type used by the military, even assuming that the grid shut down for good.[31]

Over Christmas the monitoring of coal movements continued, and Tony Benn received daily briefings on the real situation. On 29 December he addressed six questions to the Prime Minister. There began a remarkable dialogue in which the Prime Minister replied through the national press. On 31 December, unsatisfied with these answers, Mr Benn addressed a further nine questions to the Prime Minister. This exchange succeeded in arousing widespread doubt about the government's real reasons for imposing the three day week, and once the election was declared, it paid a price for this.

In an attempt to retrieve the Government's reputation, *The Sunday Times* published an assessment of coal stocks which highlighted all the government's more alarming predictions. Michael Barratt Brown, who had produced the calculations upon which the IWC based its campaign to show that the three day week was unnecessary, was denounced as having 'had little experience of energy statistics'. However, Barratt Brown's statistics were confirmed in the calculations of Dr Francis Cripps and others. These, too, were published in *The Sunday Times*. The best authorities were agreed that stocks would not fall below a possible minimum level until early or mid-April, even if the restrictions of the three-day week had never been imposed.

This evidence was lucidly summarized by Michael Meacher, in a letter which was published in the national press, and in the *IWC Bulletin* of 18 January 1974.

The latest Department of Energy statement about the level of coal and oil stocks at power stations must increase doubts as to whether a three-day working week is really necessary at all.

Firstly, energy experts now believe that if oil supplies to power stations were increased to last year's rate, then the cut in electricity use, without running down coal stocks to unsafe levels, need be less than 10 per cent, which could be absorbed without any industrial disruption at all. The Government now reveals that oil supplies at power stations have now turned *upwards* virtually to the level of a month ago, so the three-day week looks decidedly premature.

Secondly, another indication that Mr Heath was jumping the gun is his statement in the House on December 18 that 'coal stocks are now running down at the rate of about 1 million tons a week', when we now know that in fact over the four and a half weeks to that point after the overtime ban began coal stocks at power stations declined at a rate of less than three-quarters of what he claimed. How then can the Government ever have pretended that the rundown 'would reach a critical level by January/early February', when simple arithmetic showed that the 6m ton 'critical' level would not be reached till the end of March?

Thirdly, how does Mr Prior justify his scare statement on December 30 that 'when the coal stocks fell below 6m tons, the system could not be worked properly, so only 7m tons were really available'? Why did he omit to say that in the last four years coal stocks *have* been below this allegedly critical level at power stations for four weeks – not only the weeks ending February 20 and 27 1972, during the coal strike, but also those ending April 10 and 17 1970, when there was no miners' strike?

Fourthly, how is Mr Heath justified in announcing a three-day working week when coal stocks at power stations stand at 16m tons (58 per cent higher than at the same date three years before), since during the winter 1969–70 and 1970–71 stocks never even approached this level even in the best week (being mostly at *half* this level or even below), yet there was no whisper then of any need for a three-day week?

Fifthly, when Mr Heath announced the three-day week, the NCB still held 4m tons of general reserves of power station coal. This is an extra six weeks' supply at rundown rates then, enough to take the power stations through the last week of April.

Since, therefore, power station coal stocks are in nothing like so serious a position as the Government has pretended, it must strengthen suspicions that the Government is using its dire prophecies of impending disaster and the three-day week, which on this evidence was not then warranted, as a weapon to beat the miners into an unfair submission.

The Labour Party's inventory of fuel stocks generated information which greatly reinforced the weight of Labour's attack. Summing up in the Shadow Cabinet at the beginning of the new year, Harold Wilson was heard to say 'I think that we have not suffered any great harm from Tony's activities over Christmas'. Other Members of Parliament were soon able to inflict considerable damage on the credibility of official figures, and to show how irrational was the policy of the three-day week. EEPTU shop stewards made a detailed report on power station stocks which enabled David Stoddart to frame a devastating attack on the policy. It was not until 4 February that the NUM ballot of its members was declared. A total poll of more than 86 per cent showed that 80.99 per cent were in favour of strike action.

There followed a restrained, indeed, by comparison with 1972, low key struggle, in which picketing was virtually unnecessary, but was in any case restricted to six persons per colliery. The NUM executive decided to call the strike on 8 February, and Parliament was dissolved on the same day. The union was therefore concerned that no event in the strike should inhibit the Labour vote in the general election. Mr Heath had written to Mr Gormley requesting a suspension of the coal strike for the duration of the election campaign. However, the mines closed at midnight on 9 February and the general election weaved in and out of the restrictions of the three-day week, which had to be eased in order to allow for the printing of manifestos and addresses.

Committee Rooms were exempted from the three-day week order, even though they were obliged to remain unheated for their share of the time. The result of the general election on 28 February was a hung match: 301 Labour Members confronted 296 Conservatives, with 14 liberals, 11 Ulster Unionists and 12 other Independents holding the ring. When Mr Heath proved unable to persuade the Liberal leader to sustain him in a coalition, Mr Wilson moved into Downing Street. The miners strike was promptly settled in a manner acceptable to the NUM, and Britain entered the Social Contract phase of Labour administration.

The Trade Unions and 'Reform or Revolution?'

While some people claiming allegiance to Marx have been predisposed to lay too much stress on the revolutionary potential of trade unions, others, it seems to us, give trade unions too little credit for their political contribution.

Perry Anderson once contributed an important essay on trade unionism and politics, in which he adopted a strongly Leninist attitude. Trade unions, he asserted, are essentially limited in their contribution to the political development of the workers. They are not only an opposition to, but at the same time an in-built expression of, capitalist social relations. And in their opposition role their main weapon, the strike, is a negative event. The source of Lenin's thesis is to be found in the pamphlet *What is to be Done?*[32] which was occasioned by a polemic between himself and the 'economist' wing of Russian Social Democracy. His argument runs:

> We have said that the workers could not yet possess Social–Democratic consciousness. This consciousness could only be brought to them from the outside. The history of all countries shows that the working class, solely by its own forces, is able to work out merely trade-union consciousness, i.e. the conviction of the need for combining in unions, for fighting against the employers, and for trying to prevail upon the government to pass laws necessary for the workers, etc.

and again:

> . . . the spontaneous development of the labour movement leads precisely to its subordination to the bourgeois ideology . . . because a spontaneous labour movement is trade unionism . . . and trade unionism means precisely the ideological enslavement of the workers by the bourgeoisie.

These opinions are not particularly 'Leninist'. They derive directly from the thought of Karl Kautsky, then ironically known to his socialist critics as 'the Pope of social democracy'.

Anderson endorses these conclusions confidently: 'All mature socialist theory since Lenin has started by stressing the insurmountable limitations of trade union action in a capitalist society.'[33] And again:

> Trade Unions are an essential part of a capitalist society because they incarnate the difference between Capital and Labour which defines the society . . .
>
> They are a passive reflection of the organization of the work-force. By contrast a political party is a *rupture* with the natural environment of civil society, a voluntarist *contractual* collectivity, which restructures social contours; the union adheres to them in a one-to-one relationship. . . .

From this position, Anderson derives his view of the strike weapon:

> The trade union's inert adhesion to the lay-out of the social system has a crucial practical consequence. Its maximum weapon against the system is a simple *absence* – the strike, which is a *withdrawal* of labour. The efficacy of this form of action is by its nature very limited. It can win wage increases, some improvements in working conditions, in rare cases some constitutional rights. But it can never overthrow a social regime . . .

With the last sentence, we find ourselves largely in agreement; but the rest goes too far in its opposition to the syndicalist anarchist view of strikes. It has been in strike action that workers have often learned key political lessons. It has often been through strikes that the working class has restructured, or given birth to new unions. In the syndicalist phase of 1911–14 new ideas on the nature of socialism prospered and spread. Reaching into the First World War period, those ideas crystallized for many the libertarian view of socialism as a society of self-management. An earlier strike wave, in the 1830s, had as we have seen, gathered strength from and incorporated Owen's vision of a cooperative society. Moreover, while it is true that trade unionism often begins through sectoral, corporate structures, it has gone on to reform itself towards ever wider forms of association which overcome – if still partially – the occupational divisions in the workforce.

Today, no one can doubt the educational impact of the miners' strike of 1984–5, not only for the miners and their wives, but for all those sections of society which have been moved to send the money, food and other material assistance. This strike was clearly much more than an 'absence'; the miners imposed a debate upon society which it would otherwise have passed by. The transformation of the women's role in the mining and wider labour communities during the struggle represents a serious positive gain (in which it takes further their role in 1926), not to be explained in the terms set out in Lenin's early pamphlet or Perry Anderson's later essay.

Perry Anderson reached this low estimate of trade union potential in the conviction that workers alone, operating through trade unionism, are incapable of achieving 'socialist consciousness', which has to be brought to them 'from outside', by the intelligentsia. This might have been true of Czarist Russia, though this case itself requires greater debate, but how is it helpful in understanding the emergence of socialism in the British labour movement, or its development in an age of mass communications and compulsory education? From the Levellers onwards (if not indeed from the Peasants' Revolt), successive generations of oppressed and exploited people have evolved concepts of a free and cooperative commonwealth to inspire their struggles. Tony Benn has expressed the process well:

> The Levellers distilled their political philosophy by discussion out of their own experience, mixing theory and practice, thought and action, and by doing so they passed on to succeeding generations a formula for social progress from which we can learn how to tackle the problems of our time. . . . Looking back on these ideas from the vantage point of the present, and knowing that they came out of the minds and experience of working people, few of whom enjoyed the formal education available today, it is impossible not to experience again the intense excitement and the controversy that those demands must have created when they were first formulated.[34]

Did these calls come from 'outside'?

Thus, in voicing some scepticism about the efficacy of calls for the general strike as a means for a transition to socialism, we do not think it right to throw out the baby with the bathwater, and we do wish to affirm the positive role of trade unionism, and of the real contribution made by many strikes, to the evolution of workpeople's understanding of society. We also conclude, from this partial survey of mass or general strikes, that there can be no general, universal explanation of the phenomenon; each society, each historical moment, requires its own analysis and interpretation. We have found occasions when mass strike movements have carried momentous political weight with them; and we find that these occurrences are frequently, perhaps usually, not prepared and planned by any politically conscious leadership. The most extraordinary case of spontaneity was the great 1968 upheaval in France, but there are others. We have found mass strikes called from above for limited, defensive purposes, or sometimes for constitutional reform. Some of these may be formally abandoned as the constitutional implications of the action dawn on their leaders; some are beaten; others may win concessions. Some may compel a political change, as indeed was argued of that very 1973–4 British miners' strike which was the pretext for a general election and the defeat of the Heath Government. Even such an outcome however, cannot usually be prepared and predicted (Heath's abdication was voluntary; a simple political mistake), and even such an outcome leaves the question of Labour's alternative policy unanswered.

At this point, Perry Anderson's view reconnects with our own. In the event, after 1974, British trade unionism soon found itself in another set of problems with the alternatives actually imposed by the Wilson–Callaghan administrations which followed Heath's defeat.

We find no reason to go beyond the findings of Engels, quoted earlier, about the contradiction involved in the general strike as a principal weapon of advance, nor to revise Rosa Luxemburg's advice to socialist politicans, to concentrate on politics and leave the mechanisms of strike action to the social forces which alternately generate and retard it.

Meantime, it seems to us to be absolutely plain that if working people living in an epoch of universal suffrage are not capable of voting a government out of office, then they are unlikely to succeed in getting rid of it by strikes. If governments miscalculate, of course they can lose elections for a wide variety of different reasons, not excluding those arising in industrial disputes. But sensible people, if they are asked to plan a programme of actions calculated to bring about a result, will try to approach that result as directly as possible. For this reason, we think workers will be well advised to consider how they might secure the election of a Labour government and to join forces to this end. Very probably the main lesson to be drawn from the miners strike is that this is a more urgent task than ever. The danger is that the task will blank out necessary thought about what such a government should do. None the less, to the extent that political activity increases, we may well see that industrial actions, for the time being, continue to decline. All this would be perfectly predictable, if the pendulum theory were true.

Notes

1 A comprehensive, widely used text book, *Strikes*, by Richard Hyman (Fontana/Collins, 1972) contains no discussion of general strikes, and only three passing references, without analysis, to the British 1926 strike. In the same author's *Industrial Relations: A Marxist Introduction* (Macmillan, 1975) the general strike occasions only the following comment: 'The nature of ordinary strike action . . . maintains the sectionalism and fragmentation of normal union organization . . . Even in the extreme case of common action by all trade unionists in a general strike, the challenge to the capitalist class remains only partial: they attack their economic, but not their cultural and political, domination. (This explains why the leaders of the British general strike of 1926 were defeated from the outset, and knew themselves to be so).' (p. 101). K. G. J. C. Knowles, in his classic analysis, *Strikes – A Study in Industrial Conflict* (Basil Blackwell, 1952), offers a comprehensive discussion of syndicalist literature. (pp. 6–10) and a detailed examination of legal responses (pp. 110–15), together with much other information. Among the documents in *Strike – A Documentary History* by Ruth and Eddie Frow and Michael Katanka (Charles Knight & Co., 1971) is the Comintern's publication *A Striker's Handbook*, prepared by the Red International of Labour Unions. This shows how far apart are modern communist ideas, even of the 'class struggle' variety, from those of the late 1920s. In our own text book *Trade Unions in Britain* (Spokesman, 1980) in a brief discussion of the effects of 1926 upon TUC leadership thinking, we suggest that 'it is possible to imagine circumstances, such as the threat of unjustified war, or of a fascist takeover in Britain, when the TUC might be under the strongest moral obligation to consider leading industrial action' (p. 97).
2 First published 1930, 3rd edition, Allen & Unwin, 1948, pp. 126–32.
3 Harold Laski, *Authority in the Modern State*, 1919, p. 56 et seq.
4 James Plunkett, *Strumpet City*, Hutchinson, 1969. It is also the subject of O'Casey's play *Red Roses for Me*.
5 Lord Askwith, *Industrial Problems and Disputes*, John Murray, 1920, p. 260.
6 Ibid., p. 260.
7 Ibid., p. 263–4.
8 Ibid., p. 271.
9 Rosa Luxemburg, *The Mass Strike, the Political Party, and the Trade Unions*, first published in pamphlet form 1906 (see edition by Harper Torchlight, New York, 1971).
10 Max Beer, *A History of British Socialism*, first published 1919 (see Spokesman (illustrated) edition, 1984).

11 Mick Jenkins, *The General Strike of 1842*, Lawrence and Wishart, 1980.

12 Mark Hovell, *The Chartist Movement*, Longmans, Green, 1918, p. 261.

13 Mick Jenkins, *General Strike of 1842*, Introduction by John Foster, pp. 14–15.

14 Georges Sorel, *Reflections on Violence*, Collin Books, New York, 1961, pp. 120–5.

15 Friedrich Engels, 'The Bakuninists at Work', in *Der Volkstaat*, 31 October, 2 November and 5 November 1873, quoted in Luxemburg, *The Mass Strike*, pp. 8–9.

16 Luxemburg, *The Mass Strike*, pp. 44–5.

17 Ibid., p. 54. (Italics in original).

18 L. Trotsky, *History of the Russian Revolution*, Sphere Books edition, 1967, p. 51.

19 E. J. B. Allen, 'Working Class Socialism', in Tom Mann (ed.) *The Industrial Syndicalist*, 1910 (Italics in original).

20 James Connolly, 'The Axe to the Root, and Old Wine in New Bottles', from *Socialism Made Easy*, 1908, Irish TGWU edition, 1934, pp. 14–15.

21 Rank-and-file opinion recollected in interviews in the 1970s, remains divided on this point. For example: 'By keeping people well informed, we kept the situation in Coventry solid, and when the strike was called off I went down with a deputation to London to demand that it be continued, for the rank and file in our area were ready and willing to carry on.' (George Hodgkinson, Coventry Labour leader and shop steward.) 'We carried on until the end and when it was called off, there were more people out than there were at the beginning. We were let down, but it taught us a lesson. It was good training in the art of running things.' (Alf Garrard, former rank-and-file building worker.) 'Among the rank and file we had no faith in the trade union leadership, but we didn't have a real suspicion there would be a sell-out and never made any move to counter-act what the officials were doing. The rank and file did not have a real objective in front of them, what to do if they won the strike.' (Frank Hodgson, retired building worker.) 'Some of the critics have denied it, but there were signs that after nine days the strike was beginning to crack. While it lasted though, the spirit was tremendous.' (R. E. Scouller, former official of the National Union of Clerks, Glasgow.) All extracted from R. A. Leeson, *Strike: A Live History, 1887–1971*, Allen & Unwin, 1973, pp. 88–93.

22 See Margaret Morris, *The British General Strike of 1926*, Historical Association, 1973.

23 Compare this judgement with those cited by Leeson, note 21.

24 Margaret Morris, *The British General Strike of 1926*, 1973, p. 28.

25 Beatrice Webb, Diaries 1924–32, (ed. Margaret Cole), Longmans Green and Co., entry for 4 May 1926, pp. 92–3.

26 Keith Jeffrey and Peter Hennessy, *States of Emergency: British Governments and Strike-breaking, since 1919*, Routledge and Kegan Paul, 1983, gives a detailed account of the considerable and permanent organizations at the disposal of the state for the purposes, including a chapter on contemporary civil contingency planning. Cf. also Steve Peak, *Troops in Strikes*, The Cobden Trust, 1984.

27 Michael Crick, *Scargill and the Miners*, Penguin, 1984, p. 65.

28 Tony Hall, *King Coal*, Penguin 1981, p. 200.
30 IWC Bulletin, 12 December 1973.
31 IWC Bulletin, January 1974.
32 V. I. Lenin, *What is to be Done?* (Geneva 1902), Panther edition, London, 1970.
33 Perry Anderson, 'The limits and possibilities of trade union action', in *The Incompatibles: Trade Union Militancy and the Consenses*, Penguin Books, 1967, pp. 263–81. Italics in all the following quotes are in the original.
34 Tony Benn, *The Levellers and the English Democratic Tradition*, Spokesman pamphlet No. 54, published for the Oxford Branch of the WEA, 1976.

8 Class Politics and the General Elections that Will Come

If the trade unions are caught in a deep crisis, we must evaluate their options carefully. Yes, collective bargaining has been seriously undermined by mass unemployment, which has created a more adverse labour market. Bargaining has also been hedged about by restrictive laws, delicately and carefully designed to impede industrial action, and diminish its likelihood as much as possible. But no slump ever weighs with uniform severity across the whole economy: on the contrary it is the weaker who go down, and the stronger who profit from their fall. Mrs Thatcher, upon her election, celebrated the ethics of St Francis. It is doubtful whether St Francis would have approved of the carnivorous degree of competition which has evolved since the industrial revolution and has now reached feverish intensity.

Slumps are a perfect celebration of these jungle ethics. They are about the periodic readjustment of the value of capital, but at the same time they necessarily seek to re-establish or re-emphasize its power over labour. The value of capital is restored by devaluing the capital stock, because the rate of profit rises if that stock has been depreciated, provided only that the actual amount of profit does not fall. Bankruptcies, which ensure that capital stocks are sold off at very low prices indeed, provide a ratchet mechanism in this process of devaluation. The power of capital will normally be increased by the rise in unemployment, which forces down the real costs of labour, even if it fails to undermine the trade unions completely. Arising from these linked shifts in the relationship between labour and capital, productivity is expected to rise, as inefficient firms are squeezed out and intensified competition provokes rationalization. All these 'economic' processes, it is clear, are profoundly political both in their origins and effects.

However, these classic movements operate unevenly, between different sectors of the economy and different zones of the world. There are, in the jargon, a number of 'inelasticities'. Unemployed workers in Scotland do not flood in appropriate numbers to the more prosperous South East in order to wreck the wage levels in that favoured area. Still less do they arrive in sufficient numbers to cut wages in West Germany,

227

or Detroit. This inelasticity has, on balance, helped trade unions, because they have rarely been as fully vulnerable as hostile economists have predicted. But the world of multinational capitalism is one in which the purgative effects of slump can be far more rigorous than used to be the case. Thus, the British slump, deliberately reinforced by governmental actions, has demolished vast areas of manufacturing capacity.[1] Since 1979 approximately 1½ million jobs in the manufacturing sector have collapsed, partly because of the restriction of home demand through public spending cuts and tax increases, and partly because, for crucial years, the overvaluation of the pound priced British exports out of one market after another.

Since 1979 there have been 60,000 company liquidations and 33,000 bankruptcies in England and Wales, excluding Scotland and Northern Ireland. Of these, 13,500 liquidations and 8,000 bankruptcies occurred in 1984 alone. This widespread devastation forces the surviving giants to move outwards.

In February 1985, reported the *Guardian*, ICI became the first manufacturing corporation in Britain to declare profits of £1 billion earned in a single year. But the chairman of ICI, John Harvey Jones, granted a most candid interview, in which he spoke of the company's need to 'speed its withdrawal from the flagging British economy and its rapidly shrinking customer base'. Of course, there had been contraction in heavy chemicals, but Mr Harvey Jones thought that this was now probably at an end. However, he did not believe that the sectors which had been pruned back would ever resume their growth:

> The reason is grim and inescapable. Almost 80 per cent of ICI's products, which range from basic chemicals and fertilisers to medicines and space-age plastics, must find industrial customers.
>
> 'When the UK industrial base largely collapsed what could we do?' Harvey-Jones asks plaintively. 'We had either to shut down the whole bloody company or export to survive'. Scarcely half of ICI's sales and profits now generate from Britain, and half of these come from customers abroad.
>
> But exports, always vulnerable to exchange rates, can only be pushed so far. Increasingly ICI must sell to 'leading edge companies' which need advanced chemistry to fuel their own growth.
>
> 'Sadly this country does not have a very large number of world competitive manufacturing organisation. We are,' said Harvey-Jones, 'one of the few still hanging in there by the skin of our inventive teeth.'
>
> Pride and bitterness punctuate the assessment and he added finally: 'I have to go where the wealth can be created – that is right – and if the wealth isn't being created in the UK then I can buck the trend a bit – but I cannot buck the trend indefinitely.'[2]

Not only was ICI compelled to locate plant abroad in order to maintain its competitive edge in overseas markets, but it was also forced into bidding for control in overseas companies, such as the chemical division of Beatrice, one of the largest corporations in the United States: 'The buying spree is not over. ICI still has another billion dollars to spend on strategic acquisitions in the United States or Japan in areas like genetic engineering, advanced polymers and clever chemicals bought by the electronics industry.'

The processes which have been drawing ICI into overseas engagements are repeated throughout the economy. The top 50 British manufacturers increased their overseas production by a quarter in the first two years of the Thatcher administration. Their British workforce fell by half a million, while their overseas workforce increased. The abolition of exchange controls saw an outflow of £50 billion, during the lifetime of the first Thatcher administration, and by 1984 British foreign investment had reached an annual total of £15 billion. In such conditions, slump was no mild laxative for domestic British capitalism. The result is a degree of devastation which recovery will be super-humanly difficult, and that is why it will not be easy for trade unions to regain the overall initiative, even if the very unevenness of economic processes will afford them more scope in some sheltered areas than they have in others, more exposed.

Such industrial disputes as do break out will tend to have an increasingly overt political significance, if only because they are likely to become more unusual events. They are also likely to attract messy and costly legal actions, which will be calculated still further to restrict union influence. Where such strikes do erupt, their public relations will assume hitherto unimagined levels of significance. Public opinion will become a vital force in the power balance between labour and capital. This is particularly true when public employees are forced to take industrial action, often in areas where this is a most uncommon event. Here, not only the downward pressure of earnings, but the continued threat of cuts in funding and reductions in levels of service will be a continuous invitation to trade unions representing public service workpeople to seek alliances with users and beneficiaries of the services in which they work. A new political emphasis is thus likely to develop, as a normal part of this process of collective bargaining. But in wide areas of industry things are likely to be very different, as the new laws squeeze out all but the most desperate urges to resistance.

As we have been arguing throughout this book, this implies that the trade union movement needs to change gear, into concerted action on the political plane. Above all, this must involve legislative action to recover employment. During the lifetime of the first Thatcher Parliament, Labour's response became generally known under the title 'The Alternative Economic Strategy'. We have written elsewhere at some length on the problems involved in this strategy, (see the

publications of the Institute for Workers' Control from 1970 onwards)
but here it is only necessary to emphasize one thing: that each year
during which monetarist policies remain in force will be a year of further
debilitation, so that the scope for effective national remedies is being
constantly eroded. Year by year, it becomes increasingly obvious that
convergent international action has become an absolute priority for those
who seek reflation, redistribution and recovery.

Most major British trade unions have given a degree of support to the
proposals outlined by Stuart Holland in *Out of Crisis*, a programme for
European recovery elaborated with the help of socialist economists and
finance ministers from the entire arc of Western Europe.[3] The basic
thinking of this programme was summarized as the economic section
of the election manifesto of the European Confederation of Socialist
Parties during their campaign for the European Assembly elections in
1984.[4]

The core of its strategy is to link public spending and planning in a
way that can promote recovery not only by yesterday's Keynesian
methods, but also by systematic redistribution of resources, calculated
to increase demand simultaneously in the depressed areas to which new
aid would go, in the impoverished and low paid sections of the
community to whom priority assistance would be given, and in the
public services whose growth would also reinforce a multiplier effect
from the bottom upwards. Orthodox Keynesians, who are beginning to
recover their voices, silent for so long during the early years of Mrs
Thatcher's rule, have more recently argued that growth is the key to
the maintenance of social equity.[5] But the *Out of Crisis* project, while
affirming the need for growth, insists that redistribution itself can be
a crucial means by which such growth can be secured and sustained.

Redistribution can move resources from richer to poorer, from
developed to less developed regions, from private to public services and
from men to women. Depending on its extent, it can often stimulate
precisely the most depressed sectors. Slum clearance, for instance,
means work in the construction industry, stimulating demand at home
for materials which are largely home-produced, and employing a large
workforce. Increases in the consumption of the poor attract less imports,
too, than do increases in luxury consumption.

From the simplest areas to the most complex, a variety of attempts
have been made by national governments to pursue policies not
dissimilar from those advanced by, say, Mr Peter Walker, or the alliance
of senior politicians in the Employment Institute which was launched
in April 1985. Tentative efforts were made in the first years of the Social
Contract under Harold Wilson after 1974. Bolder experiments were made
under President Mitterand in France. The hazard is always the same.
The growth of consumer demand sucks in imports which contribute

to someone else's recovery, but which damage one's own balance of payments. In due course, there arrives a deputation from the International Monetary Fund, and recovery policies give place to retrenchment, disillusion and defeat. But were there, in Western Europe, several socialist or Labour governments committed to the same expansionary policies in convergent action involving planned growth, public intervention and serious reallocation of resources, things could be different. Adverse trade balances could be underwritten by joint agreement of those whose economies were benefiting from them. In place of beggar my neighbour, the current rule of slump, we could enter an era of better my neighbour, and the beginning of the new recovery.[6]

Naturally, these interesting ideas appeal to trade union leaders, who favour the maintenance of the post-war consensus which established the welfare state, bargained corporatism and all the other institutions which entered crisis while Mrs Thatcher's forces were grouping themselves for the kill. But the redistribution which will really guarantee sustained recovery is not simply a redistribution of payments; it is a redistribution of social power, inventing new forms of democratic planning which can truly begin to socialize the entrepreneurial function. Post-war indicative planning has not succeeded, and the expansion of corporate institutions has not extended the democratic reach, either of trade union members, or of community organizations, anything like as far as educational advance implies they should go. At the turn of the century pessimists argued that there was an iron law of oligarchy, which meant that the best we could hope for was that benevolent governors might displace less kindly ones. 'Socialists may triumph, but socialism never', was the watchword of Roberto Michels.[7] But Michels wrote at a time when English schoolchildren were being sent to work at the ages of 12 or 13 and literacy among working people was often rudimentary. The socialist parties studied by Michels set up higher academies for the training of 'orators'. Today's party schools teach more accessible and democratic skills. The mass media, for all their power of centralization, transmit information on a scale which was inconceivable even in 1945, let alone in 1900. Today's workpeople have already shown themselves quite capable of elaborating the most audacious social plans, co-ordinating the work of professional consultants with the irreplaceable insights of shop floor workpeople themselves. It is certainly arguable that the creative capacity of these workers is the main unused economic resource as we enter an age of computers and robotics. The trade unions should not therefore seek to re-enter yesterday, looking again only for access to high level planning decisions and centralized consultative bodies. Planning should reach to the top, but needs to begin at the bottom. Leaders need to emphasize their accountability as their principal qualification.

During the 1930s, planning was a concept almost completely dominated by models established in the Soviet Union. After all, had not the first and second five year plans brought that country from rural backwardness into advanced modern industrialism? The British expositors of Soviet successes were John Strachey or Sydney and Beatrice Webb. Strachey, in his most popular work, *The Nature of Capitalist Crisis*, saw such planning as the key element in his political analysis. He even went so far as to write: 'If it were true . . . that the fascists are the agents of a separate class, built to set up a workable economic system, which would end the present chronic state of crisis . . . then there would be a great deal to be said for the fascists'. This judgement flowed from the not unreasonable assumption that 'the master question' was 'whether the occurrence of crisis is accidental to or inherent in the capitalist system'. If slumps were accidental 'we shall certainly work for their gradual elimination by appropriate reforms. For who would be so mad as to recommend the scrapping of the system itself if the catastrophes which it is bringing upon us were remediable'.[8]

From their more systematic Fabianism, the Webbs arrived at a different focus on Soviet planning examples. The Communist Party, they thought, exercised through Gosplan and its related institutions, a 'vocation of leadership'.[9] Many other Fabians who were far more agnostic about Soviet institutions than the Webbs, none the less found this an entirely acceptable doctrine. After all, it required a high degree of professionalism, concentration of power and virtually unlimited authority for the elite in charge. Thus, throughout the 1930s, staunch anti-communists like Herbert Morrison consistently cited Soviet industial management methods as the justification for bureaucratic models of public enterprise. Morrison repeatedly sought to establish that the roots of his reform of London Transport could be traced to the Russian experiment.[10]

Communist doctrine also contains more radical models, however. It was Lenin who posed the profoundly disturbing question, 'Who – Whom? *Who* plans, for *whom*?

British civil servants or Soviet cadres have shown in a wide variety of situations that they are capable of organizing remarkably efficient operations on a grand scale. Central planning can succeed. But from the British ground nuts scheme in West Africa to the bizarre episode in Riazan Oblast,[11] central planning has also demonstrated a built-in tendency to muddle, waste and disorder on a heroic scale.

In 1957 Nikita Khrushchev launched a major policy initiative to improve Soviet agriculture. He began to insist that the Soviet Union could overtake the United States in the production of meat, milk and butter, within a mere three or four years. Such rash optimism almost cost him his job within a month, and so, in order to vindicate himself, he weighed in very heavily behind the Riazan Oblast committee when it sought to double meat production (and more) in 1959. The result was disastrous. The slaughter of livestock soon ran ahead of local capacity to maintain replacement rates. Farm managers bought in cattle from as far away as the Urals. Funds earmarked for machinery and development had to be illegally diverted in order to take in more and more livestock purchases. Even the tax system was converted to a meat standard. Meat, milk and butter quickly disappeared from all the shops in the Oblast, but it fulfilled its target by quadrupling meat production. The first secretary of the Oblast became a Hero of Socialist Labour, and received the Order of Lenin. The people of Riazan, starved of meat, watched their farming industry struggle to the point of collapse. When the inevitable inquiry was set in motion, too late, the unfortunate Hero of Socialist Labour shot himself at his office.

Cautionary tales like this may be multiplied on a large scale. One Soviet nail factory, finding itself in difficulty with the production of its quota, beat all its plan targets by manufacturing one two-ton nail, which, if not much use in the construction industry, weighed enough to earn everybody's bonus.

None of this argues that all centralism brings disorder. As President Reagan's advisers continuously assure us, Soviet military production is widely admired in the United States. The Chinese, by a prodigious concentration of resources and expertise, progressed from the detonation of a conventional nuclear weapon to the capacity to manufacture hydrogen bombs in the span of three years, a remarkably shorter time than that involved in the United States of the Soviet Union, both of which took ten years to make the same 'progress'.[12]

The problem with centralization is that it focuses the need for control inwards, placing impossible demands on the small group of those people who have become ultimately 'responsible'. Once industrial take-off has been achieved, and a complex modern society is in being, it is more and more difficult to administer all economic matters from one unchallengeable centre. That is why planning must base itself on the steadily increasing involvement of the widest democratic constituency, including workpeople and their trade unions, at every possible level. The same workpeople are, of course, also consumers, although their interests as consumers are more difficult to organize. All planning involves a process of matching needs to resources. Democracy is the process by which a large number of social needs are given the possibility of making themselves known. The interests of consumers in the housing, health, education and wider social services may thus be established in a proliferation of pressure groups. In the private sector of consumption, market pressures may be reinforced by public controls over standards, quality and accurate information. These operate in a different way from the pressure groups, by establishing checks and balances rather than by extending representative influence and power. But the simplest device among all the others open to popular planning is that of direct workpeople's involvement, either in a system of planning agreements in which trade unions negotiate with their managers on a wide range of management objectives, or in the development of workers' alternative plans such as that pioneered by the shop stewards of Lucas Aerospace.[13]

Shop stewards' corporate plans have involved a study by employees of the resources, output potential and outlets for products of the companies in which they work. Normally, when such plans have emerged, this has been in firms involved in the arms industry, when it has been threatened by changes in patterns of military spending. Such workers are often trained in the use of high technology, as were those at Lucas. The call for socially useful employment rather than redundancy is exceptionally poignant in such circumstances. The Lucas plan itself began as a mode of resistance to redundancies: but it became far more than that. In addition to bargaining about wages and conditions, the Lucas stewards began to make claims about the social use of labour, about the direction of collective efforts, the social objectives to be pursued by the entire corporation.

They developed proposals for 150 new products. Some of these related to the needs of welfare services, and would have been financed (like the new kidney machines which were proposed, or the hob cart for the victims of spina bifida) by the appropriate parts of the National Health Service. Others were designed for sale on the open market. Among these were a range of wind generators, and a hybrid power pack which made possible non-polluting engines. This pack involved a very small internal combustion engine which charged a stack of batteries operating an electric motor. The most famous of the Lucas projects, the road rail car, has been taken up by British Rail in prototype, and may be observed racing up and down branch lines in remote rural areas. In all 1,200 pages of such blueprints emerged from a truly unprecedented effort of consultation by the Lucas shop stewards.

First they wrote to 180 leading authorities and institutions, seeking advice. How could the Lucas workforce, with its given skills, its age, the levels of its training, and the standards of its actual equipment, be redeployed into continued and useful effort, after the retrenchment of military production? Only four people from this exalted list of experts offered actual practical assistance. At this point, writes Mike Cooley, 'we then did what we should have done in the first instance: we asked our own members what they thought they should be making'. A questionnaire was sent to all the shop stewards' committees in the combine, and the result which emerged was six volumes covering a new project range, and containing detailed engineering drawings, costings and technical details.

The Lucas project emerged during the Wilson–Callaghan administration, and attracted virtually unanimous support from the Labour Party Conference, together with almost total indifference at the level of government. The stewards were nominated for a Nobel Prize by workers' organizations in Germany and Sweden, but in due course Mike Cooley was dismissed by Lucas, and abandoned by the leaders of his trade union, the AUEW/TASS. A prophet is not without honour . . .

To some degree the career of Mike Cooley encapsulates what has happened to the argument about industrial democracy in Britain. Evicted from his job, this most creative shop steward took refuge in the Greater London Enterprise Board, set up by the local government in London to initiate economic development. This pioneering institution has since been imitated by a number of other local authorites, including those in South Yorkshire and the West Midlands. Similar initiatives were undertaken at a lower level by the councils in Cleveland, Lancashire and West Yorkshire. The GLC established GLEB under outside directorship, while some of the other enterprise boards were set up under the direct control of elected members.

Local enterprise boards devoted themselves to industrial rescue, the establishment of co-operatives and new forms of enterprise and the protection of employment. They are 'not a utopian strategy for the long term, to be pursued under ideal conditions, with a committed Labour Government. They are designed to function, here and now, in the present . . . and so, when London saves 120 jobs in a furniture factory, or West Midlands saves a foundry, it is not just a little investment decision: it is the propaganda of practice'.[14]

As more and more local authorities follow the initiative of Mike Ward and the GLC, the trade unions will become increasingly familiar with the challenge and opportunities offered by local planning mechanisms: this can only be helpful. But the process must be joined to reciprocal exchanges, both at national and international level, if it is to be properly effective.

The Development of Industrial Democracy

The argument for company law reform to increase trade union involvement in industrial decision-making was given a notable impulse by European draft legislation. The British TUC was pushed into a long discussion as a result of the preparation of a draft statute for the structure of a European limited company. This stimulated the TUC to advance its own proposals for industrial democracy, which, if they had succeeded, would have raised collective bargaining to a new level.

The commitment to formal structures of industrial democracy, enabling accountable trade union representatives to be elected on to the boards of companies, reached a high point in the earliest years of the Labour government of 1974 onwards. The TUC had been persuaded of the need for counter proposals to put against the draft for a European company law, which sought to generalize a modified version of the German system of co-determination.

British trade unions objected to German 'Mitbestimmung' on three grounds of principle. First, they believed that any elections for worker directors should be held through the established trade union machinery, in order to avoid a situation in which the workers' voices could be divided through divergent or even contradictory channels of representation. Secondly, they objected to the intrusion of company works councils which might undermine the unique representative role of the British shop steward system.

Thirdly, the unions did not wish to participate in a minority role: they saw workpeople's involvement in company boards as an extension of normal collective bargaining in which there are two possible 'votes': 50–50 or 100 per cent. Fifty–fifty is a 'failure to agree', and constitutes a veto. A hundred per cent is an agreement, on which consensus harmonious action is possible. Most radically, the TUC insisted that this 50–50 board, with its enshrined veto power for the trade union side, should assume legal supremacy in company law, overriding the authority of the shareholders' meeting. With a wealth of supporting arguments, the TUC prepared a succession of drafts for industrial democracy laws, and when the Labour government came to office it was pledged to legislate along these lines. The most significant apostasy of that government was its refusal to do any such thing. Instead Harold Wilson set up the Bullock Commission to report on how such legislation could be framed, and then procrastinated for long enough to ensure that action on its recommendations became impossible. Harold Wilson was undoubtedly influenced to follow this course of action by some quite blatant threats which came from the City and the CBI, of a 'strike of capital', should the TUC proposals be enacted.

The actual proposals of the Bullock Commission were an important dilution of the TUC's original policies.[15] Notably, Bullock recommended the creation of an intermediary group of directors to be nominated by consensus of both shareholders' and employees representatives, and to hold the balance between the two groups. This, the famous '2x + y' formula, was much discussed at the time, but it did not actually persuade any employers' organizations of the acceptability of such a reform. Indeed, they maintained a strenuous lobby against the whole idea of industrial democracy by legislation. By contrast, the Bullock compromise was often cited by trade unionists as a reason for cooling their ardour for reform. The most important proposal of the Bullock team tended to be submerged beneath the commentary on the idea of an intermediary 'y' group of directors. In fact, basing itself no doubt on the strategic sense of Jack Jones, certainly the most far-sighted trade union leader of his time, the Commission had devised an arrangement of joint representative councils to co-ordinate the trade union input to company board elections. These joint councils would have provided a framework up to the company level which would have been a most notable legislative contribution to the development of trade union influence and unity, by generalizing and facilitating through legal authority the emergence of the equivalent of shop steward combine committees.

The TUC's proposals for legislation on industrial democracy were an attempt to secure legislative expression for a vast secular movement based on full employment. The growth of plant bargaining and of workplace initiative by shop stewards was founded on the decisive fact that employers were competing for labour. Attempts to subordinate shop stewards to managerial interests were recurrent throughout the whole period of post-war industrial relations, but they met with only the most ephemeral success. Full employment was the continual refresher of trade union independence, the stream from which trade union initiative was constantly renewed.

Collective bargaining might be thought to have reached its highest point in this movement, which foundered in the rejection of Bullock's proposals. Now it has fallen far below that peak.

It is quite clear that the British unions were right to believe that shop stewards' organizations, working during full employment, had at least as much power as the worker directors in the German system of Mitbestimmung. However, Mitbestimmung is an institution fixed by law, and this means that it is equipped with a ratchet which maintains it in being even during times of economic adversity. Accordingly, today, it is by no means clear that British shop stewards have not been pushed some distance behind their German colleagues, by the weight of mass unemployment.

The force of institutional arrangements can be measured in a British experience, as well as in Germany. Industrial tribunals in Britain, while far from perfect in their functioning, have succeeded in restricting unfair dismissals, even though unemployment has reached unprecedented levels. Without idealizing these institutions, it is clear that their influence is not confined to the court room. Fear of what they might do persuades many employers to behave better than they would wish to have to behave, and restrains some delinquents by encouraging them to negotiate in order to avoid the judgment of the tribunal. Without the tribunals, few can doubt that there would be far more arbitrary dismissals, far more capriciously carried through. That is to say, there is something for the use of the legal ratchet mechanism. It is difficult, however, simply to revive Lord Bullock's proposals, although parts of them are certainly worthy of revival. Company law reform re-enters the agenda through another EEC initiative, for opening the books of (particularly) multinational companies to trade union scrutiny. This initiative, known by the name of its initiator, Vredeling, represents a typical EEC response, a lowest common denominator, but it could, for all that, stimulate renewed debate in Britain and elsewhere. In this debate, the Confederation of British Industry and the British government will find themselves increasingly isolated. At a time when all kinds of sanctions have been taken against trade union independence, Vredeling's hypercautious proposals have been stonewalled, while both governments and employers sing hymns to the 'progress' of 'voluntary' development of 'employee participation'. Such progress is not very visible.

To link the development of planning agreements and popular planning networks with company law reform is not at all a difficult task, when construed at the purely intellectual level; but it is rather more difficult in practice. Unions will need to study the rapid growth of planning agreements in Greece, Spain and elsewhere, in order to evaluate the contribution they make. Planning agreements as a control mechanism within multinational corporations will, in any case, presuppose international trade union cooperation. The term 'planning agreement' has now entered every European language, but we still await any detailed study of the working of the concept. As for linkages across frontiers: at this level they have hardly begun. If trade unions are to make their effective contribution to the recovery of employment, then the growth of constructive industrial democracy is quite imperative, in order to reach into cooperation of this kind. Mass unemployment is so awful that people find it hard to concentrate their minds on how things ought to be: but the problem will not simply go away, and indeed will get worse until an alternative politics can win strength to impose itself.

Most political campaigning relates to existing institutions, parliaments or local authorities. But international campaigning has no adequate institutions around which to focus. The limits of the European Community are exposed in the wisecrack by one of its opponents, that its title contained three misrepresentations: it was not European, nor economic, nor a community. Certainly the EEC leaves out an important part of that Europe which must learn to cooperate if it is to seize the initiative for economic recovery. Further, the institutions of the Common Market are grossly distorted in that it gives much less weight to employment policy than to the Common 'Agricultural Policy'.

There is no reason, however, why trade union and Labour movement cooperation should exclusively polarize around the EEC or any other existing international forum. On the goals of reflation, redistribution and regeneration, trade unions could easily define common objectives which could be set within the framework of convergent national policies both by unions and sympathetic governments. This is broadly the approach of *Out of Crisis*. But the growth of local authority enterprise in Britain is also matched by an existing tradition in many European countries. Cannot trade unions participate with towns in encouraging local planning, and trade between regional enterprise units? When first trade unions met across frontiers, they established a new institution, albeit, for a long time, a fairly unstable one. If urban and regional planning bodies were brought together with the trade unions, their meeting could be more than simply propaganda. This is the significance of the Russell Foundation's appeal entitled *Europe Against Unemployment*, launched from Britain in the first half of 1985 (see appendix 8.1).

This appeal seeks to provide a means for linking actions at the most primary local levels with a national and international convergence of planning policy. The aim is to restore full employment.

As we said in the opening chapter of this book, there are two parts to any approach to this goal. On the one hand, it is necessary to secure economic recovery; on the other, there have to be systematic reductions in working time, in the hours of the working week, in the length of the working year, and in the span of the working lifetime. To maintain the capacity to organize for participation in planning, unions will need to inspire their members with confidence that they can also win serious improvements in this other field as well. Moreover to prevent the erosion of their base by unemployment, they will need to claw back, by legislative means, some of the powers they have lost in the adverse labour market.

International action of the kind proposed in the Europe Against Unemployment appeal has, therefore, many precedents, from the International Working Men's Association onwards. It calls, however, for the overcoming of inertias and practical obstacles which have always seemed particularly daunting for the insular and unilingual British. But these deterrents are more apparent than real. Transport facilities are now such that the efforts required to stage meetings and conferences involving representatives from the whole continent of Europe are today no greater than those facing the Victorian trade unionists who travelled the length and breadth of Britain to constitute national trade unions, the TUC and Chartist conventions and national rallies. In the USA the distances involved in running nationwide political and trade union functions have always been no greater than those required to encompass the territory of Europe.

It is true that, at the other end of the Victorian railway journey, the delegates who assembled all spoke the same language; but the problem of multilingual assemblies of trade unionists, socialists and municipal authorities can be overcome; there are many precedents to encourage this conclusion. Poles, French, British, Germans and Italians combined more than 100 years ago, and found means to communicate together in the First International. Trade union secretariats already function effectively in Europe, handling the language problem as they have developed. And most recently, the European Nuclear Disarmament Conventions of the 1980s have proved that translation and interpretation facilities can be provided, even by a voluntary movement with the most limited finances.

Moreover, the cultural imperialism which elevated the English language to top place in international discourse, while its origins are to be deplored, makes the British contribution to international dialogue the easiest to accomplish. This is not to encourage complacency in Britain: we have to demand that language courses, in French, German, Spanish and Italian be added to the curriculum of trade union education if we are to be seen to take the international discussions of our future campaigns with proper seriousness.

If international cooperation is now urgent, the success of any trade union strategy needs to be measured by its capacity to involve wider and wider participation by members. It is within this spirit that it is necessary to develop a whole series of political campaigns, deeply rooting them in every workplace.

Minimum Wages

The more restricted becomes the scope for conventional industrial action, the more necessary becomes the option of political organization. As we have already argued, compulsory political fund ballots challenge this process, but they also reinforce it. If any unions lose one ballot, they will need to institute another. The more successful they are in campaigning for legislative reforms on matters which are close to their members' interests, the more confirmed becomes their members' political commitment. Large scale campaigns for a legal minimum wage, or for shorter working time will teach trade unionists important lessons. Who favours their interests, and who opposes them? Politics in such campaigns are not about remote and abstract, not to say dogmatic, notions, but about real and necessary issues.

In 1985, a former Labour Leader, James Callaghan, took issue with an article by a trade union officer in the Party's newspaper, *Labour Weekly*.[17] Dealing with the impending abolition of the Wages

Councils, and the gross deterioration of the legal protection of low paid workers as a result of the nullification of the Fair Wages Resolution, Mr Callaghan argued that a national minimum wage had become an unavoidable response for the Labour Party. This argument has, of course, a long history, but Mr Callaghan is essentially right, that whatever might have been the case during the years of boom, the conditions of the low paid during a prolonged and intractable slump have become a major scandal, and require priority action from any reforming government.

At the beginning of 1984, the Trade Union Congress had to revise its guidelines on low pay. Basing itself on the notion that anyone receiving less than two-thirds of the average male manual earnings is in jeopardy, the TUC recommended that negotiators treat £98 a week as the figure below which low pay is defined. For a family, a weekly income of this much may well hover very close to the official poverty line. None the less, very many workers receive far less than this, including innumerable governmental employees.

The gap between the highest and lowest paid people has been constantly widened through Mrs Thatcher's years of office. Partly this results from generalized economic pressures in which the weakest have gone to the wall. There has been an insistent propaganda from the more neanderthal ministers blaming unemployment on 'high wage rates' and insisting on the withdrawal from ILO conventions designed to protect poorer people.

Not only ministers have been seeking to end the vestigial protection for low paid workers. A *Times* Leader[17] claimed that Wages Councils 'tend to price young people out of jobs' and should therefore be done away with. A clear refutation of this unedifying argument is quite simple: the earnings of young people have fallen relative to those of adults since the middle 1970s, while youth unemployment has risen rapidly and continuously. Wage cutting has been illegally imposed in the Young Workers' Scheme, which we discussed in Chapter 1. Employers who are willing to do this do not have to show that the young people in question are newly employed, still less that they are undergoing any training. The subsidy is available on the sole understanding that the young people receive only the lowest imaginable pay. The House of Commons Public Accounts Committee reported in December 1983 that 77 per cent of the jobs which qualify for a Young Workers' Scheme subsidy would have been necessary whether or not the subsidy was available. The small number of jobs created, over and above these, were costing the government almost £5,500 apiece. The easiest way for employers to qualify for a subsidy is to cut the pay of young people already on the books, or to set on new young employees while getting rid of older ones.

The Times refers to a research paper of the Department of Employment which suggests that a 10 per cent cut in the wages of young people might produce up to 100,000 jobs for young people. But 80 per cent of these jobs would be created by displacement of older workers. In fact, low pay produces low demand, and itself contributes to the spiral of decline and slump.

The government's own view was encapsulated in a White Paper of 1983 (Cmnd 9111) on 'Regional Industrial Development':

> Imbalances between areas in employment opportunities should in principle be corrected by the natural adjustment of labour markets. In the first place, this should be through lower wages and unit costs than comparable work commands elsewhere. Wage flexibility, combined with a reputation for good work and a constructive attitude to productivity and industrial relations, would increase the attractiveness to industry of areas with high unemployment . . . The Government believe that wage bargaining must become more responsive to the circumstances of the individual enterprise, including its location. Their policies of privatisation, together with a reduction in the power of trade unions to act against their own members' interests, should help to achieve this.

This is a very open attack on the trade union principle of the rate for the job (the common rate), as well as another typical expression of that government belief that workers are 'pricing themselves out of work'. Mrs Thatcher herself has abrasively enunciated this belief, as in this extract from a 1980 pronouncement: 'If excessive wage demands are granted, one of two things will happen. Either workers price their products out of the market and lose their jobs, or, if they are in a monopoly industry and can hold the country to ransom, end up destroying the jobs of others'. Novice students of economics could identify the flaws in this argument as a useful, if not too difficult, early exercise.

A very large proportion of the low paid are women, and 1½ million of them are public service employees. No doubt this accounts for the strong traditional support in the National Union of Public Employees for legislation to establish an official minimum earnings level. However, other trade unions have been slow to support this call. One reason for their reluctance is that women workers are less fully organized than men, and inadequately represented on the governing councils and in the annual conferences of unions in which they make up a large part of the membership. But a more acceptable reason for trade union reluctance to seek legislation on pay levels is quite simply that many unions feel that such legislation might remove the pressure on low paid workers to belong to a union. If such workers felt that their earnings were protected solely by government intervention would they see the necessity to continue to pay trade union subscriptions? This argument has, over many years, been heard in the debate among farm workers. They are covered by a Wages Council, which they often cite as a sufficient reason to explain the difficulties of maintaining trade union membership in their industry. But, whatever the explanation in such particular cases (and low-level unionism in farming has other causes), a *general* statute on minimum pay, for which the trade unions sustained a public campaign, would have a different effect on trade union consciousness; it would bring the issue out of the obscure, marginalized areas of Wages Council industries, into the centre of political controversy and debate, the position which it occupies in countries like France.

From the point of view of the Labour Party, this timidity on the part of affiliated unions has been a liability. Legislation would have been the quickest way to win support among legions of presently apathetic and non-political low paid workers. Hundreds of thousands of women's votes would mobilize themselves in its favour.

On 12 April 1983, a Bill was tabled in the House of Commons by Michael Meacher, Stuart Holland and a number of other Members of Parliament. It offered an ingenious solution to the problem which had for so long divided the unions. The Bill would establish a 'minimum fair wage', which at the time in question it fixed at £100 a week, based on a normal stint of 40 hours. Employers would be required to enter into negotiations with appropriate trade unions in order to implement this fair wage. Employers of part time workers would be compelled to concede a basic hourly rate proportionate to the minimum full time wage.

Negotiations would begin within 12 months of the passing of the Act, and would need to be completed within two years of that time. The Act would only apply to the wages of employees who were represented by a TUC-affiliated union at relevant negotiations. This stipulation at once removes the main trade union objection to a legal minimum wage, since it preserves the union's crucial space in representing its members' interests.

Of course, employers have always argued that a national minimum would squeeze out many jobs, by pricing inefficient companies out of their markets. The Fair Wage Act would meet this argument by providing for government financial assistance to companies which could not otherwise implement the new law. If the implementation of the Act would lead to redundancies or the closure of the company, then financial assistance would be made available subject to an economic audit according to Treasury criteria, which would be agreed with the Departments of Industry and Employment and the appropriate trade unions. If the employer was reluctant to apply for such assistance, then the trade union would be empowered to require him to do so, or alternatively to apply themselves for assistance on the basis of the conversion of the company to a cooperative or municipal enterprise.

A new British law to establish a compulsory basic wage would bring Britain into compliance with the European Social Charter, which lays down that 'all workers have the right to a fair remuneration, sufficient for a decent standard of living for themselves and their families . . . the exercise of these rights shall be achieved by freely concluded collective agreements, by statutory wage fixing machinery or by other means appropriate to national conditions'. Statutory machinery has operated in France since 1950, and in the Netherlands since 1945. In Belgium, there is a national minimum wage agreement between the trade unions and employers' organizations, within the framework of the National Labour Council, which is a statutory body. All three countries have linked their minimum rates to the Consumer Price Index, but only in France and the Netherlands are there arrangements to modify the national minimum alongside general living standards.

Numerous analysts have commented on the influence of minimum wage legislation in France. Obviously Mitterrand's promise to raise minimum wage levels by 10 per cent under the existing French legislation played an important part in the changeover which brought him to office. The promised measure was duly introduced in June 1981. The new larger minimum immediately benefited more than one-third of the labour force in the clothing industry (although less than one-tenth had been covered by it before the increase). In the field of personal services the new minima covered almost one-half the labour force after the increase, although less than one-quarter had been protected before. In Britain, previous minimum wage protection has always been piecemeal, so that the absence of a statutory national figure has made it very difficult to generalize the protection of low paid workers.

The only significant improvement which is needed by the Fair Wage Bill is that it should state a clear and precise hourly minimum when it is prescribing for part time workers. In every other sense, the Meacher/Holland draft provides a perfect instrument for dealing with that crucially significant part of Britain's economy which is directly attributable to low pay.[18]

As we have already argued, low paid workers will not respond simply like donkeys to the carrot offered by a political campaign for a national minimum. They are intelligent, and often well-educated people. They will observe not only who helps them, but also who hinders them.

Shorter Working Time by Law

There is a classic example of a campaign by trade unionists for political solutions to industrial problems. It was born in the heyday of the new unions, towards the end of the last century, and, we should never forget it was linked with a major development of labour internationalism. The first modern May Day demonstrations were summoned around the international demand for a legal eight-hour day. Responding to a call of the American Federation of Labour, the Paris Congress, which constituted the Second International in 1889, proposed that the 1 May 1890 be the occasion for worldwide demonstrations for shorter working time. The London May Day demonstration was an extraordinary success, and as a result there emerged a pressure group for the 'legal eight hours'.[19] There was an unremitting campaign to persuade the TUC to support legislation bringing in an eight-hour day. Tom Mann became known all over the country as the most persistent advocate of this cause. His first pamphlet was called *What a Compulsory Eight Hour Day Means*,[20] but he was soon diversifying to explore the possibilities of local political action to enforce reductions in the working day. Sydney Webb followed Tom Mann into print, with a major study entitled *The Eight Hours' Day*.[21] William Morris was involved in a joint appeal by the different socialist groupings to centre attention on an eight-hour Bill. During this campaign, throughout the early part of the 1890s, Liberal voters among that relatively small part of the working class which was enfranchised were forced to think and think again. The eight-hour agitation drew support from working people, but it divided politicians along a distinctly radical axis. Trade unionists learned about the fickleness of their traditional alliances, and became steadily more ready to rely on their own resources.

There can be no doubt that this agitation played a major part in turning over the ground in which the new Labour Party was later to grow. Of course, in the last years of the century, the unions were strongly on the defensive as a result of an outbreak of provocations orchestrated by the employers' organizations. But the Second International was still emphasizing that the eight-hour day was the most crucial demand of all the parts of its immediate programme when it conferred in London in 1896. The engineers' lock-out the following year, while responding to the attacks of the employers, still felt able to make this call their main priority, thus joining an offensive of their own to the defensive manoeuvres they were forced to undertake. Once people had decided to try to found a committee for the representation of labour, they discovered that employers' onslaughts, such as that of Taff Vale, could actually assist them in their work. But the eight-hour movement had established the need for separate representation in a constructive way, and without this example the opening years of Labour history might have been altogether different.

No doubt it is time to reinvent this movement. Perhaps our middle-term strategy, to be reached partly by legislation of longer holidays, and partly by collective bargaining, is for a working year of 1,000 hours.

In 1981, the TUC adopted a motion moved by Clive Jenkins of ASTMS instructing the General Council to campaign for a limit on the number of hours worked annually, reducing the working week 'by statute to a maximum of 35 hours', providing a 'minimum holiday entitlement of six weeks per annum, plus sabbatical leave after a stipulated number of years for all employees' and reducing 'the qualifying age for retirement pensions to 60 years'. In an eloquent support for this case, Clive Jenkins showed that engineering workers in Sweden were, at the time, working 1,500 hours annually, while in Belgium and Germany they were working 1,600 and 1,700 hours respectively. But 'the British engineering worker is working 1,902 hours a year.'[22]

We must face it that there are a number of difficulties about implementing the call for a statute to fix a 35-hour week. Even though unemployment waxes, institutional overtime in British industry never wanes. In December 1982, while 3 million people were already out of work, British manufacturing industry worked 9.66 million hours of overtime. In December 1983, this figure had risen to 11.36 million hours, whilst the incidence of short time had fallen from 1.61 million hours at the end of 1982 to 0.46 million at the end of 1983. If it became magically possible to outlaw overtime, overnight a quarter of a million new jobs could be created. The number would increase as working hours were reduced. Negotiations have been tending to secure reductions in agreed working hours, even though these are often not reflected in reductions in actual hours worked.

The TUC has been carefully monitoring progress and publishing a regular progress report. By 1983, it had monitored 57 separate agreements, reducing hours by varying amounts from 40 down to 39 and 36½. Only one agreement was reported implementing a 35-hour week, in the exhibition industry, but this does not take effect until 1987.

The killer in this process is, of course, overtime. Overtime is concentrated and does not fall equally across the labour force. Workers who are doing overtime are, thus, normally, doing far more than the average hours of overtime. From April 1981 to April 1982, the average weekly hours of overtime per male manual worker actually rose from 4.5 to 4.9, having fallen the previous year. But average overtime hours per male manual overtime worker rose from 9.5 to 9.7 during the same period. The following year both these statistics fell, back to 4.7 and 9.3 respectively. The TUC is well aware of this problem, which continues to be intractable. Indeed, in February 1984 it pointed out the fact that the percentage of workers who do overtime has actually been rising since 1981 from 46.8 to 49.8. The small decline in the number of overtime hours is more likely to reflect the depression than the results of trade union limitations. And in their scrutiny of these figures, the TUC tell us that 'the tendency . . . for the percentage of people working overtime to rise from April 1981 must be a matter of concern'.

The agreed basic weekly hours have been slowly declining, and manual male workers now average a 39.2 hour week, compared to 39.9 hours which they would have expected to work in 1979. The following conclusions have been drawn by TUC researchers from the movement of working hours during recent years: men who are manual workers work a lot longer than other people. They average a 44 hour week, of which five hours are overtime. But the average is misleading, because half the manual male workers do not work any overtime, which means that the other half who do, average 9½ hours of it a week. Women manual workers average 39.7 hours, of which only one hour is overtime. Only one-fifth of these women workers get any overtime at all, and so they average 6 hours of it a week. Non-manual working men work some 38½ hours, of which 1½ are overtime; but only one-fifth of these people actually do work overtime, which means that those who get it average 6 hours a week. Non-manual women workers are on a 36½ hour week, of which only half-an-hour is overtime, and in fact only 12 per cent of these women get to work overtime at all, and they average 3 hours a week.

Between 1979 and 1983 the total hours worked by men who were manual workers declined by 2⅓, of which 1.6 were accounted for by a decline in the availability of overtime. Decline among other groups was very much less significant.

The TUC's campaign, and the efforts of affiliated unions, have effectively broken through the barrier of the 40-hour basic week, and it is clear that legislation could make a major contribution if only the unions could agree on how it should be framed. The problem is extremely simple to state, and very difficult to solve. Trade unionists will not say thank you for a law which cuts their earnings, and if overtime is forbidden then approximately half the male manual workers will be much worse off unless they are compensated for its loss. There is a very strong need for parliamentary draftsmen to consult with the TUC, if the Congress resolution of 1981 is to be implemented.

During the Referendum on British membership of the EEC, and then again in the first elections for the European Assembly, according to those who favoured Britain's adherence to the Common Market, a cornucopia of benefits was expected to open. Perhaps the most prominent among these was the benefit of increased holiday time. It was pointed out that

Europeans enjoyed far better holiday entitlements than British workers: that they had longer annual vacations and more of them; that their statutory holidays outnumbered ours, sometimes by two or three times. The same TUC resolution of 1981 which sought a statutory 35-hour week also addressed the problem of holiday starvation which afflicts workers in British industry. But when we look at the problem with care, it seems very clear that legislation to standardize holiday entitlements is very much easier than legislation on weekly hours to be worked. Basic annual holiday entitlement in France and the Netherlands run at 5 weeks, and in many enterprises in Italy this is also true. Ninety per cent of workers in West Germany have obtained six weeks or more annual holiday.

The TUC's official objective of six weeks holiday is in fact a modest one, although it would represent a substantial improvement in the conditions of most workers. It would be relatively simple to legislate a statutory holiday entitlement of six weeks. It would even be feasible to legislate to enlarge the size of the labour force in every firm by an amount commensurate with the increase in holiday entitlement. To invent an example which embodies the principle simply: if we were to legislate to give every person an additional month's holiday, it might well be possible simultaneously to require every employer to expand his or her labour force by ten per cent. This would at once create some two million jobs, even allowing for the fact that some smaller employers would slip between the mesh on a net which would have to be loosely stung. Any such large redeployment of formerly unemployed people would liberate vast sums of dole money which could be used to ease the burdens of those employers who fell into resultant difficulties. Here a similar principle could be invoked to that we have already discussed in connection with the 1983 Fair Wage Bill. Of course, some people will argue that a month's additional holiday is a dramatically overgenerous improvement in conditions. In that case, we could opt for a fortnight's additional improvement, and a five per cent increase in the size of labour forces. Indeed, we could create a sliding scale, upwards or downwards, aimed at directly facilitating work sharing without loss of pay.

The Campaign for Shorter Working Time in Western Europe

In West Germany, the trade union campaign for the 35-hour week was to become the most severe and important struggle in which that hitherto quiescent labour movement had engaged since 1945. British trade unions promised solidarity with it. The German unions case was developed with characteristic comprehensiveness. They argued the job creation potential of a shorter work week, calling for commensurate new jobs to replace the hours 'lost' by the reduction in working time. They also pointed to its beneficial effects on health and safety, and on the equalization of domestic duties within family life as male workers in particular obtained more free time. They looked forward to the liberating effect upon social awareness of a decisive breach in the customary trade union goal of 'eight hours work, eight hours sleep and eight hours play'. The German metalworkers strike of 1984 makes a pointed contrast with the British miners strike, not only because it won an important breakthrough, but also because it was oriented outwards at winning public opinion as a major strategic objective.[23]

In Western Europe, there is a widespread debate, amounting to a ferment, over the reduction of working time.[24] Much of this movement has received governmental and EEC support. In September 1984 the European Parliament passed a resolution, moved by the Socialist group, calling on the EEC Commission to 'support forthwith all trade union and management initiatives likely to provide industries, individual undertakings and regions with suitable approaches to the reorganization and reduction of working time'. It also called for the 'opening of a European Commission Inquiry into the structure of the working week in Europe and possibly the creation of an observation centre whose role would be to provide information'.

Many agreements, however, have been made bilaterally through union–employer negotiation. The objective is always clearly related to the creation of new employment. Not all the agreements are unambiguous in trade union terms; some reductions in working time have been paid for by loss of wages, or by wage freezes. Not all have led directly to increased employment. But there is in this trend the basis on which to build a concerted multinational trade union and labour campaign as a major contribution to full employment through work-sharing.

In Germany the trade union federation DGB adopted the 35-hour week policy in 1978. This was followed by a strike and lock-outs in the steel industry, which lasted six weeks. The settlement, which was adopted also by most of the private sector, introduced a standard six weeks annual leave entitlement which is now applicable throughout a large part of German industry: but the working week of 40 hours was retained at that stage. The engineering industry took up the campaign in 1984 with the largest post-war German strike, lasting seven weeks. The settlement provided for a cut in the working week to 38.5 hours from April 1985, without loss of pay.

IG Metall, the union which led the strike, regards the objective of the 35-hour week as an absolute priority, surpassing any advances in pay. The employers' opposition was fierce, and was endorsed by the government, both parties arguing that reduced working time would increase labour costs. They countered with offers of flexible working time, early retirement, part time work, and job sharing.

The arbitration award which ended the conflict provided that each company could negotiate its own interpretation of the terms; hours could vary between 37 and 40, but must average 38.5. Overtime up to 10 hours per week, with a limit of 20 hours per month, was permitted; this would normally be compensated with overtime rates of pay, but time off in lieu could be negotiated. An early retirement scheme was included in the deal, under which workers with 20 years' service might retire at 58 on 70 per cent of gross earnings, about 75 per cent of former net pay. The printing industry subsequently adopted the same terms.

The progress in West Germany over holiday entitlement in the early 1980s was spectacular (table 8.1). About 94 per cent of all employees covered by collective agreements in 1982 were entitled to additional holiday pay on top of their basic pay entitlement during annual holidays. It took the following forms; 42 per cent received a percentage of their basic holiday pay, averaging an additional 46 per cent; 33 per cent received a lump sum, averaging £148.50; 19 per cent received a fixed daily amount, averaging £6.05 per day. Ninety per cent of workers received a '13th month's salary', equivalent to 65 per cent of a month's salary, and 54 per cent of employees received full salary beyond the statutory six weeks' period in sickness. In 1983, the German government introduced legislation granting employees the right to opt for early retirement at age 59, through agreements negotiated by the trade unions. The following year, early retirement at 58 was supported by government subsidy. The employers' costs in pension payments are subsidized providing they take on unemployed people as replacements. Minimum early pension levels are at least 65 per cent of former gross earnings, or about 70 per cent of net earnings. The subsidy covers 35 per cent of the pension costs, up to 65 per cent of former earnings. Retirement at this age remains voluntary.

The Belgian government had set the pace for reduced working time linked to job creation in 1983, when it set a deadline for company or

Table 8.1 Improvement in holiday entitlement in West Germany

No. of weeks holiday	Percentage of employees		
	1980	1981	1982
3 but < 4	5	4	4
4 but < 5	22	19	13
5 but < 6	69	52	45
6 weeks	4	25	38

industry level agreements to cut working time by five per cent, with accompanying increases of three per cent in employment levels. Where no agreement was reached, companies must pay a penalty into a newly created Employment Fund. In the first few months, a total of between 50,000 and 60,000 jobs had been preserved or created, and agreements were made covering more than one million workers, embracing more than 90 per cent of the private sector. Volkswagen in Belgium provided 18 days additional holiday, equivalent to a reduction of average hours to 37 per week, accompanied by a three per cent employment increase. The Caterpillar company provided four more days holidays, and provided for retirement at 55. One hundred jobs were created. In the insurance sector, the working week was reduced by stages to 36 hours in 1984, and in textiles, the week was cut to 37 hours and 20 minutes. In 1984, the Belgian Cabinet approved a Bill granting 240 hours paid leave per year for training, and an additional 160 hours for more general education. By April 1985, average hours in Belgium were down to 38.5, and still falling. In addition, paid leave has been granted for workers temporarily replaced by an unemployed person; the employer receives £144 per month in state aid under this scheme. The worker's leave in such cases must be for periods of six months to one year.

The Dutch trade union movement has now taken over the lead from the Belgians in the shorter hours movement. Their key demand for 1985–6 was the 36 hour week. The printing industry has already achieved this target while 32 per cent of the overall workforce is now below a 40 hour week. Government support for the moves is strong. In February 1984, the Dutch Cabinet announced that it might propose legal measures to bring down working time in 1985–6, although hoping that this could be achieved earlier by negotiation. It argued that a planned reduction of ten per cent in hours by 1986 was essential to cut unemployment. The engineering industry had made a tentative start during 1984 by agreeing 26 extra half-days 'free time' from 1985, although the agreement provides for workers to forgo part of their price-indexed wage increases to pay for the deal. The Philips company introduced 26 additional half-days leave from 1 January 1985.

The French government has initiated a number of measures. In 1982 it decreed that men should have the right to retire on full state pension at age 60; a full pension is 50 per cent of pay based on the ten best years of earnings. It decreed a 39-hour week affecting 15 million workers in the private sector, a move seen as a first step towards the 35-hour week. Those on shift work should achieve the 35-hour week by 1985. Compensation for the loss of hourly earnings is subject to industry-level negotiations, though many of the agreements signed do in fact provide full compensation, and the statutory minimum wage is fully protected by law. At the same time, a fifth week's holiday was introduced, again by law, for all employees. In 1983, the French Cabinet took further steps to cut working time in order to increase employment. It extended financial incentives to employers to recruit staff for 30-hour week jobs, and extended parental leave to fathers as well as to mothers. The government is encouraging phased early retirement in particularly arduous jobs, a measure to be accompanied by the recruitment of the young unemployed.

The Swedish LO demanded the 38-hour week in 1985 for double-day shift workers, and an additional three days leave for all workers. The Danish movement, involving revulsion against pay levels as well as the claim for 35 hours, generated a general strike wave in March and April of 1985, which produced the largest industrial action since the war, mass demonstrations on an unprecedented scale and the nearest thing to civil disorder which the peaceable post-war Danish society has ever witnessed. Some 300,000 workers were on strike or locked out, and were met with uncharacteristically visible hostility from government, employers and police. Private manufacturing was chiefly affected, but food, petrol and oil distribution were also halted, as well as public transport. The dispute reached the proportions of a general strike at the end of March with its extension into the public sector. There it was led unofficially by left-wing shop stewards who expressed the widespread social opposition to the government's monetarist policies. Thousands stayed out for several days after the strike's statutory termination by government decree in early April.

The Danish system of centralized collective bargaining is normally a ritual biennial affair, practised continuously since 1899. After agreement between unions and employers, the settlement becomes legally enforceable. When major conflicts arise in this process, the government steps in with a compulsory solution. The last previous occasion for such intervention was in 1973. The unusual feature of the 1985 dispute was that the average worker would have been better off with the employers' final offer than with the unions' demands, at least in terms of take-home pay. For the unions demanded a cut in the working week without seeking full hourly wage compensation. Their demand was for a 35-hour week (a reduction of five hours), though they were eventually prepared to settle for an immediate fall of two hours. This was to be coupled with a substantial pay increase for the low paid, but no increases for the higher paid. The unions' whole case was grounded on the need to generate employment through reduction of working time. The employers' final offer was for a cut of only half-an-hour per week, and the government ended the crisis with a statutory award of a one-hour reduction by the end of 1986, combined with a two per cent wage increase. The law was used to force the strikers back to work.

The European Trade Union Institute (ETUI) has attempted to distil general lessons from all these experiences.[25] It finds that throughout Western Europe the unions' goal is the 35-hour week, although some have demanded restrictions on overtime, longer holidays or other forms of reduction in annual hours. Progress is piecemeal, but the ETUI claims that the overall effect upon employment is favourable. New jobs have been created, existing jobs under threat have been preserved, and more part time jobs and training places have been brought into being.

European governments have shown varying degrees of appreciation of the connection between hours reduction and employment creation. Most have been markedly interventionist in the process, in sharp contrast to the British government's determined *laissez-faire* attitude. Of course, while the Danish government's hostile response shows the closest affinity with Mrs Thatcher's approach, all the administrations share, by conviction or compulsion, a common ambivalence deriving from the dominant monetarist emphasis on 'supply-side' solutions to the labour market 'problem'. There is a discernible general trend towards the 'deregulation' of the labour market, which matches the British government's relaxation of laws and state practice in the fields of health and safety, employee protections, welfare provision and other statutory provisions, as well as the tendency towards forcing workers to pay for hours reduction with reduced hourly earnings, or with pay freezes, statutory incomes policies and the like. As in Britain, trade union membership figures are falling generally, and sustained industrial action leading to unambiguous victories are commonly difficult in these circumstances.

The conclusion must be a reinforcement of the general theme we have emphasized through this book: without international coordination of national policies and campaigns elevated to a *political* level, the drive for full employment in Europe and the reduction in working time will founder on the rocks of national isolation, governmental resistance and the superior power of employers, deriving from the integration of multinational capital.

Restoring Union Rights

In most trade union offices, a main purpose of political action will be the restoration of trade union rights. Our arguments throughout this book have supported this objective, and there can be no doubt that countervailing action is urgently necessary. The 1984 Trade Union Act is a direct assault on Article 3 of ILO Convention 87, which is entirely specific on this matter:

Workers' and employers' organisations shall have the right to draw up their constitutions and rules, to elect their representatives in full freedom, to organise their administration and activities, and to formulate their programmes. The public authorities shall refrain from any interference which would restrict this right or impede the lawful exercise thereof.

A number of other ministerial decisions contravene ILO regulations, and it is entirely arguable that the ban on trade union membership which was imposed on employees in the GCHQ at Cheltenham is actually illegal. At the top level, there will be a queue of cases in the international courts, and even if these courts are far from perfect, it is doubtful in the extreme that they can be more biased against trade unions than are domestic British judges.

Appeals to international courts, however, while abundantly justified, will not prove to be an adequate defence. The British unions must mobilize in the electorate if they are ever to regain their strength: and first they must win their own section of the electorate for agreed common proposals. To the extent that union members feel that their organizations are responsive, accountable and representative, they will feel disposed to maintain the traditional autonomy of those bodies from government regulation. But it will be difficult for unions to win support for motions which actually render them less democratic. For this reason, the unions will need to consider rather urgently how to frame their own constructive proposals.

The very fact that the Conservative government has been so merciless in its onslaught on political pluralism and so determined to reduce trade unionism to a shadow, means that it becomes not only possible but also to a degree necessary for the trade unions to address themselves to the problem of company law reform. This is possible because Mrs Thatcher has removed many taboos, and provoked people to think more radically. It is necessary because the weakening of trade unions by mass unemployment as well as legislative encroachments will mean that they will not easily resume some of their traditional roles while unemployment remains at record levels. The British Conservatives registered the quite unjustifiable claim that trade unions are a favoured type or organization because they have hitherto been entitled to certain immunities for behaviour in restraint of trade. How a trade union might operate without such immunities is not easy to imagine. However, this onslaught by the Thatcher team has distracted people's attention from a far more powerful privilege, which is enjoyed by every major capitalist organization: the principle of limited liability. The capacity to avoid personal responsibility for debts incurred on one's personal initiative is, by any count, a remarkable advantage. Well over a century ago, the argument for this degree of licence was heard in the absence of an organized mass labour movement. Now it is time to reopen the question. As a modest interim step, the principle of limited liability should surely be contingent upon an affirmative vote of employees, at regular intervals. The easiest way to make this effective would be to require every company to submit to the Registrar an annual statement of satisfactory labour relations, with its audited accounts. Such a statement would need to be endorsed by the responsible trade union organization involved. Failure to submit the statement would automatically revoke the privilege of limited liability, thus rendering all shareholders responsible in full for any failure by the company in which they held investments. This measure would partially redress the imbalance in company law which renders directors ultimately accountable to shareholders but not to employees, and it would strengthen trade unions during the period of their convalescence, while they recuperated from the gross debilities imposed by monetarism.

The Labour movement throughout Europe is being tested by a crisis which is as much political as economic. Attempts to resolve this crisis by arbitrary means can only succeed in making in worse. If the movement can keep its head through these present adversities, it can bring about a notable advance in the democratic organization of industry and society. Surely, it is quite unthinkable that an age of microcomputers, lasers, and widespread robotics will for long conform to the prejudices of the more backward Victorians? There is a future in which human capacities can grow to match and outpace the results of invention. Already this future lives in the imaginations of multitudes of people. How long can it be prevented from asserting itself in public order?

APPENDIX 8.1   EUROPE AGAINST UNEMPLOYMENT

Unemployment is laying Europe waste.[26] With 20 million people out of work, the number of direct victims has become intolerable: a common scandal. But there is every reason to believe that this number is growing steadily, while the indirect sufferers already include whole populations.

The direct victims enter poverty for long periods of time, and in some age groups and regions, they stay poor, permanently. Such people are forced outwards to the margins of society. There they live a kind of twilight life, without hope of personal betterment, and without any of those social links that might bring collective improvement. In a world in which men travel to the moon, Europe contains many areas in which a fifth or more of its citizens are in want.

The indirect victims of this wasting disorder are counted in further millions. Low paid workers in declining industries gain no improvement, even while their wages are too small to allow decent existence. Often employees in public services are similarly squeezed. Restriction breeds further restriction: as the economy declines, so public spending is cut over and again, each time aggravating the general decline.

Unemployment seeds fear, and this fear breaks up individual personalities and tears apart the fabric of human society. It spawns violence and mental breakdown, riot and repression.

First among the sufferers are young people, women and racial minorities. Four decades of European progress in education are now abruptly reversed in a cataclysm in which vast numbers of school leavers discover that they are completely unnecessary: that their skills and knowledge have no economic value, and that their generation has become a social problem. Hard won advances in the conditions of women workers are brusquely checked as the labour market shunts their employment prospects into casual or part time occupations, ill protected by trade unions or social conventions. The condition of migrant workers and ethnic minorities is deeply menaced, as they lose the chance to find work and suffer the worsening of xenophobia and heightened community tension.

For individual people unemployment may bring despair or even suicide. For societies, its effects are equally poisonous: within the climate it establishes sprout the seeds of authoritarianism and militarism. Democratic institutions become difficult to maintain when multimillions of the citizens are excluded from constructive economic life. The social base of trade unions and other voluntary associations is often undermined, and fear breeds fear, reinforcing tensions between states, and heightening military power. Previous great slumps have commonly exploded into war: although the world knows that such an outcome today would put an end to human evolution.

There is no reason to believe that unemployment is unavoidable or foreordained. A mere fraction of the ingenuity which has transformed our technical capacities could rearrange our social rules in a way which would guarantee a useful role for all our people.

Of course, action by governments can improve or worsen this condition. If all, or even some of the European governments were willing to act together in order to reject mass unemployment, there is no doubt that conditions could be radically improved. But this is not a problem which can be left to governments. Because it concerns everybody, it needs action by all of us. Just as economic collapse threatens our democratic institutions, so economic recovery calls for an enhancement of our power to respond through democracy. Those who are still employed have a special responsibility to help their fellows who have been squeezed out of work. It is understandable that insecurity breeds fear, but this can only be dispelled by acting together in mutual support. Ideas about economic recovery and action for employment are needed at all levels of society, and from all relevant social organizations.

The work which is necessary requires us to find ways of joining needs to resources, of restructuring institutions to regain the democratic initiative in the global economy. As the slump has deepened, want and waste have faced each other out. Europe must discover an answer to this evil process; an agenda for the recovery of output, production, incomes and trade and for the regeneration of work and hope, not only in our corner of the world but also in the underdeveloped countries and among the victims of a dreadful world-wide crisis of debt which threatens to breed famine, turbulence and war. We must find ways to replace the policies of 'beggar my neighbour' by those which seek instead to 'better my neighbour'.

A part of this agenda involves those social organizations which both shape and voice public opinion. We think that political, religious and cultural associations, trade unions and public authorities need to establish an open European forum from whose platform it will be possible together to generate the self-confidence for renewal. At the same time, there are innumerable democratic bodies which have it in their reach to initiate practical actions to develop prospects of employment, and to overcome the scourage of enforced and unwanted idleness. Trade unions are already concerned to establish coordinated moves to establish safer and healthier working conditions, shorter working lifetimes, longer holidays and more educational facilities at work. Local municipalities are often concerned to encourage industrial development, international contact, and improved trade in their own areas, and may find joint action across frontiers a valuable aid in this process.

Proposal: Joint Action for Jobs

Joint European action on the remedies for unemployment would give scope for all such interests to work together, reinforcing every positive example by healthy imitation and support. This, therefore, is what we propose, beginning with a series of conferences and working parties which may be a starting point for widespread, common initiatives. These could be linked by a common rubric: Joint Action for Jobs.

Such conferences must be international, because the present trauma of monetarism is itself world-wide, and more, because the growth of private multinational power has itself been very largely responsible for a marked loss of democratic national controls over economic policy. Our response must operate at the same level as the crisis itself. But the wider it ranges across frontiers, the more it must draw upon, and stimulate, the initiatives of local communities, since these are the agencies through which our peoples can begin the work of regeneration.

Therefore, we do not believe that the difficulties in agreement of international policies are an excuse for inaction either nationally or locally. We think it necessary for Europeans to consult with one another, not in order to discover reasons why action must be deferred until all are able to move as one, but rather in order to overcome passivity, to support each initiative that shows itself, and to create a sense of overriding priority, against which the actions of governments and others in authority may be judged. There is a considerable effort of new thinking, which asks insistent questions about the future of our social lives and personal relationships, in the context of our changing environment. If Europe is to recover wisely, and in unity with the peoples of the rest of the world, we must examine these ideas.

At the same time, the millions of workless people who have been evicted from active influence over many of our democratic processes must be able to find a platform from which to explain their needs, and a movement within which they may recover their hopes.

We circulate this appeal for signature. Those who believe that European meetings on this theme could be a first step towards more coordinated progress invite others to join with them in exploring how such contacts may begin. All those groups and individuals who are concerned with this most desperate challenge are invited to help, by bringing their examples and their problems to a common forum. Daunting though this task may be, it will help us to face it together.[26]

Notes

1 Cf. John Hughes, *Britain in Crisis*, Spokesman 1981.
2 James Erlichman, 'The Imperial Imperative', in *Guardian*, 19 February 1985.
3 Stuart Holland, *Out of Crisis, A Project for European Recovery*. Spokesman, for IPSE Forum, 1983.
4 Manifesto of the Confederation of Socialist Parties of the European Community, 9 March 1984.
5 Thus, the statements of Mr Peter Walker, from within the Cabinet, and the pressure group, Conservative Centre Forward, around Mr Francis Pym, from outside it. Within the same overall perspective, there is the announcement of a new Employment Institute under the intellectual influence of the Social Democratic Party.
6 These, broadly, were the arguments of Neil Kinnock in *New Socialist*, No. 16, March 1984.
7 *Political Parties*, Dover (Constable) 1959.
8 John Strachey, *The Nature of Capitalist Crisis*, Gollancz, 1935, p. 342.

9 Sidney and Beatrice Webb, *Soviet Communism: A New Civilisation*, Longmans, 1944, pp. 262 et seq.

10 Herbert Morrison, *Socialization and Transport*, Constable, 1933, pp. 208-10.

11 Roy and Zhores Medvedev, *Khrushchev - The Years in Power*, Oxford, 1977, pp. 94 et seq.

12 Nie Rongzhen, 'How China develops its nuclear weapons', *Beijing Review*, 29 April 1985, 15-18.

13 Cf. Hilary Wainwright and Dave Elliott, *The Lucas Plan*, Allison and Busby, 1982. Also Ken Coates (ed.) *The Right to Useful Work*, Spokesman, 1978.

14 Mike Ward, 'Local economic strategies', in *Planning the Planners* (ed. Tony Topham), Spokesman, 1983, p. 86.

15 *Report on the Committee of Inquiry on Industrial Democracy*, HMSO, Cmnd 6706, 1977. Cf. also Ken Coates and Tony Topham, *A Shop Steward's Guide to the Bullock Report*, Spokesman, 1977.

16 *Labour Weekly*, 11 April 1985, p. 12.

17 *The Times*, 20 December 1983. Cf. also Low Pay Unit, *Who Needs the Wages Councils?*, 1983.

18 See Ken Coates, Michael Meacher and Walt Greendale, *Task Force Against Low Pay*, Institute for Workers Control Pamphlet, 1983.

19 Cf. Allen Hutt, 'The hours of labour', in *Marxist Quarterly*, II, 1 January 1955, 2-13.

20 Reprinted in *Archives in Trade Union History*, published by the Institute for Workers Control, 1968.

21 Sidney Webb and Harold Cox, *The Eight Hours' Day*, Walter Scott. 1890.

22 TUC Report, 1981.

23 International Metalworkers' Federation, *The 1984 Collective Bargaining Dispute*. (IMF, Geneva, 1985).

24 Data in this survey are derived from Incomes Data Services *International Reports*, 1982-5.

25 The ETUI has issued two relevant reports: *Practical Experiences with the Reduction of Working Time in Western Europe*, and *Collective Bargaining in Western Europe, 1983, and Prospects for 1984*.

26 This text was drafted by Ken Coates on the basis of extensive discussions within a committee of economists, parliamentarians and local councillors, which began to meet regularly from the end of 1984 onwards. This committee has subsequently become known by the title 'Joint Action for Jobs'.

9 Afterword

In 1980 we published a descriptive account of British trade unionism. At that time, 1½ million people were lined up in dole queues, and the Thatcher administration had thrust its way into office after a shrewd campaign of denunciation of the hardships involved in such an unheard-of statistic. In fact, Saatchi and Saatchi had organized their publicity around a somewhat smaller total, during the declining years of Jim Callaghan's government.

We shared in the apprehension and unease, aware already that things were no longer as they used to be. We concluded our book with these words:

> With widespread unemployment, poverty, already endemic, became more and more acute.
>
> In this context, all the principal achievements in the field of welfare provision and humane social organisation, established during the decades following the Second World War, became objects of bitter contention. The postwar decades had previously been marked by a consensus. This broad social agreement assumed continuous improvement in living standards; growing social provision in the fields of education, housing and health; and greater involvement by trade unions in the regulation of an increasingly liberal society. The architects of this consensus would be dismayed by the Britain of 1980. Marked authoritarianism, increasingly obtrusive and arbitrary police powers, surveillance, and frenetic preparations for an impossible war: all marked an end to the postwar settlement, whose dreams had turned into nightmares.
>
> If anyone remains free to write an updated version of this book in 1990, it will very possibly record events which have hitherto been unthinkable. No-one can with certainty predict the outcome of the desperate period into which we are entered: and we do not wish to end this book on a note of vapid optimism. But if the British Trade Unions still need an expositor at the end of the trials which are about to be encountered, then there will remain a real hope that the goals of liberal civilisation, of brotherhood, sisterhood and mutual support, may yet prevail.
>
> If, however, the unions were in fact to be powdered between the pitiless grindstones of official repression and economic ruin, those who dared

260

remember them at all would remember also the democratic promise which they held out, and the large freedoms which were always rooted in their ample support. Books would be burnt, and witches soon after them, on the evil day when the British Trade Unions were compelled to close their offices.

Educated working people may be relied upon to make all these most dire events quite difficult to achieve.

Now, halfway through this terrible decade, we are encouraged to think that the grounds for hope have not yet been eroded, even though there has been a flood of troubles turbulent enough to drown all but the most determined hopes. There were always those who thought that there would be resistance, and that this would inevitably give rise to an abrupt upheaval. Certainly the government sought to provoke, and then draw out, the miners' strike. It succeeded beyond any rational expectation, provoking a struggle in which the mining communities endured

Table 9.1 Results of union ballots on the retention of the political fund

Union	For		Against	
	(No.)	*(%)*	*(No.)*	*(%)*
SOGAT	91,760	78	25,947	22
ISTC	28,633	87	4,404	13
FTAT	11,410	72	4,269	28
UCW	102,546	75	33,337	25
NCU	77,183	81	17,757	19
GMB	448,426	89	54,637	11
APEX	39,465	73	14,380	27
BFAWU	19,954	90	2,237	10
AUEW	238,604	84	44,399	16
EETPU	140,913	84	26,830	16
NUR	71,907	87	10,580	13
PLCW/TWU	2,242	75	697	25
ASLEF	19,110	93	1,491	7
TSSA	22,975	70	10,017	30
NUS	6,179	87	963	13
Ceramic and Allied Trades Union	17,967	77	5,383	23
National Union of Scalemakers	460	77	135	23
TGWU	511,014	7	119,823	18

Note: The turn-out in these 18 ballots averaged 51.7%. Unions which held general secretaryship elections in the same period as their political fund ballots all had higher turn-outs in the latter. Political fund ballot turn-outs were 50% higher in workplace balloting than in postal balloting.

sustained suffering in a manner which can justly be described as heroic. But unnoticed, there has been as significant a testimony to the power of democratic ideals, in the quiet but unshakeable commitment of British trade unionists. Nowhere is this more plainly apparent than in the first results of the political fund ballots, conducted in the wake of a completely unprecedented campaign against trade unions and all their works, but above all against their political commitments. At the time this book goes to press, eighteen unions have balloted more than 4.3 million members. Nearly 82.4 per cent of those voting have supported the maintenance of political funds. The complete results to date are given in table 9.1.

This set of results follows an unprecedented campaign, during which both leaders and activists have been involved in a remarkable discussion with rank and file members. A measure which intended to bring about irreparable splits and divisions, by playing the different levels of union organization one against another, has decisively backfired. The trade unions' political links emerge immeasurably stronger than they were before, and unions have polled far more decisively than they did in the years after 1913, when political funds were first set up. Provided they build upon their unity, there is now little doubt that the unions will shortly see the downfall of those who have wrought such damage and misery among them.

What may then be built on the ruins of Mrs Thatcher's radical dystopia remains to be determined. It is this uncertainty which calls for new politics, a new internationalism and steady nerves, and which invites the British labour movement to meet the greatest test of its long history. We see no reason not to believe that the best pages of this history are yet to be written.

Index